Bordering
Religions / *Concepts, C.*
and Convers.

SERIES EDITORS

Kathryn Kueny, Karen Pechilis, and James T. Robinson

MOTHERHOOD AS METAPHOR

Engendering Interreligious Dialogue

JEANNINE HILL FLETCHER

Fordham University Press NEW YORK 2013

Fordham University Press has no responsibility for the persistence or accuracy of
URLs for external or third-party Internet websites referred to in this publication
and does not guarantee that any content on such websites is, or will remain,
accurate or appropriate.

Fordham University Press also publishes its books in a variety of electronic
formats. Some content that appears in print may not be available in
electronic books.

Library of Congress Cataloging-in-Publication
Data is available from the publisher.

Printed in the United States of America
15 14 13   5 4 3 2 1

First edition

To Francis and Elisabeth
Virginia and James
In Gratitude for Roots and Wings

CONTENTS

PREFACE

In my first book, *Monopoly on Salvation? A Feminist Approach to Religious Pluralism,* I set out to discover what difference it would make to bring feminist theoretical and theological insights to bear on contemporary discussions of religious difference. It seemed that the theologies being offered were stuck at an impasse of seeing persons of different religions either as fundamentally 'the same' or as radically different. To this discourse on religious pluralism, a field dominated by male scholars, I brought the feminist theoretical consideration of our hybrid identities as a way of recognizing that each of us encounters our others with a dynamic mix of 'sameness' *and* 'difference'. The multiplicity of who we are provides a multitude of possible sites of encounter, but nevertheless many things about our others remain inaccessible to us—they fundamentally remain 'mystery,' although we can encounter one another in solidarity and friendship.

Because the theological discourse on religious pluralism has been dominated by male scholars, *Monopoly on Salvation?* has been well received as an alternative *feminist* approach within the landscape of approaches to religious diversity. And yet, about three-quarters of the way to finishing that work, I realized that the methodology I had employed fell short of the feminist methodological frameworks in which I had been trained. That is, while I brought to bear a new feminist theoretical framework to a previously masculinist discussion, I was nevertheless working with male-centered traditions, men's voices, and men's experiences. The resources I had available to me for thinking about 'interreligious encounter' were resources that had been formulated along the lines of malestream knowledge, where women's experience simply was not captured in historical writings or put forth as example of interfaith exchange. While the first book made its contribution, I realized that a more thoroughgoing feminist methodology might change the landscape more radically. With the research of this book I set out to ask the question: What difference would it make if it was women's voices and experiences that constituted the data of interreligious exchange?

Committing to a more thoroughgoing feminist methodology in drawing from women's voices and women's experiences, I now had a more daunting task in front of me. For while a range of men's voices and experiences in interfaith contexts were available to me in published works of missionary documents, doctrinal statements, or historical accounts, in published works little was available that took women's experiences as central. The original research for the book, then, was necessary before I could draw out from these experiences for theological consideration. For the theology that follows, I took three sites of women's interreligious encounter as my starting point. First, I attended to the experience of Catholic women of the Maryknoll order in the mission fields of China (drawn from research at their archives in Ossining, New York). Simultaneously, I began an ethnographic investigation of an interreligious dialogue group of women in Philadelphia, with interviews conducted over two years. In addition to these explicitly 'religious' sites, I was compelled by my foremothers in feminist theology to recognize the secular space of the women's movement itself as data for the consideration of women's interfaith encounter.

What difference *does* it make when women's voices and experiences are taken as the point of departure for theological investigation? In the pages that follow I suggest several aspects of a distinctive approach to encountering our religious 'others': an approach that is fundamentally relational, grounded in friendship and the messiness of actual human lives; an approach that resists compartmentalizing 'sacred'/'religious' over against 'secular'/'nonreligious'; an approach that insists that our religious orientations must be accountable to the practical, material, and social outcomes that they engender. The insights in these pages have come almost exclusively from listening to and culling the theological reflections from women across the faith traditions of the world. To them, in their courage, their particularity, and their persistent mystery, we owe significant debt and apology for having not considered the possibility of their deep theological knowledge before.

ACKNOWLEDGMENTS

As the dedication indicates, I am profoundly grateful to two sets of parents who have mothered me into authorship of this book. Francis Schüssler Fiorenza nurtured in an unbelievable way the scholar I have become as he mentored me from a young graduate student to who I am today. The methods of Elisabeth Schüssler Fiorenza have been among the most formative in shaping my feminist theological orientation. Francis's confidence in me and Elisabeth's feminist methods provided the tools with which I found my own theological voice. The role these academic mothers have played in my scholarly development built on the foundation laid by my mothers of origin, Virginia and James Hill. Traces of their living influence and deep wisdom are found within these pages; I am sure my sense of mothering comes from them. Without these mothers in my life, this work would never have been birthed forth. For both sets of mothers I am grateful for both roots and wings.

The reader will find in the pages that follow a commitment to the idea that who we are as human beings never exists in isolation but is fundamentally relational in its formation and instantiation. It is fitting, then, that this opening acknowledge the countless mothers who have brought this book into being. The institutional home of Fordham University provided numerous resources for growing the research of this book. I am especially grateful to Dean Nancy Busch, whose awareness allowed child care to be included in a research budget that provided the initial grant for work in the archives of the Maryknoll Sisters (2005). Ellen Pierce was a friendly guide into the world of the Sisters in their letters, diaries, and other archival material. Fordham's Graduate School of Arts and Sciences also provided funds to support the interviews of the Philadelphia Area Multifaith Women's Group (2007–9). In the interviewing process, the collaboration with Mara Brecht was invaluable; as an epistemologist, she provided the gift of her reading of chapters 5 and 6. Mara and I are both indebted to the women of the Philadelphia group for their hospitality and welcome into their sacred interreligious space. The final draft and theological culmination of this work was made possible by a research leave from Fordham and a grant from the Carpenter Foundation. My thanks to James Wilson and Celinett Rodriguez, who shepherded my work in the Office of Research. I am grateful to the many wonderful colleagues at Fordham whose advice and friendship have nurtured my scholarly self; and to Eric Meyer, who read chapters in their final form with tremendous care and incredible insight. My colleagues in the Dorothy Day Center for Service and Justice at Fordham have helped me see the necessity for applying my scholarship in the direction of the needs of our world, precisely the world we actually live in here in New York City and the Bronx. To my institutional family at Fordham, and the external support I received from foundations such as Carpenter, I owe a great debt. Words cannot express how incredibly transformative my most recent research leave has been in bringing together the many strands of my thought written over seven years. It has only been through this external support that I have finally, this year, found ways to address the calculus of concern attendant to both work and family. I look forward to returning to the company of Fordham as the future of who I am unfolds.

I am grateful to the wider network of theological exploration and religious studies in the academy for the testing of ideas together. My interreligious colleagues from my earliest graduate school experience to more recent colleagues have stayed with me also in a profound way: Amira Rosenberg, Neelima Shukla Bhatt, Julia Watts Belser, and Homayra Ziad. Their friendship has informed many dimensions of my thinking, and I met each through the specific multiplicity of our identities as scholars. The ideas in this book have been shaped by other scholars as well. Presentation of elements of this book in a variety of venues, including sessions at the annual meetings of the American Academy of Religion and the Catholic Theological Society of America, provided tremendous opportunities for collaboration and feedback. The cohort of scholars from the AAR's Luce Summer Seminars in Theologies of Religious Pluralism and Comparative Theology furthered my investigations at crucial stages. The prayerful exploration of these themes with the committed Christian women religious of RSHM, who have become sisters to me, provided the opportunity to see the import of this project. Refining my thought for its more practical purposes, I am indebted to discussions with the community of the Network of Sacred Heart Schools (RSCJ).

As my work came together from out of these disparate endeavors, the mothers of my closest theological community helped me integrate and shape this manuscript. These colleagues of the New York–Nashville Workgroup in Constructive Theology—Michele Saracino, Bradford Hinze, Roger Haight, John Theil, Elena Procario-Foley, and Paul Lakeland—mothered me both professionally and personally. Their reading of chapter 2, and Michele's reading also of chapter 3, gave me courage to pursue this creative endeavor.

I have been mothered also by those who have helped me to be a mother: Chandra Budi and Earl Samms, Sarah Dueth, Sophie Botross, Sinitra Siengsanaoh, Meaghan Carlstrom, and the moms of Paulus Hook. Namaste to the community at Shiva Shanti, Rutherford, who embraced and mothered me bodily. My sisters and my brother have helped me to see that becoming a mother is but one node of relationality, and that there are many types of relationships that are lifelong and sustaining. My closest friends suggested motherhood might be theologically significant. And the entire Fletcher family demonstrated what it looks like to begin the process of widening our scope of mother-love.

As I seek theological insight in the everydayness of our human existence, my work as a theologian could not develop in the direction it has without the relational horizon of investigation made possible by Owen, Ella, and Thea. I love you. Finally, all of who I am is forever being mothered by my husband, Michael, for whom I am forever grateful.

Many thanks to Fortress Press for permission to reprint "A Christology of Motherhood," which first appeared in *Frontiers in Catholic Feminist Theology*, a collaboration of this workgroup.

MOTHERHOOD AS METAPHOR

Introduction: We Feed Them Milk

THEOLOGICAL ANTHROPOLOGY
AS A LABOR OF LOVE

We feed them milk, we feed them love, we feed them hatred.
Whatever we feed them they will eat and they will become.[1]

She was reflecting on her participation in interreligious dialogue and considering the importance of the work through the lens of her experience as a nursing mother. The point this young Muslim woman was illustrating was that in the same way we nurture the next generation with material sustenance, we also shape them emotionally and relationally, for better and for worse. Perhaps this is the heart of the theology offered in the following pages: that our theological thinking and our religious outlooks shape the way we think about ourselves and our world; they are what we 'eat' and what we will become. For too long we have eaten the fruit of a knowledge that has shaped us to think individualistically or, if communally, to extend the boundaries of our community only as far as our own faith. The knowledge we must eat is what might shape us anew for lives radically intertwined with persons of difference.

The Fruits of Theological Anthropology

The most fundamental theological fruit that Christians have ingested and that shapes their understanding of themselves might be situated under the heading of 'theological anthropology'—that is, a faith perspective on what it means to be human. Of course, Christian theology has offered ideas about the nature of God and the person of Jesus Christ, and many within the Christian community are willing to concede that these are faith perspectives situated within the horizon of divine mysteries (and therefore eluding our grasp of them). Yet Christians might not quite as easily recognize the way faith traditions have shaped our fundamental understanding of human nature and who we are as human beings. Deeply intertwined with the understanding of God and Christology, traditional Christian theological anthropologies have drawn on a series of scriptural resources, including the creation accounts of Genesis, Jesus' teaching on the nature of the human person, and the letters of the New Testament (Paul's and those attributed to him) to present a portrait of who we really 'are' as human beings. Since the premises provided in these accounts are often taken for granted, it is necessary to look closely at these classic texts. But Christian theological anthropology has always also been intertwined with articulations of philosophy and other of the humane sciences contemporary with it. So too in our age. If the resources of the Christian tradition are to continue to provide insights into the nature of our human condition that might positively inform Christian self-understanding, they must be fruitfully engaged with the many different resources of our multi-religious world.

Recognizing the importance of our particular context as site for theological reflection, we might follow the methodology of Karl Rahner, who insisted on beginning with humanity in its distinctive settings as the starting point for considering what the Christian tradition has to say about our human condition. Or, as he describes his method: "We should rather acquire enough theology so that, starting with experience and with a description of the existentiell human situation, we can talk about the *matter itself* without using [the particular language of theology]. Only at the end would we have to indicate that this very actual reality of one's own life and one's own situation is called 'original sin' [for example] in ecclesiastical language."[2]

Rahner suggests that we hold the theological and Church-informed ecclesiastical language of the Christian tradition at bay just long enough to investigate our actual human existence before applying the theological terms. He was convinced that a close examination of the texture of our human experience would provide the richest resource for thinking theologically. Only after interrogating the matter at hand would we then return to the language of theology and apply key terms to describe the reality that we were experiencing. The method of this book will follow Rahner's pattern. It will consider 'the matter itself'—namely, our experience of being human in the world, taking women's experiences from across the religious traditions as the starting point. It will do so first without using particularly Christian theological vocabulary. Only then will

I ask whether there is Christian theological vocabulary that speaks to these particular experiences and whether/how we will proceed theologically with the Bible and tradition to create new theological language for our future humanity.

This investigation cannot (obviously) consider 'the matter itself' in abstraction or in comprehensive scope. It will necessarily be circumscribed by a series of experiences particular to the new interreligious context that is my concern. The chapters that follow share a common framework in two parts. In each of the three parts, the first chapter details historical/archival/ethnographic evidence of women's experience in interfaith contact through letters, diaries, public speeches, and interviews of women in interfaith settings. In the second chapter in each part, the theological insights from these experiences are culled and they are placed in conversation with modern theological anthropology (with Rahner taken as conversation partner). As will become evident in the unfolding of this exploration, I do not think we can consider 'the matter itself' without recognizing the frameworks and interlocutors that shape our very attention to the material. And yet, through new research with heretofore unheard women's voices, the possibilities for engaging these formative sources might emerge.

> I think that because of my experience in the women's interfaith dialogue . . . I associate it with the profound connections among women. . . . Much of what I value in this group is that I am getting to experience in this group are these really powerful women, that I might not have. So I think that is one piece, that I have learned the power of women, the power, the strength, the resiliency, the role people play in their family lives and you know that sort of thing. . . . I think 'intimacy' is a word that I have come to really appreciate in a different way. Because it's probably as close a term to being a faith experience as well as human experience, and how many people are lucky enough to experience a really deep intimacy in their lives? Right? So with whom do we allow ourselves to experience that deep intimacy? And do we even really seek that? For me, you know, it became a question of a sense of intimacy with God.
>
> Ava[3]

She suggests that her experience as a Jewish woman in interreligious dialogue provided profound understandings of what it means to be human and what it means to be in relationship with God. How do we consider 'the matter itself' as Ava has articulated it—human intimacy and relationality (our experience of love), human courage and resiliency (our potential for making choices), human knowledge of self, other, God (the foundational experiences of knowing)—in light of the theological tradition that is our heritage?

Paralleling the categories surfaced in Ava's reflection, Rahner, too, described humanity with these basic categories: our ability to know, our ability to make free choices, and our ability to love. With the first quality, that of knowing, Rahner describes the human being as 'person and subject' characterized by self-understanding and an awareness of the world. He writes, "Man experiences himself precisely as subject and person insofar as he becomes conscious of himself as the product of what is radically foreign to him."[4] This subject is situated in the world with 'freedom and responsibility' for self-creating, which Rahner describes when he writes that "being a person, then, means the self-possession of a subject as such in a conscious and free relationship to the totality of itself."[5] In Rahner's view, the human being, as knowing and free, is responsible for himself: "He is left to himself and placed in his own hands not only in his knowledge, but also in his *actions*."[6] Rahner presents us with three basic categories: we are knowers, we are doers in freedom, and we are lovers. Yet as universal as these categories seem—surely all persons in some manner participate in knowledge, free will, and love—their universality will be tested with the actual experiences of women in the many religious traditions of the world as the women give texture to the concepts of knowledge, freedom, and love in a variety of contexts. The challenge will then be to ask whether there is sufficient vocabulary within the Christian theological tradition to aptly name this reality in its diversity.

Our investigation will, almost exclusively, take as its focus the lives and experiences of women to pursue a Christian theological anthropology. The working presupposition here is that what has been counted as 'knowledge' about the nature of human existence and endorsed as 'theological insight' has largely been the product of male experts and has not taken into account the distinctiveness of experiences and understandings as they are conditioned by gender. For the better part of Christian history, theological anthropology has been written by male theologians who necessarily reflect from their own (male) experience toward theological insights in light of the received tradition. They have offered a variety of reflections on what it means to be human from out of their lived experience, reflections that both are representative of their individual experience and resonate with the wider experience of persons in the world.

From out of their experience they offer symbolic expression, interwoven with the Christian theological tradition, that invites others also to reflect on their lived experience. It is not surprising, then, that scripture and Christian theological reflection have tended to present theological anthropology from the perspective of the male as norm. After all, for most of the tradition's history, it has been male theologians and philosophers who have been given the task of reflecting on our human condition. Whether willfully or inadvertently, this has too often had disastrous effects on the lives of women. The experience of my foremothers in the faith have repeatedly illuminated this for me, from Elizabeth Cady Stanton to Elisabeth Schüssler Fiorenza: A hermeneutic of suspicion must guide attention to the sources that are authoritative in the Christian tradition. "It is evident," she wrote, "that some wily writer, seeing the perfect equality of man and woman in the first chapter [of Genesis], felt it important for the dignity and dominion of man to effect woman's subordination in some way."[7] Recall, she insisted, that the story as we have it has been formulated by the historical winners.[8] As a feminist methodology, this theological anthropology will think from the experience of women to see if corrections might be made to this damaged and damaging history.

Theological Anthropology and the Experience of Women

When the history of Christian theology offers reflections on theological anthropology derived solely from men's experiences, it misses rich opportunities for opening new understandings of what it means to be human. Thinking with the perspectives of women and thinking with those of men need not be mutually exclusive. Rather, diverse theological perspectives are like lenses through which we might gain a perspective on the prism that is human nature. Depending on what lens or perspective one uses, a different dimension of what it means to be human comes into view. Further, just because the experiences that gave rise to these reflections were grounded in the particular subject-positions of male experience does not mean that they are altogether exclusive of women's experience. Rather, it means that they are partial representations of human experience; they may be helpful in illuminating also the experience of other subject-positions but, importantly, they are not exhaustive of what it means to be human.

The same applies to a theological anthropology that might emerge from women's experiences. In what follows, I will pursue a theological anthropology grounded in women's experience of motherhood, women's struggle for rights, and women's interfaith dialogue. But just as the reflections offered in the tradition of theological thinking are grounded in particular experiences, so too are these experiences particular. They are not the unique experiences of *all* women, in the same way that they are not identical to the experiences of men.[9] Yet that is simply the nature of any theological reflection: It emerges out of distinctive human experiences, interwoven with the faith tradition, and it offers an invitation to view one's own experience through them. What follows is an invitation to consider what it means to be human and to shape our human lives toward the future. Food for thought, milk for human becoming, the metaphors and insights that emerge from these women's experiences provide a rich starting point for a theological anthropology. What we will find is a challenge to the modern theological anthropology we have received, as relationality precedes the individual, constraint challenges our freedom, and interreligious knowing is recognized as a new form of sacred knowledge. These features that emerge from the varied experiences of women offer both a variety of ways of thinking about ourselves as human beings and new resources for engaging the theological traditions.

In the past forty years—that is, in the course of my lifetime—the study of women in religion has emerged. The women's movement, feminist theory, and women's studies have profoundly altered the landscape of our social and historical understanding of women and the religious traditions they engage. But do our Christian theological anthropologies yet *think* from the experience of women? Or, taking masculinist sources of the tradition as foundation, do they continue to only nod vaguely in the direction not only of sexual difference but of women's diversely gendered experiences? It is the purpose of this theological anthropology to think from the experiences of women in their many and great diversities. A Christology of motherhood, the creative rereading of Genesis, and an eschatology that envisions the repair of religious divisions are the constructive writing forward of the tradition that this investigation will offer.

While a feminist approach indeed includes the experiences and issues of 'women', to compensate for masculinist research that has ignored women as the subjects of study, it is not enough for a feminist methodology to simply include women's experience as neutral data. Rather, the principle distinguishing a feminist theological methodology is that it includes with it an inherent critique. As Rita Nakashima Brock explains, "In examining patriarchy, feminist theories expose the structures, such as class, race, region, religion, sexuality, and nationality, that subordinate and oppress women."[10] With this critical element in mind, Elisabeth Schüssler Fiorenza helps to make a crucial distinction when she explains, "In contrast to both academic women's studies and gender studies [which use only women or gender as their lenses], a critical feminist hermeneutic focuses on the systematic analysis of wo/men struggling to change patri-kyriarchal structures of oppression."[11] In the words of Enid Sefcovic and Diane Theresa Bifano, feminist scholarship is 'mission'-oriented in that "it often comes from a stance of cultural critique" and seeks "justice and equality."[12] Feminist theory and theology have been interested not only in drawing women's voices into the sphere of consideration but also in transforming the contexts of those experiences especially as they negatively impact women. That is, feminist theory and theology have an advocacy agenda. As a feminist methodology, this text will investigate how Christian feminist theology impacted by interreligious engagement has articulated its advocacy for women's rights and human well-being.

Theological Anthropology and the Experience of the Religious 'Other'

[The Christian missionary] accepts [converts/pagans] as they are, which is to say, as God made them, as original sin warped them, and as four thousand years of paganism have left them.

J. E. Walsh[13]

In addition to experiences that are excluded through the male-normative construction of theological anthropology, Christian theological anthropology has tended to exclude the insights of other faiths and the many wisdom traditions of the world.

For the better part of Christian history, theologies have been constructed with little explicit reference to the insights gleaned across religious boundaries. It is as if Christians have been reluctant to think theologically with the wisdom traditions of the globe. Nowhere is this more clear than in the construction of a Christian theological anthropology. It is as if Christians know all they need to know from Genesis to Jesus—as if those provide the only answers to who we are and who we might become. Surely, theological anthropologies have been drawn across religious–secular divides, especially in the modern period, when philosophical resources have increasingly gained a hearing as sources for theological understanding. But there has been a reluctance to draw on the theological insights of explicitly alternative faith traditions. The story of Christian theological anthropology has been told as if the Christian moved through the world oblivious to the many and diverse stories that orient humanity to the world.

And yet in our globalized world the encounter with religious differences is, for many, an everyday reality.[14] We do not live within the Christian story as if its sources were the only ones with which we routinely engage. Rather, Christians live and move and think and wonder and become in a world filled with great philosophical, theological, and practical diversity. Our thinking about what it means to be human might be better situated in the broader sphere of the many sources of the self. The methodology of this book, then, aims to consider the life practices and religious worlds of my neighbors of diverse faiths also as resources for thinking about what it means to be human.

This methodology proceeds, then, in an 'inductive' fashion, in contrast to the 'deductive' approach I have inherited. A deductive approach begins from the first principles of scripture and doctrine and from these general principles deduces the particular understanding of the nature of the human person and the nature of our religious 'others.' Yet too often this deductive approach has been applied to the detriment of our religiously other neighbors. They are seen, first and foremost, as 'other than Christian' and in light of the theological anthropology outlined through Christian scripture and teaching. The result is that they are first 'other' and only secondarily site and substance of what it means to be human. The deductive application leads us to believe that the mystery of our being human has already been figured out and that it no longer remains mystery to us, that we need only apply our revelatory Christian insights to illuminate the mystery (of ourselves, and our 'others') at hand. Proceeding inductively, from the experience of the particular interreligious encounter 'on the ground', provides new resources for theological thinking. The foreclosure of mystery might be opened up anew with an inductive approach in which we wrestle with the very details of the human experience as witnessed by our friends of other faiths and return only then to formulate a theological reflection. As Maryknoll Sister Julia

Hannigan recalls from her time in the Catholic mission, "When I first went to China, I believed that without Baptism one cannot be saved. . . . I think that was my original desire—to spread the Faith and to see that people would be saved. 'To save souls,' I think that's how we said it. . . . But in this particular setting, I myself, began to have a deeper appreciation of other religions. This one Chinese lady, the mother of the Catholic doctor, was a beautiful person."[15] Offering insight into a religious imagination that had been transformed, she reflects, "That was when I became more tolerant of other religions."[16] The inductive method of this work invites us to consider our neighbors of other faiths as beautiful persons in all their complexity and to theologize from there.

Bringing to Light Everyday Experiences

Theological anthropology emerges as we reflect through the lens of our religious traditions on the myriad experiences that make us who we are. "I just made this walnut cake."[17] But those experiences do not come pre-packaged or set aside from the everyday world (pause . . . waiting for tea to boil).[18] What it means to be human is found in the everyday, in our moment-to-moment existence in the beauty and tragedy of the profane and secular world. "I don't know how strong you like your tea. The scones are homemade."[19] It is in and through these moments that we *are* who we are as human beings; it is the everyday that profoundly shapes our self-understanding. Theological anthropology takes root, then, not elevated from the world and looking in on ourselves, but in changing diapers, and doing laundry, and commuting into work, and riding the subway, and welcoming a friend, or teaching a class, operating on a sick patient, or waiting in line for food stamps. "And this is something you should taste, it's very delicious. And if you like it, you can . . . I am going to fix this for you."[20] It is in these moments that we succeed or fail as a human community. In the mundane, and the everyday, we feed to one another milk, and tea, and scones and salad, and love and hatred. What we feed one another we will eat . . . and we will become.

> I have been reading Adler's sermons. He says so well what I have long thought and believed—viz., that religion is life. How much happier life would be, if we made more of man and this world and thought less of future states of which we know nothing.
>
> Elizabeth Cady Stanton[21]

If religion is life, embedded in the everyday, we might find both the insights and the challenges of religion in the everyday. Among the most pressing questions facing persons under conditions of globalization in the twenty-first century is whether and how we are living our everyday-ness and sharing our future with persons of other faiths. With the increasing contact of persons across faith traditions in a world where information and people move swiftly through globalized systems, the possibilities for thinking together across religious traditions about what it means to be human presents itself with marvelous opportunity. "The group has been a circle of faith. . . . It has been a consistent reminder for me that I need to touch other people of faith, people who are traveling the same road and asking the same questions."[22]

This Theological Anthropology: A Labor of Love

I have thought about this work as not merely an academic exercise but, indeed, a labor of love. I recognized the importance of bringing to voice the experiences of women in various religious traditions for rethinking a Christian theological anthropology, but I have also admitted the possibility that their voices might never be heard. Uncertain as to whether this work would make a difference to anyone but myself, I had fallen in love with the Chinese women of Maryknoll, and the North American, Egyptian and Indian women struggling for rights, and the women of the Philadelphia Area Multifaith Dialogue Group bringing forth a better world. It is in love with them that this labor has been possible; it is this love that propelled the labor. The women I have met also labor in love. The women of Maryknoll were propelled by love—a love they thought they had to bring to China, but which they found there in friendships and life-long relationships. Women of the early feminist movement embraced the struggle in solidarity with other women for the love of generations to come. And the women of Philadelphia persevere in their interreligious dialogue simply because of love—their love for one another and creating a world more loving and more humane.

> My large room with a bay-window is the literary workshop. In the middle is a big library table, and there Susan and I sit *vis-à-vis*, laughing, talking, squabbling, day in and day out, buried in illegible manuscripts, old newspapers and reams of yellow sheets. We have the sun pouring in on us on all sides, and a bright wood fire in the grate, while a beautiful bouquet of

nasturtiums of every color stands on the table with a dish of grapes and pears.[23]

I have no live Susan B. Anthony with whom to sit vis-à-vis and talk, laugh or squabble as I do my work. But, the women whom I have loved in this endeavor are like Susan to me. So, too, are the women of many faiths who have accompanied me on my theological journey—Neelima, Amira, Julia and Homayra. Just as the two companions of early feminist theological thought, and the committee of *The Woman's Bible* endeavored to bring forth new knowledge among a community of women, so too these women of Maryknoll, of the secular women's movement, of Philadelphia, and life have been my conversation partners and my guides. With them I, too, seek a more just and humane world.

The cause of a more just and humane world is one shared across religious lines and with those who hold no specific religious affiliation. And, sadly, it is also a cause that must be turned inward. That is to say, our religious traditions themselves are the site of oppression, dehumanization and hatred. This often is at the expense specifically of the religious other, but there is also a parallel set of exclusionary ideas and practices that are directed internally against persons on the basis of sexual difference. The cause of feminist theology, then, drives this investigation bringing to light the voices and experiences of some among the excluded, simultaneously offering them for how they might expand our understanding of what it means to be human *and* how they might challenge it. In the words of Julia Ward Howe, spoken at the World's Parliament of Religion in 1893:

> I think nothing is religion which puts one individual absolutely above others, and surely nothing is religion which puts one sex above another. . . . And any religion which will sacrifice a certain set of human beings for the enjoyment or aggrandizement or advantage of another is no religion. . . . Any religion which sacrifices women to the brutality of men is no religion.[24]

Nothing is religion which does these things, and yet every religion in some way has done these things. Perhaps nothing is religion since each has been mobilized to put oneself above others.

The future of our religious traditions, however, is that they *might* be mobilized to bring forward a more humane and just world. In the vision of Elizabeth Cady Stanton,

"Equal rights for all" is the lesson this hour. "That cannot be," says some faithless conservative: "if you should distribute all things equally to-day they would be in the hands of the few to-morrow." Not if the religious conscience of the people were educated to believe that the way to salvation was not in creed and greed, but in doing justice to their fellow men.[25]

With Elizabeth Cady Stanton, we might embrace the theological commitment that the way to salvation is not in creed or greed, but in doing justice. But, the doing of justice itself does not fall from the sky. It is visioned and enacted from out of our particularity—a particularity that is shaped and transmitted in and through our religious traditions. From my perspective as a Christian feminist theologian the story of Jesus of Nazareth remembered in the New Testament *can be* a story that visions justice. In the investigation that follows, I aim to do two things: to bring to light the as-yet-unwritten histories of women's interfaith encounter as a site for doing theology, and to think with the resources of the Christian tradition to write the story forward in a trajectory of justice. In all of this it will become clear that my methodology insists on our religious traditions as important frameworks for encountering and organizing the data of 'reality', and as discourses themselves that are constructed by our human interaction with that reality. Theology is, after all, a profoundly human endeavor, as we seek to bring to light and to life the mystery that Christians call 'God.' May we be honest in our recognition that the project of Christian theology has not always been a project that enables human loving-kindness and justice, may we be gentle in our care for ourselves past and future, and may we be bold in our pursuit of a more humane world. Sisters, into your hands I commend my Spirit.

PART I

In Mission and Motherhood

1 Encounter in the Mission Fields

ENGENDERING DIALOGUE WITH WOMEN OF CHINA

The Mission Imagination

"Pagan Babies—Save Them for Christ Through Maryknoll."[1] So, the caption reads on a promotional poster (circa 1929) that helped shape American Catholics in their imaginings of people of other faiths. With a pagoda in the background and the silhouette of two Chinese youngsters in the foreground, the idea of the religious other as 'pagan' all but erased their distinctive humanity. The specter of paganism cast long shadows over the people of China as the American Catholic public was urged to commit their concern through prayer and financial support. "Every Catholic student should know what the Church is doing in the Orient," reads another poster from the same era: "How Christ's soldiers are fighting the forces of paganism."[2]

A small group of American women religious helped shape the Catholic perception of Chinese religious 'others' through their work with Maryknoll, a religious order established in 1911 as the Catholic Foreign Mission Society of America. In the order's beginning, the Sisters played primarily a supporting role in the organization, often serving as stand-in cooks for the young seminarians and, more notably, helping to produce and distribute *The Field Afar*, a magazine styled after the popular magazine *Life* and designed to spread information and encourage the support of Maryknoll priests.[3] Assembling the materials to be sent to press, the women of Maryknoll participated in the shaping of the religious imagination of the readers as the magazine encouraged donations with the advertisement "$5 will provide for the adoption of a Chinese baby, thereby rescuing it from paganism."[4] These efforts were promoted as desperately needed, as the publication page of *The Field Afar* announced that "in seven large areas of the Orient—in South China, Japan, Manchukuo, and Korea—Maryknollers are laboring among 20,000,000 pagan souls."[5] Indeed, the work of Christian missions in China was described in the magazine as being amid a "sea of paganism."[6]

While the women of Maryknoll had a hand in shaping the American religious imagination as they passed along the information transmitted to them by the American priests in China, they in turn were shaped by these same currents of thought. Viewed as the 'religious other' from afar, Chinese persons of native faiths stood as anonymous shadows in need of the saving power of Christianity. When the Maryknoll women were finally enlisted to help convert 'pagan' women, the imaginations of these newly college-educated women were captured by the uplifting, expansive, and ultimate goal of doing God's work of saving souls. As Mary Rose Leifels articulates it, "I felt we were there to get souls."[7] Sister Rosalia Kettl recalls that she entered the mission field "to save souls in heathen lands." In her oral history (1981) she reflects, "I just hoped that I could win many souls for Christ in the terminology of that day."[8] The theological horizon of Christian inclusivism heralded by Vatican II was still many years off, and the concern for the souls of the unconverted continued to be driven by the idea "Outside the Church, no salvation."[9]

But, when they came to know the Chinese women in their daily encounters with them, the Catholic women recognized more than isolated souls needing to be saved. No longer anonymous pagans, the Chinese women became their friends. While the endeavor to enlighten pagan peoples propelled Christian conversions in this era, the story of the Maryknoll Sisters is one of a different sort of conversion. Entering the field to rescue native women from their pagan practices, the American women saw their potential converts as empty slates on whose hearts the gospel was waiting to be written. Entering the homes of the Chinese women, they encountered persons with complex lives, whose hearts were already filled with hospitality and overflowed with relationship. The Christian women were even offered the opportunity to appreciate the religious practices of non-Christian forms. Becoming friends with the women of China, the Maryknoll Sisters in the first half of the twentieth century found their theological presuppositions challenged, and changed. The conversion was theirs.

While the study of Christian missions is only rarely identified through the category of 'interreligious dialogue', it is one of the few places where we have records of women's interfaith engagement. Surely, the framework held by the Christian Maryknoll Sisters was not the neutral arena of comparative discourse on religious matters that many envision of interreligious dialogue today. Nonetheless, in order to share their Christian faith, the women of Maryknoll needed to undertake processes similar to those necessary for interfaith dialogue today. They needed to get to know their dialogue partners in all their complex humanity; they needed to understand the social location of their 'dialogue partners', and they needed to articulate clearly, in language their partners could understand, the basics of their faith. In the process, the Christian Sisters 'wrote the faith forward', allowing their inherited tradition to be shaped by the encounter. The investigation of women's interfaith engagement through the experience of Maryknoll Sisters in China provides resources also for thinking about our interfaith engagements today; and their commitment to fostering relationships provides a resource for thinking anew about the Christian interfaith encounter. We also gain access to the most fundamental aspects of our human condition, as interfaith dialogue reveals as much about our humanity as it does about our faiths.

Maryknoll Women in Mission

As Penny Lernoux writes:

> As the [Maryknoll] seminary grew, so too, the women's work. Wanting his small group to be self-sustaining, [Father James Edward] Walsh established a farm with livestock and fruits and vegetables planted by the seminarians. In addition to office work, sewing for the seminary, and making its bread, the women fed the animals, drew water from their rain-filled well, did the laundry, cared for the gardens, and picked and canned so many vegetables and fruits that they came to hate the sight of beans and berries.[10]

Although at least two of the four original women-helpers had successfully completed their college studies at Wellesley and Smith, the initial experience replicated the gendered expectations of society as the women were responsible for the home-care of male priests who would enter the public realm. Or as Margaret Shea (Sister Gemma of Maryknoll) recalls, in the family of Maryknoll, "the woman's part was quite naturally ours."[11] While the women were integral to the life of the organization, the structure of Maryknoll separated men and women to distinct roles and separate lives.

The same pattern of gendered separation structured the work of the male priests who entered Maryknoll's mission field in China. Although the women's movement in China is recognizable as early as 1914, traditional segregation of women and men continued to shape the settings in which the Maryknoll priests undertook their mission.[12] It would be the mark of impropriety for a woman in China to be conversing with an unknown man, and to be willing to do so publicly with foreign male missioners was incredibly unlikely. While gendered expectations were not the only reason why conversions would come slowly, the segregation of women and men was identified as a key obstacle in the success of Maryknoll missions. It wasn't long before it became clear that a greater degree of participation by these women as full members in mission was essential to the organization's success. Sister Mary Imelda Sheridan writes:

> Bishop [Francis] Ford realized on his own mission journeys that any plan for the conversion of souls would be incomplete if it did not provide women Apostles for the evangelization of women. He was convinced back as far as 1919 that owing to social conditions in China where there was at that time such a distinct line of separation between the sexes, that the training of Sisters for the direct apostolate was indispensable. . . . However, it was not until 1934 that his plan was effected. . . . And He sent them two and two into every town and village teaching the Word of God.[13]

The Catholic Sisters were to serve as representatives to Chinese women in places where Catholic priests could not go.

Under the initiative of Bishop Ford, the women of Maryknoll were empowered to encounter Chinese women. But Ford also continued to shape their imagination regarding just what sort of women they would meet. For example, he served as mentor to the Sisters and led retreats where he engaged their work in China. In one such retreat, Ford considered Jesus' words from the New Testament, "This is my new commandment, that you love one another." From the retreat diary, we see Ford's view of the religious-other in his own words:

> [This] is the Christian Commandment. You notice that very strongly in a pagan country. In China there is no conception of the idea of love for one another. Mothers sell their daughters; if they have any love for them at all,—they sell their daughters. If they are very practical, they simply

destroy them. Fathers will bargain over the price of a child as if it were a pound of meat. Wives are cast out and others taken in on a whim. They haven't what we are accustomed to, love.[14]

From Ford's reflections we see that the religious other was not merely painted as an unknown shadow but even portrayed as a known evil. To argue that the Chinese have no conception of love could not help but inform the negative expectations of the Sisters. Given the way the Maryknoll women were shaped by the theological currents they encountered, it is not surprising that one of the first Maryknoll women in Chinese mission wrote home to her family: "Please pray that we learn the language soon, for indeed there are countless opportunities here for planting the seeds of Faith in many hearts that now have such hard and loveless lives. Christian charity needs to shed its light into this pagan darkness."[15]

"Hard and loveless lives," women living in "pagan darkness" and needing the salvation that could only be offered by Christian women—this was the portrait of Chinese women held in the religious imagination of Maryknoll Sisters, shaped by sermons, promotional posters, and glossy magazine pages. Shaped by these sources and sharing in this outlook, the American women of Maryknoll stepped into this portrait only to find a very different Chinese woman.[16] The Chinese women the Maryknoll Sisters came to know were multi-relational, keepers of promises, and complex companions. While the shadow of paganism proved difficult to shake, the women of Maryknoll nevertheless were provided the opportunity to get to know some of the women of China and to call them friends.

The Apostolate of Friendliness: In the Fields and among Families

To meet with these women they would come to call friends, the Maryknoll Sisters undertook a unique form of mission practice, which, as one historian notes, "revolutionized the role of religious women in the work of evangelization."[17] As Lernoux describes it: "In the early 1930s, the Sisters expanded to the northeastern section of Kwantung province, where the Hakka people lived. In contrast to earlier missions where the Maryknollers were engaged in traditional institutional work, such as schools and orphanages, they pioneered a new approach by going out to the people, often living for weeks at a time in the homes of the villagers."[18]

They would walk through Chinese villages in full habit, dressed from head to toe in a long dress and head covering, their primary aim being to meet other women and talk about their faith. Their main objective was to weave themselves into the lives of ordinary women in order to share with them the gospel message they so dearly loved.[19] In the mid-1930s this was still a bold thing for American women to do—to be so far away from home, independent of family responsibilities, engaging in the work of faith. But it also was not an easy project. Under Ford's direction, the Sisters recognized that there was much they needed to do in order to be in a position to share their theological witness with the women of China. As Sister Paulita Hoffmann recalls:

> [Ford] said, "Learn their language and learn the way they do things. Find out what they're doing—then you've got an in with them. Then you understand what they're talking about! You understand what their life is all about. Then you can relate . . . what Christ is telling them in their daily life to what it is. You can tie up the gospel with what their lives are if you know them."[20]

The Sisters took to heart the method of encounter outlined by their mentor. Indeed, going out into village and countryside required a process of inculturation that first necessitated a textured understanding of the lived experience of those they would meet. As Hoffmann further explains, "We [had] to be the ones to put ourselves into the rhythm of their lives, to understand their lives and then work, be with [them,] and in the midst of [their lives, bring] the word of God."[21]

In her description of mission work, Sister M. Marcelline describes the Kaying mission of 1938, writing that "we have dedicated ourselves in a special way to the women of Hakka China." As part of a "triple aposto-late" that included also teaching and visiting, the primary contact of Maryknoll women in this interfaith encounter came to be known as "the apostolate of friendliness." Sister M. Marcelline describes it in this way:

> First, there is the apostolate of friendliness, through which [we] hope to radiate Christ's love, that powerful magnet that draws souls to Him, pro-vided we, ourselves, put no obstacle in the way of its action. It is often just a smile—a smile imbued with the Message, or a friendly hand, sensibly conveying our yearning spiritual interest, that has been the means of getting a soul engaged in the search after the true God. Or again, it was

a friendly word, perhaps answering the question so often put to us, "Why did you come to China?" . . . Having heard us, some have gone away untouched; others have listened, and rejoicing have answered the call, while we went on, believing in the apostolate of friendliness, as the best first contact that we know.[22]

Prior to engaging in any theological conversation, the Sisters first offered friendship and friendliness. They had to open themselves to relationship and the many complex dimensions of the women's lives in order to be in a place to engage theologically. And, while the Maryknoll women were empowered by their roles as missionaries and encouraged by Ford as their mentor to meet Chinese women in their daily lives, they were also empowered by the warm reception they received from the women of China. In entry after entry of the Sisters' diaries, there seems a natural air of encounter such that the apostolate of friendliness reflects the extending of friendship by the Chinese women as well. In a letter home, Anna Mary Moss recalls, "At a pagan home last week the woman showed two of us all around her Chinese cottage and then through the garden and ended by sending the Sisters home with the biggest turnips in the garden, enough for our dinner."[23] And as is recounted in the Sisters' Kaying diaries:

And so when Sister Rosalia and A Yn Tsi found themselves off on a wild goose chase into a village which had never heard of 'so and so,'—they were inclined to feel rather helpless, and so decided to sit down on the side of the road and see what would happen. And happen it did for along came two little maids carrying their heavy bundles of firewood from the hills, and going into their village they spread the news far and wide of the strange sight they had seen on the hillside. And soon after an old lady waved at us from her ancestral home at the foot of the hill, and then the family appeared from everywhere, and we were their welcome guests. And an hour later, we left with reluctance, our hearts warmed by their friendliness and our two little maids running to give us their gift of berries they had picked on the hillside. . . .

September 9, 1936

In one house, we discovered a little boy of five, who had been baptized 'in foreign,' although his parents still remain pagan, for some strange reason. The little girl-mother, a sweet little lass of no more than nineteen, seemed quite taken with the Sisters, and promised [sic] to come and visit us soon—and so we left with hearts warmed by the simple hospitality and with a feeling that we were their friends.

November 6, 1936[24]

The apostolate of friendliness clearly relied on the friendliness of Chinese women.

Because women in the Chinese countryside were responsible for much of the farmwork that supported their families, this meant that the American Sisters often went to the fields as the first point of contact. In the writings of Maryknoll Sister Mary Rosalia Kettl—whose memoir *One Inch of Splendor* is announced for sale in *The Field Afar* for $1.00— Chinese women emerge from out of the shadows and into the sunshine of fieldwork and friendliness.[25] Kettl captures the apostolate of friendliness: "'And how is the field work today?' we called across the watery embankment, while our rubbers slipped perilously over the soft mud. 'How wonderful it is that the rain has come!' Sometimes the chats were quite prolonged. We had plenty of time, and the women were most friendly."[26]

Even the most casual encounter with Chinese women in the fields provided the opportunity for an appreciation of the commitments among women's lives, as Anna Mary Moss writes from China to her father in America (1935):

> This is surely one science the Chinese have down to perfection. They work very hard during this season. And they all help each other. We stood on the paddy around Mrs. Lim's little field watching the group of women transplanting the rice for her as she was ill and unable to do it herself. They chatted good-naturedly with us, all the time working skillfully with both hands, pulling up the tender shoots, wrapping them in bundles with straw, and the[n] throwing them up on the paddies to be transplanted elsewhere.[27]

As the Sisters began to weave themselves into the lives of Chinese women, the portraits in their imagination began to transform. They find the women to be, instead of blind and in joyless darkness, "good-natured," "welcoming," and "naturally religious."[28] In the memory of Sister Rosalia Kettl, "and so we just went around, I would say, visiting in a way that we knew how, we would just go to a home and see a group of women sitting there and we would go in and we were it seemed as though we were always welcome."[29]

Drawn to the mission fields for the express purpose of converting Chinese women, the simple fact of being present in this non-Christian context provided a unique opportunity for Christians of the era to encounter non-Christian peoples. While the primary setting was in the direct outreach to the women of Hakkaland, there is evidence of ongoing relationships with non-Christians who supported the very practical day-to-day workings of the mission enterprise. Efforts of conversion were a primary aim, but they were by no means the only style of relationship Maryknoll women undertook as they lived and worked among non-Christian peoples. As Lernoux describes it:

> Their convent was actually a rented part of a peasant home, usually one or two rooms, from which the Sisters would go out to other villages. While one stayed at the "convent" to provide religious instruction for those in the area, the other traveled with a Chinese woman catechist to preach the Good News, walking four, five, sometimes thirty miles a day to meet with Chinese women in outlying regions.[30]

The 'peasant homes' that the women rented as their home base were often the homes of non-Christians. And as the women continued their efforts of evangelization, they met the native women in their own arenas—that is, in 'pagan homes.' And so the Maryknoll women also encountered people of other faiths in their practical relationships, which were often sustained over a long period of time. Sister Mary Rose Liefels recalls:

> I remember my first mission trip, I think it was with Sister de Lourdes. We remained a week or more away from the Yeungkong Center and lived at a pagan's house in Sheung Yeung. This pagan, Mr. Ew was very friendly with the Fathers. He was the principal man in the village it seemed and the wealthiest. The Fathers not only stayed there during their mission visits to the Christians, but said mass in his main room, and he was pleased to have the Sisters remain there on their visits.[31]

Following the paths set by the Maryknoll fathers, the Sisters lived and prayed in 'pagan' homes, and as they extended their evangelization efforts they did so having been welcomed into 'pagan' households as well. The livelihood of these Catholic women in mission relied on the kindness and hospitality of non-Christians.

In addition to witnessing the way the Catholic women were welcomed by the non-Christian Chinese, the diary descriptions of home visits also reveals the way the Maryknoll Sisters encountered the women of China not through their religious identities alone. That is, while interested in their religious practices, they met the women in their everyday practice. By visiting them in the home and adjusting the mission practice to the living responsibilities of the Chinese women, the Maryknoll Sisters met the women in their embedded complexity. In her memoir, Sister Mary Rosalia / Mary Martha Kettl writes:

> We arrived at the household of the Liou's, a pagan family. . . .
>
> Here we entered, and immediately came upon women engaged in domestic tasks. One was feeding chickens. . . . The women looked up from their work and greeted us. They were plainly a bit curious, and one seemed a little frightened. It was an unusual occurrence to have visitors, especially queer-looking foreigners such as we appeared to be. But on the whole they were friendly and soon came crowding around us. Out of the rooms and halls came other women, among them the one for whom we were looking, Fout Bac Me. . . .
>
> And so, there in the main *tong* of the house of the family of Liou, in view of the swinging lanterns and the green of the rice fields, we sat and tried to grow into the life of those about us. There was a crowd present. One woman squatted on the floor and joined in the talk while her fingers busily plied the needle on a dress she was making. Another brought vegetables which she was cleaning in preparation for the noonday meal, and one busy housewife raised clouds of dust by vigorously sifting the husks of wheat through a huge bamboo sieve. Some stood by with babies strapped to their backs or sleeping in their arms. One woman picked up the crucifix on my rosary and asked what it meant. The gathering was a happy, informal one.[32]

To 'grow into the life of those about us' required that the Sisters be present not just as dialogue partners but as friends woven into the fabric of daily lives: dressmaking and vegetable cleaning, food preparation and child care. Honoring the responsibilities of their new friends, Sister Mary Rosalia Kettl describes the way this encounter was structured to meet the native women in the multiplicity of their lives. This approach would have an advantage over other mission strategies of the day. Kwok Pui-lan describes Protestant women in the nineteenth century engaged in mission work who also aimed at meeting Chinese women. And yet,

> women who could afford the time to participate in religious activities were those relatively free of household duties. Older women could come

to religious meetings and even accompany missionaries on itinerations; young girls before the age of puberty would join the Sabbath schools and station classes. Nineteenth-century missionary reports often lamented that married women would not afford the time to attend religious activities or to come to station classes.[33]

Quite different from mission practices that would require the disengagement from family responsibilities (and therefore would be impossible for most women), the encounter of Maryknoll was structured to meet women in their embedded lives. This not only brought them into the vibrant lives of 'pagan homes' but out into the fields as well, and it continued as Chinese women agreed to learn more about the Christian faith that Maryknoll women were so eager to share. As Lernoux describes it,

> the Sisters' work followed the seasons. During planting and harvesting times, the peasant women only had free time at night after the supper had been cooked, the animals fed, and the children bathed. So the Maryknollers would often accompany them in the fields or the kitchen, teaching them a rudimentary catechism and talking about their hopes and woes as they picked peanuts together or prepared the evening rice.[34]

Maryknoll Sister Paulita Hoffmann recalled that "because not many women went to school, everything had to be learned by rote. So I sat out with them in the fields, digging sweet potatoes . . . or picking the peanuts off the stalk," and in this setting she would share the basics of the Christian faith.[35]

In approaching this interreligious encounter with a recognition of the complex distinctiveness of the women they would meet, the Maryknoll Sisters were challenged to transform their mission practice. Not only were most of the women they encountered illiterate, but the language they spoke was specific to their everyday concerns. The Catholic Sisters understood that, to meet women in their lived experience, they would need to adapt not only their missionary approach but also their teaching style and language. The challenge of speaking theologically with the Chinese women was an issue not only of translation but also of the multiple levels of language native to the Chinese context. There was the literary language, a spoken language used in schools, and a colloquial 'earth language'. This last layer was the only language the women, who had no formal school education, knew. Bishop Ford's suggestion to the Maryknoll Sisters was to "go into the Kitchens—get the womens' [sic] daily down to earth expressions, stories, etc., and incorporate it" into their teaching.[36] As Paulita Hoffmann explains,

> every word would have to be said in their colloquial language. . . . So you really had to . . . explain the characters so that they would understand the meaning of those prayers. The Mass prayers the same way, they were very literary. . . . Then you had the catechism which was in Pai Hua. So that was more understandable. That was understandable to students but not to the women from the kitchen! Because that's not what they spoke!
>
> Then you had tutom. And what was 'tu' is the language and 'tom' was the earth language. Well, the tutom was the way, woman-to-woman, would speak over the back fence. You know, "how is your kitchen stove?" and "I burn this and I burn that, and I burn fire." It's a completely different language!!
>
> So we studied the catechism, we studied the doctrine and all those. Bishop Ford, I guess about the second year the sisters were there or the third year, he said, "You know, we're never going to get to these people until we get into their kitchens. And the women are in the kitchens. The women really have the feel of the sentiment of the children. They instill knowledge into those children—into the heart. And we won't know them until we get into (he always used the word kitchen) the kitchen."
>
> What he meant is that that was the heart and the center of the real core of their thinking that governed them. So he said, "We could talk all this beautiful language about the doctrine and they wouldn't understand it." But he said, "You have to use their examples, you have to use their language, to have to [sic] use their words to take the concepts of the doctrine and put it into that." So he said, "You sisters have to do it. You're the only ones here."[37]

And the Sisters did. They made a book of Christian stories on the commandments and the stories of Jesus in 'earth language', creating, in effect a 'Hakka Catechism.'[38] From reflections on this endeavor, we see elements of the theology that structured this encounter:

> Slowly, in the simple language of these women folk, we told them of God who loves them, who gives them the rain for their fields and the light of the sun for their work. He it is who gives to them the beautiful young daughters and the strong agile sons which the scrolls described as the 'hope of the household.'[39]

We often think of interreligious encounter to be a meeting of foreign religious identities conversing over the details of doctrine. But the

Maryknoll encounter calls to mind a meeting at the heart of a different set of concerns—that is, the daily workings of the kitchen, the everyday practices that are the rhythm of our lives. Ford had an insight, that the heart of the lives of the Chinese women was in the workings of family and relationships and responsibilities; and Rosalia Kettl extended that insight to recognize God present there—in the rain of the fields and the sun of their work, in the beautiful daughters and agile sons. In Kettl's own theological understanding, the women were not waiting for Christians to bring God to them in the separate realm of Sunday mass or catechesis. God already met these women in the rhythm of their lives.

A Dialogue among Women

As the Maryknoll Sisters aimed to expand on the witness to God present in their lives, they further introduced Christian teachings and prayers and the fundamentals of the catechism. But, speaking women-to-women and aiming to connect with the relationships that structured women's lives, the Sisters realized that the catechism they had translated did not hold any specific teachings on women. When faced with a lacuna in resources for Christian understanding, the Sisters wrote the faith forward by preparing a 'lecture' on women in society (the last in a series of twenty-five catechetical tracts prepared for the women of China). Arguing a fundamental equality among the sexes, the teaching reads:

> Women like men are created by God, woman has a soul, body joined to become a human being the same as a man. Men have ears, eyes, hands, feet, he can walk, move, see, h[e]ar. Women are the same they have ears, eyes, hands, feet able to walk, move, see and hear; men have intellect, emotions, women are the same they have an intellect and emotions. Men have free will, women also have free will. Men want to study, want to [gain] abilities, obtain wisdom to enable them to truly attain blessings and a better life. Women also want to study, want to gain abilities, obtain wisdom to enable them . . . to enjoy a better life. As men, they too want to share in the benefits of this life. Because people were created to live in this world and enjoy the good blessings so after death they could enjoy the joys of heaven, this was the original purpose of God in creating mankind. Regardless of man or woman all were to enjoy this, no division of man and woman—no division of people, sexes, all were created *EQUAL*.[40]

This feminist theological sentiment is witness to the growing women's movement in the early twentieth century. Both in their teaching and in

their mission endeavor, the women of Maryknoll in China were challenging the gendered roles of American society, where expectations continued to define women's place as influencing the home. Like many of the
mission women who transgressed the social boundaries that might have
kept them in America or Europe, the women of Maryknoll often saw
their mission work attending to women's perceived subordination in
Chinese culture.[41] Many of the Sisters recall this element as a distinctive
gift of Christianity. When asked in interview, "Do you think your work
among the Chinese women helped to improve the role of women among
the Chinese?" one Sister responded:

> Oh . . . decidedly Sister. Because it gave the women a status in their own
> families. They were looked upon now. "You're Christian and I'm Christian,
> my husband and my sons . . . we're all Catholics and we're all the same."
> So I think it really raised them. I also think it helped the daughters-in-law
> a great deal in a family where there was a Catholic marriage or a Catholic
> married into a family. See, because once the family is Christian then we
> look at each other from a completely different viewpoint.[42]

A comparison with the Confucian ethos and family structure affirms
that the Christian outlook may have changed familial relationships. As
Kwok Pui-lan reports, with the introduction of Christianity in China in
the nineteenth century, "the Chinese gentry saw the introduction of a
new religious system as iconoclastic, threatening the social fabric of the
traditional order. The Christian teaching that all human beings are brothers and sisters before God, for example, would undermine hierarchical
social relationships in the family and society. Some of the anti-Christian
writings accused Christianity of upsetting the established social order
stipulated by Confucian teachings."[43]

Catholic missionaries and native Chinese alike may have perceived
Christianity to transform the social order with respect to women, but the
actual introduction of 'women's status' to the Catholic catechism reveals
a more complex reality. In the Hakka manual prepared by the Sisters, it is
clearly stated that "all were created EQUAL" (emphasis in the original).
And yet the teaching continues: "In their relations there has to be order.
The wife should obey her husband because truly he is bigger than she
is—all important things, and difficult things, the man should take
care of—the woman should handle the minor things of the family."[44] The
Hakka Catechism reveals a complex tension between raising women's

status and defending traditional gender roles (both Christian and Confucian). As they attempted to communicate the 'Christian' stance, there is evidence that the women of Maryknoll were being shaped by multiple and perhaps conflicting sources.

While the women's movement addressed the 'women's question' primarily in relation to men, the application of the idea of 'Christian equality' also points toward the more complicated relationality that structured the Chinese women's lives. For social relationships were governed along not only gendered lines but several axes of relationality, not least among them being the relationship between mothers-in-law and daughters-in-law. Paulita Hoffmann explains:

> And then you have mothers-in-law and daughters-in-law, and so help me God. God help me, you know, here we are, you know, and I can kneel next to my mother-in-law and I can receive communion just like she receives communion; and I can sit in the sodality meeting just as she sits in the sodality meeting; and I can hold up my hand to vote just like she holds up her hand to vote. Before that—um-umm [no]. You know, *I* represent the family and carry the keys and I dole out the rice; but now well it's a different situation. We have personal value, and I think those things were stressed; and when we realize that, you know, we're all brothers and sisters our Father who art in heaven! God help me, you can't change anything from that.[45]

The Chinese women with whom the Maryknoll Sisters wrote their faith forward were embedded in responsibilities that took on a variety of shades and revealed the diversity of relationality that constituted them. Woman was not 'woman' only but possibly mother-in-law or daughter-in-law, mother, daughter, wife, and more.

Speaking 'woman-to-woman' demanded that the Sisters of Maryknoll write the catechism forward in order to discuss the Christian view of women. Further, their direct encounter in the lives of Chinese women provided the platform from which they challenged their received tradition. For example, it is clear that the social arrangement of multiple wives/concubines did not fit the nuclear-family model brought in by the Western framework and Catholic teaching. As several of the Sisters recall, it was a practice that stood as a roadblock to conversion. The Western Christian perspective insisted that this practice of polygamy (or concubinage) was contrary to the gospel.[46] Julia Hannigan recalls that "the

[Church] law that a man couldn't take a concubine—that was a stumbling block, too, for some."[47] And as Mary Rose Liefels recalls, many of the 'pagan homes' in which the Maryknoll Fathers and Sisters stayed were headed by polygamous householders. The same Mr. Ew who hosted the Fathers and Sisters in Sheung Yeung, and in whose home the Fathers celebrated mass, "had several wives, according to pagan customs."[48] And though Mr. Ew's first wife and some of his sons were baptized, Mr. Ew does not appear to have had any intention of converting. Paulita Hoffmann reflects, "Well, I think concubinage—you know, like having a second wife, that was a problem that was hard for a lot of them."[49]

But, the Sisters' embeddedness in the lives of Chinese women allowed them to consider this situation from women's perspectives. Sister Julia Hannigan recalls an exchange with Bishop Ford during one of their many retreats:

> I think I remember that once there was a question about a concubine who wanted to be a Catholic and I think he said that if she would break-off relations with the man, she could be baptized. And I think I said, "Suppose she is not willing to do that?" I remember he seemed startled at my question and raised the little cap he wore—a habit I noticed in him if you took him by surprise.[50]

Hannigan in her recollection of the exchange goes on to comment that Bishop Ford did not have any easy answers and that native customs often were the source of challenges to Western expectations. In Ford's mission practice, he encouraged the missioners to consider things from the Chinese perspective. As Hannigan recalls, "he told us, 'the customer is always right', meaning the Chinese to whom we were (in a sense) selling the good news of the Gospel."[51] The encouragement to see things from the 'other's' perspective allowed Maryknoll Sisters the opportunity to consider the experience of Chinese women not merely as Western Christianity would dictate it but from out of the complexity of the women's lived experience.

A more intimate knowledge of the complexity of actual women's lives allowed the Maryknoll Sisters to gain a new understanding of Chinese women and even possibly to communicate this to Americans back home. Rosalia Kettl writes of a Chinese Christian woman who

> kept the Faith in spite of the fact that, when her husband brought her to his ancestral village in China, she discovered waiting for her a first wife

whom she had not known existed. The husband [was] a villain of villains, who kept the whole household dancing with bellowed orders. The two wives soon became friends, for they evidently believed that in union lay strength.[52]

While most mission materials viewed the situation of multiple wives from the perspective of Church teaching and/or from the perspective of the husband and first wife—shunning all but the first wife and demanding that, as a precondition of his conversion, a man cut off social, sexual, economic, and familial relationships with any additional wives—Rosalia Kettl reads the situation differently. In an unusual turn, the two women are not pitied and shunned but appreciated for the solidarity and friendship they show to one another under adverse conditions. Through her writing, Kettl offered to the American religious imagination the opportunity to glimpse the situation from the perspective of the wives themselves.

The complexity of living in an extended family made 'conversion' to Christianity a complicated practice. Because the Maryknoll Sisters continued to desire the salvation of souls, it is not surprising that the language and literature of these Christian women communicates repeatedly the disappointment they experienced at the refusal or inability of their new Chinese friends to reject 'pagan ways' and convert wholly to Christianity. Forever encouraging the relinquishing of the age-old practices that punctuated Chinese women's lives and tied them to family members, friends, and society, the Maryknoll diaries are filled with recognition that the complete disengagement with native religious practices was a difficult process and full conversions successful only to a limited degree. In 1938, Sister M. Imelda writes from Rosary Convent in Kaying that "it was a disappointment to see a well-kept pagan shrine in the house, but it evidently belonged to the other members of the house."[53] Indeed, and by their own description, the women of Maryknoll set out to save souls, to win them over for Christ, to achieve conversion of the other. And at times, this desire was disappointed when their Chinese friends continued to carry out the practices that in Christian eyes appeared as 'pagan superstitions'.

Unfortunately, the negative assessment of pagan practices and the compulsion toward conversion often blinded the American Christian Sisters to the complexity and necessities of native women's lives. In the following snapshot, we hear Sister Rosalia Kettl experience the disappointment of a Chinese friend who participates in pagan practices that would form a roadblock to conversion. Yet, read against the grain, we hear more clearly the complex lives where economic and material necessities made conversion not merely theologically impossible but materially unappealing.

> Van Bac Me, too, returned to her home after a week or so of instruction. There it was that a Sister found her one morning, sitting before a small mountain of superstition papers, coloring them and pasting on silver tassels, for this was her means of livelihood. These papers are the back-bone of pagan worship. They embody all the things that pagans believe of the after-life, and are in great demand. To burn paper houses, money, clothing, and so on, at the grave is supposed to guarantee the deceased all his necessaries in the next world. The pasting and coloring of these papers is turned over by the shops to villagers who do the work in their homes. So Van Bac Me sat laboring at her stacks of yellow paper. When, in the catechumenate, the study of the First commandment had brought out the fact that all connection with these superstitions is barred to Catholics, Van Bac Me had made her decision. She had gone away, and she was not coming back—that was evident. It was a sorrow to us, but we resolved to keep her in mind and to visit her now and then. There will come a day when her hands can no longer work, and then God will still be waiting for her.[54]

At face value, this entry can suggest a blindness to the economic con-straints and agency of Chinese women. Yet it can also be read against the grain to access an understanding of some of the economic realities and agency of Chinese women who chose not to convert to Christianity, as Van Bac Me's decision against Christianity is a reasoned one.

Transformed by the Encounter

In theologizing about Christian missions, there may be a tendency to envision the catechetical process as a one-way endeavor: from Christian missionaries to their native converts. Given the intense missionary aims communicated in writings to home congregations, it is also tempting to envision the catechesis as streamlined toward theological understanding and to read the above entries as a single-minded pursuit of Catholic Christian doctrine whether in the fields, in the homes, or in the convent. But in the writings of the Maryknoll women, we get a sense of the way communications in mission contexts were woven more complicatedly in the actual lives of the people. Catechesis was frequently 'disrupted' by the living concerns of the women in courses of religious instruction. Sister Miriam Louise recalls from Kaying in 1939 that

> [catechism] classes frequently ended in stories galore about the pig which was to be butchered at the funeral of one of the catechumens present [*sic*]; about Precious Virtue, the one and only grandson in the world; or the six green vegetable seedlings which some one is raising to further substantiate the year's income—prompted by an old lady who has stolen away from school to be sure that her lone chicken is still being cared for, while she is at the Women's Church (as they call the sisters convent) studying the principle means of saving her soul.[55]

If we imagine a one-way catechetical process, we envision the native women learning much about Christianity but the Christians learning little about their interlocutors. The diaries of the Maryknoll Sisters tell a different story. They tell of catechism that moved excruciatingly slowly through the rhythms of Chinese women's lives, punctuated by living concerns about family, fields, economic challenges, and the multiple dimensions of women's lived situations.

Being woven into the intimate lives of women in China allowed the Maryknoll Sisters a chance to reshape their religious imagination and to challenge inherited teachings. While the Christian theology of the day insisted that pagan darkness ought to be dispelled by the Christian light of salvation, and that any person once introduced to the gospel would prefer Christian forms of worship and practice, the Maryknoll experience allowed some of the Sisters to appreciate the native religious practices and the reasoned decision of persons *not* to convert. In the new religious imagination of the Maryknoll Sisters, the Chinese women were not blank slates on which to write the message of the Christian gospel. They were complex human beings embedded in networks of relationships with material, social, emotional, and religious needs that were already being met by native forms. Sister Julia Hannigan recalls getting to know the mother of one of the Catholic doctors educated at Jesuit University in Shanghai. Hannigan remembers that

> his mother, who was a Buddhist, I believe, used to come to most of our Holy Days Celebrations at the Church. . . . One day I said to her, "What are you doing coming to a Catholic Church—you, a good Buddhist!" She said, "Sister, you know I made a promise to my parents that so long as

I had two hands to burn joss in front of our ancestral shrine, I would do it, in their memory. And I couldn't do that if I became a Catholic. . . . So I give my children the freedom to belong to whatever religion they want to. And I will keep my promise, as long as I have two hands, to burn joss."

Hannigan reflects that "at that time, I don't think the Church allowed Catholics to burn joss in front of Ancestral Shrines. . . . Nevertheless, her willingness to allow her children to do what they wanted, knowing that when she was gone, her children would not be allowed to burn joss in her memory, impressed me!"[56]

Julia Hannigan offers a window into a religious imagination that had been transformed. She recalls:

That was when I became more tolerant of other religions. . . . When I first went to China, I believed that without Baptism one cannot be saved. . . . I think that was my original desire—to spread the Faith and to see that people would be saved. 'To save souls', I think that's how we said it. . . . But in this particular setting, I myself, began to have a deeper appreciation of other religions. This one Chinese lady, the mother of the Catholic doctor, was a beautiful person.[57]

Far from being a loveless woman isolated in her pagan darkness, this particular Chinese woman, as Sister Hannigan recounts, was a keeper-of-promises, embedded in relationship to her ancestors and in relationship to her children—a woman who negotiated the diverse religious responsibilities in changing contexts, keeping the promise to her parents to maintain the ancestral shrine but providing freedom for her children even when it meant no shrine would be kept for her.

Rosalia Kettl describes a similar experience of getting to know the *people* even if she was not changed by their religious views:

I think the Chinese naturally are very religious people. You see very young people here in the temples, worshipping, but it is always, except for their funerals when they make a lot of noise and things like that everything is very quiet, and the whole atmosphere is one of like an individual interior living of what they believe, and I think you know that effects—even though you know we believe in our own interior spiritual life—I think that this atmosphere has helped me a great deal.[58]

The atmosphere of interior living accessed by being in the constant presence of the other and coming to see their embodied and embedded practices provided a distinctive means for appreciating the 'other'.

But this appreciation of the 'religious other' was not only the experience of Maryknoll women looking back on their time in mission. From the files of the archives, we see that it was an experience among the earliest Maryknoll women in mission. A caption on an otherwise unmarked photograph from the archive file of Anna Mary Moss reads: "This woman is a pagan, but a very good friend." In this telling inscription, this Catholic Sister, who was engaged in the task of evangelization, mission, and conversion, attempts to communicate something deeply positive (the woman pictured is 'a very good friend') from out of a nonetheless conflicted religious relationship (she is, after all, still a pagan). While the religious imagination of the day encouraged one to believe that being pagan left one in joyless darkness and misery (indeed, language that Anna Mary Moss herself employs in some of her early letters), the religious imagination of Maryknoll women demonstrates that the failure to adopt Christian ways and the decision to remain 'pagan' did not capture all of who the Chinese women were. Even if they chose not to convert, Chinese women could be appreciated as agents, economic participators, embedded in relationships, committed in their promise keeping. In the religious imagination of Maryknoll women, Chinese women could be both 'pagan' and 'friend'.

Paulita Hoffmann in a personal interview indicated that the experience of friendship with the non-Christian women of China changed her theological outlook. Expressing in her oral history that her goal in mission was "to save souls," in getting to know her neighbors of other faiths she could recognize their complex humanity and their deep religiosity. She confided that through this experience she realized that she could not believe in a God who would abandon these women. Knowing them, she said, she now knew something new about God. The experience of women of other faiths as 'friends' allowed the Maryknoll Sisters to challenge the theologies they had inherited. Having gotten to know so many women in China in their complex humanity, with their personal qualities in intimate relationship, who nonetheless chose not to convert to Christianity, Sister Hoffmann indicated that her understanding of God's relationship to diverse peoples had changed. Knowing her 'pagan friend', she realized that she could no longer believe that the Catholic faith was the only true way to experience God. Knowing this friend, she realized that "God could not possibly *not* be in relationship with her."[59]

In the examples of Rosalia Kettl, Anna Mary Moss, and Paulita Hoffmann, we see that interreligious encounter does not necessarily lead to understanding the 'other' even while it does offer the opportunity for appreciating her. The complex and interglossing system that is a religious tradition is not an easy field for comprehension. Indeed, as I have argued elsewhere, following George Lindbeck, religious traditions, like cultures and languages, are so holistic and comprehensive that unless we inhabit those traditions we cannot fully understand them.[60] In the preceding examples, the Maryknoll women did not pretend to understand the religious practices of their friends or those they came to know. They did not suggest that they had come to an understanding of the religious beliefs or systems or of why their friends preferred another religion to Christianity. In Kettl's appreciation, she underscores the difference between the forms of interior spiritual life represented by the Chinese people, and so she does not argue for an 'anonymous Christianity' in the reflection she undertakes. What all of these entries communicate is that an 'other' is known in personal relationship and that knowing her as friend has changed theological thinking, reshaped the religious imagination, and brought a new understanding of God.

That interreligious encounter might change our perceptions of the 'other' is a fundamental reason why interfaith dialogue continues to be a pressing concern. In considering how persons of different worldviews might live together in their difference, Kwame Anthony Appiah suggests that changes will come not so much from live debates over philosophical and religious differences but rather from getting to know one another in our all our complexity. As Appiah notes, social practices and ideologies change less from reasoned arguments than from getting to know people who hold different views.[61] This seems to have been the case with many of the Maryknoll women in China.

In the end, for many of the Maryknoll women the interfaith encounter that was their life in mission allowed them to see the women of China as friends. Compelled into mission in China for the purpose of 'saving souls', they grew into relationship with women of native faiths and toward an appreciation of them as complex human beings *and*, as Sister Hannigan recounts, "began to have a deeper appreciation of other religions."[62] We might also press on toward a theological reading of these interreligious encounters. What does it mean that it is the Chinese women whose hospitality provided the first point of engagement for the 'apostolate of friendliness'? The Chinese women offered their lives, their stories, their homes as the first point of contact for the mission work of Maryknoll Sisters. It is *their* hospitality and *their* friendliness that shines through in the Sisters' diaries. What does it mean that it is the Chinese 'pagan' who is 'welcoming the stranger', as the New Testament enjoins on all Christians? What does it mean that the heart and core of life and meaning is 'in the kitchen' for these Chinese women? The Christian virtue of hospitality and the sharing of a meal finds expression first and foremost from these 'pagan' women's lives.

It is no wonder, perhaps, that the Sisters are transformed theologically by their encounter. Paulita Hoffmann reflects: "I really think the Hakka Chinese people are some of the most beautiful people I have ever met! They're easy to get to know, they are friendly, they are sincere, they're happy and they take you in as part of the family—real part of the family. And they give, they give proof of deep respect, affection, regard, of real friendship."[63]

Rosalia Kettl comments:

Well, I think you know we in the West, we always think that being Catholic, you know we're always talking about perfection and—all these things that go with living a Christian life and so on, and we find that the Chinese very often can out-strip us in virtue, you know they're much more patient, and we really don't have that monopoly on virtue, you know, we really don't have it at all, just because we happen to be Catholic.[64]

Or, in the words of Paulita Hoffmann, once again, the Sisters often found a revelation of their own religious belonging in the life and practice of their interreligious 'others':

[We taught them] the knowledge of Jesus Christ. He was there all the time. They knew it. He was with them but they didn't recognize Him. They couldn't name Him. He was there but they didn't name Him. And then when they had an opportunity to listen to the doctrine they accepted it.[65]

This theology of the 'unknown Christ' echoes the approach of Karl Rahner, and it is not unproblematic from a twenty-first-century perspective. But from the perspective of women in mission in the middle of the twentieth century, the recognition of virtue and 'Christ' in the lives and practices of the Chinese women provides a reading of the encounter as one of genuine transformation. Perceiving the 'other' as inhabiting hard and loveless lives, the Maryknoll Sisters were welcomed into homes to share in relationship with their non-Christian friends. Unexpectedly, they found there the gifts that they themselves had sought to give: friendship and Christ.

A Different Dialogue

While not unproblematic in the construction of the 'other' that Maryknoll writings of the early twentieth century often convey, there is an important realization here even for twenty-first-century people. In our globalized world, we are increasingly encountering people of diverse faiths. We hold in our own religious imagination what it must mean to be 'Buddhist', 'Hindu', 'Christian', 'Jewish', 'pagan', or 'Muslim.' But the actual encounter with people of other faiths demonstrates, as it did for the Maryknoll women, that persons cannot be reduced to their religious identities. The construction of interfaith friendships, even if one does not understand the religious perspective of the 'other', is an important model that Maryknoll women in mission offer for persons even today.

The Sisters of Maryknoll invite twenty-first-century Christians to do the same. In our globalized world we have increased opportunities to get to know people of diverse faiths as friends. Yet given the challenges of understanding across religious differences, it is unlikely that most Christians will have the opportunity to study and understand the religious perspectives of friends of many faiths. However, we are invited to reshape our religious imagination and our theological thinking not by ever more study, textual analysis, and religious comparison but by appreciating the complex humanity of our friends and by trusting that they, too, could not possibly *not* be in relationship with God.

It is only recently that women's voices in interreligious dialogue have been investigated as the site of a different sort of religious encounter and exchange. Some of the initial conclusions that have been drawn suggest that women's participation in interreligious dialogue is different from mainstream religious exchange. One way of explaining this is by recognizing the unique location of women in religious traditions as being on the margins and therefore more willing to transform the faith in the process of conversation. As Chung Hyun Kyung concludes, interreligious dialogue among the male leaders of religious traditions perpetuates androcentric interpretations. She writes: "So-called, all higher world religions are patriarchal and are institutionalized under the patriarchal light. So we have patriarchal Buddhists and patriarchal Christians having interreligious dialogue, and we have nice patriarchal conclusions there."[66] But as Pamela Dickey Young and others have suggested women's experience within their traditions brings a different perspective. Young writes that "women, by their very presence in interreligious discussions, often question the 'official' stances of their traditions."[67] This seems to be the case in the Maryknoll expressions that ask after theological insights from out of women's experiences, questioning the teachings on multiple wives from the wives' perspectives, and challenging the official stance of Catholic theology from out of the experience of Chinese women as friends.

But there is a further suggestion made by those who study women's interfaith engagement—namely, that in the encounter, women have been willing to bring forth something new in their traditions by way of conversation with other faiths. "When I look at our women's religious experience very critically," Chung Hyun Kyung comments, "it is not a religious pluralism. It is sometimes syncretism, sometimes symbiosis, and sometimes a synergetic dance of many religions in our daily lives."[68] Indeed, something different can be seen when we look at interreligious dialogue not from the perspective of abstract theological exchange but from the lived reality of daily lives in encounter.

The structure of these interreligious encounters provides witness to the relationality that is fundamental to our human existence, our human condition. The Maryknoll encounter in China reminds us of a foundational premise for interreligious dialogue: We meet one another in multiplicity. We meet not as 'religious others' alone but in the complex embeddedness of our lives. That we meet in multiplicity holds the further illumination that we *are* in multiplicity. The nature of the human person is that we are complex, structured by the wide variety of relationships that create us. It is to that insight into our human condition that we now turn in chapter 2.

2 We Meet in Multiplicity

INSIGHTS FOR THEOLOGICAL ANTHROPOLOGY

What the mission strategy of the Maryknoll Sisters demonstrates is that in order to meet the 'other', we must meet in multiplicity. We meet one another not merely as 'religious others' but in a complex multiplicity constituted by relationship and responsibilities. This indicates not only that a meeting can be forged in this multiplicity of relationships but also that, as human beings, we are constituted in this way. To meet the other requires both the building of relationship and an awareness of the variety of relationships and responsibilities that constitute that person. In contrast to modernity's stress on the individual as the site of agency and identity, the fact of human existence illumined by the Maryknoll women in mission and their Chinese friends is that we are not isolated individuals but that our very 'self' is found in the web of relationships and responsibilities that form the fabric of our lives.

I'd like to pursue a move from historical evidence of interfaith encounter to theological insight through the working out of a theological anthropology. In part, this is because I think we learn as much about what it means to be human as we do about 'religion' when we look at interreligious exchange, dialogue, and encounter. And further, following the method of Karl Rahner, I want to affirm that the everyday experiences of our humanity can be illuminating for theology. Rahner invites us to suspend the terms of theology and start instead with experience of 'the matter itself' and to bring theological language to bear only after having examined our lived experience.[1] Such a method is essential for bringing to light the insights gained by women and others marginalized by traditions that have not considered their unique experiences as revealing fundamental dimensions of humanity and divinity. Rosemary Radford Ruether explains that "women must be able to speak out of their own experience of agony and victimization, survival, empowerment, and new life, as places of divine presence and, out of these revelatory experiences write new stories."[2]

Or in the words of Mercy Amba Oduyoye, "When we have learned more about our humanity, perhaps we will also be able to understand what God is telling us about divinity."[3] To see what women's experience illuminates about the human condition, the contrast with modern theological anthropologies is key.

Modes of Theological Anthropology

In the modern West, theological anthropology has been shaped by philosophical currents that emphasize the individual as a primary locus of identity. In Linell Elizabeth Cady's description of modern philosophical, social, and political trends, "The primary accent in the liberal vision falls on the individual abstracted from the relations through time and space that in any way limit or define him or her. The freedom and autonomy of the individual self are inviolate."[4] Quoting Iris Marion Young, Cady writes, "in this modernist ideology, 'the authentic self is autonomous, unified, free, and self-made, standing apart from history and affiliations, choosing its life plan entirely for itself.'"[5] In Cady's assessment, the result is that the autonomous individual in rational independence is the privileged way of identifying what it means to be human. The human person is first and foremost to be a free individual, making autonomous choices and independently directing one's self in the world.

The theological anthropology of Karl Rahner follows this pattern of privileging the independent individual. Constructing a theological anthropology with the resources of philosophy, Rahner pinpoints the fundamental characteristics of human being: "Man is person and subject."[6] Unpacking the meaning, Rahner insists that the most fundamental reality is the individualized self (person) comprised of spirit and matter and therefore capable of self-reflection and self-direction (subject). Underscoring the relationship to God in Spirit, Rahner privileges freedom and responsibility as fundamental human qualities, located distinctively in the individual subject.[7] This individual subject has the ability to move outside him- or herself in knowledge and love and so is also conditioned by the external realities of the world. So Rahner does recognize the relational aspect of humanity when he witnesses that the human person is social and "intended for community with other persons."[8]

Nevertheless, while there may be external realities that impact and shape the human person in his or her concrete life expression, there is a more fundamental reality that precedes this shaping. This more fundamental reality is the individualized self. Through a philosophical reflection on what is at the ground of our human experience, Rahner explains that "to say that man is person and subject, therefore, means first of all that man is someone who cannot be derived, who cannot be produced completely from other elements at our disposal."[9] His theological anthropology privileges the individualized subject who precedes the encounter with others and the world.[10]

But feminist insights question whether this individualized person ought to have priority in our theological anthropology. Instead, we are encouraged to ask whether the sociality and intersubjectivity of relationship aren't more fundamental. From a feminist perspective, the human condition isn't first that of solitude from which one then enters community; rather, sociality is primary in our human experience. In Luce Irigaray's feminist psychoanalytic approach, the solid subject of modernity is introduced to the fluid viscosity of postmodern thought.[11] The 'self' is not the solid subject acting out projects of discrete actions but rather constituted by a fluid relationality. Irigaray writes:

> You are moving. You never stay still. You never stay. You never "are." How can I say "you," when you are always other? How can I speak to you? You remain in flux, never congealing or solidifying. . . . These movements cannot be described as the passage from a beginning to an end. These rivers flow into no single, definitive sea. These streams are without fixed banks, this body without fixed boundaries. This unceasing mobility. This life— which will perhaps be called our restlessness, whims, pretenses, or lies. All this remains very strange to anyone claiming to stand on solid ground.[12]

Irigaray conceives the human person as always one constituted by the persons one encounters. "She herself enters into a ceaseless exchange of herself with the other without any possibility of identifying either."[13] Privileging relationality as the foundational human condition, Irigaray puts forth an anthropology that cannot be reduced to the individual. Rather, the self is constituted by relationships, where the boundary between self and other is permeable. Catherine Keller extends this understanding from a process perspective, describing our radical relatedness:

> I cannot exist without in some sense taking part in you, in the child I once was, in the breeze stirring the down on my arm, in the child starving

far away, in the flashing round of the spiral nebula. . . . I am not a separate and enduring substance but an event in which the universe composes itself. . . this subject does not precede its own experiences but arises from its relations.[14]

'I' am an event, constituted by the multiple relationships that form 'me'. I am an event constituted by 'others'.

Return then to the preceding exploration of Christian women in interreligious encounter and the stories of Maryknoll Sisters in mission. Viewed through a feminist lens, the fundamental condition of the women—their 'self' and self-understanding—was constituted by relationality. The Chinese women were not isolated individuals to be encountered and converted. They were embedded in their native religious and social practices and in relationships of economic and family responsibilities that intersected with them. Chinese women met Christian missionaries from within diverse social locations within the family (wives, second wives, daughters-in-law, mothers-in-law, daughters, mothers, and more), often inhabiting them simultaneously. Meeting the women of China in their embedded relationality allowed the Maryknoll Sisters to witness the multiple forms of relationality that structure human lives. At the same time, the Chinese women welcomed the Maryknoll Sisters into new forms of relationship and new understandings of themselves. Their lives reflect how fluid and dynamic networks of relationship form our self-understanding. Their example shows how our religious 'others' also shape our selves.

Motherhood as Site of Multiplicity and Insight into the Human Condition

In the writings of the Maryknoll Sisters in China, one of the key familial positions that introduced them to the multiplicity that their friends experienced was the subject-position of mother. Recall Kwok Pui-lan's insight that other missionary efforts could not encounter most women because of their familial responsibilities as wife and mother. As we saw in the preceding chapter, the Maryknoll Sisters met the women of China in the context of their familial responsibilities—in the fields and in the kitchen. When the Maryknoll Sisters invited their Chinese friends to participate in catechesis, with a view to conversion and the practice of the Christian faith, the Chinese women continued to bring their particular lives and responsibilities to their participation in this new faith. Many of them arrived at catechism class with baby in tow and the concerns of the home were not left at the door. As the Sisters recall:

> The opening of a catechumenate here in the interior of China has all the attending excitement of the opening of a kindergarten—and more. Youngsters bring with them their childish pranks; the young and middle aged women, with little ones tied to their backs who add noise and general disturbance to the class, insist on recalling the memory of their mother-in-laws [sic] at home; while the old ladies are ever interspersing the doctrine with their reports of various conditions of eye, ear, nose and throat, and physical well being in general.[15]

In the living space of catechesis, doctrine mingles with embodiment, and faith and family cannot be disentangled. In the 'dialogue' of the catechumenate, "There were mothers with babies. Babies cry. Occasionally these broke up a class, or set up a howl just at a moment when we were using all our powers of expression to put across our meaning in this Oriental tongue."[16] As the Chinese women extend themselves in the relations of this new faith practice, they continue in their role and commitment as mothers. "The little ones come to Mass with the mothers on Sunday after the first couple of weeks, and the feeding schedule goes on as usual in a very modest, hardly noticeable way."[17] "All the mothers bring their babies with them on Sunday. . . . One is a little clown and performs all during Mass."[18] Mothers reminded the Sisters of the ongoing relationality that constitutes our humanity.

To probe our relationality, I propose that we enter the examination from precisely this node of relationality: the social position of 'mother'.[19] In the traditions of psychology and child development, it is the mother who forms the first relationship that structures the 'self'. Yet, as we see from Sister Miriam Louise's description, the women who entered this interreligious space as mothers did so simultaneously as daughters-in-law. This subject position was sandwiched between 'the little ones tied to their backs' and the mothers-in-law who structured their home life; simultaneously, these mothers were in relationship with other women in the village catechumenate and with the Sisters as well. All this relationality was included in the extension to relationship with the Christian faith. This reminds us that relationality within the subject-position of 'mother' is not simply a child-bearing role but encompasses a multi-dimensionality of relationships that, in this case, included simultaneous relations between mother and child, wife and husband, mother and mother, mother-in-law and daughter-in-law, mother–child dyad and celibate religious sister, and others. Through the experience of these women, whom we have met through the interfaith encounter of Maryknoll in China, 'motherhood' emerges as a metaphor for our human condition in its multiplicity of relationality.

At the outset it is important to underscore that 'motherhood' is a *metaphor*—that is, a symbolic way of articulating a fundamental characteristic of *all* human beings. Selecting motherhood for this purpose entails two simultaneous gestures. First, it recognizably offers symbolic expression rooted in the lives of actual women.[20] A critical approach to theology demonstrates that what has counted as normative for humanity and has been offered as a theological anthropology was conditioned by the social location and contexts of male theologians. That is not to say that the theological anthropology thus produced did not provide insights to be more widely distributed beyond their context but only that the theologians' particularity as male theologians disclosed some realities of the human condition and not others. Motherhood as a point of departure might illumine new realities of the human condition. Yet, at the same time, as metaphor, 'motherhood' does not see the biological role of mother as requisite for all women or 'motherhood' as inherently female.[21] Here is the second point, equally important: While the symbolisms may be rooted in the subject-positions gendered female, the experiences they describe are not bound by gender or biology. The actions and relations engaged as 'mothers' provide content that can be applied to human beings regardless of biology and gender. While articulated in symbolic language rooted in women's experience, motherhood is more widely applicable— by invitation—to humanity at large.

By beginning with the mothers in Chinese mission, we underscore an insight into the human condition: that we are constituted by our relationality. As we move through the world, humanity is not found as the collection of isolated individuals. Rather, we have been formed by and continue to be formed in relationship with others. The 'self' exists in multiplicity, forged out of a diversity of relationships.

The Human Condition: Multiplicity and Relationality

I did not know this part of who I was until you came into being. I was never so stretched in my relationality before you needed me. I have never been so overwhelmed by what I did not know—life-and-death knowledge, critical knowledge for keeping you safe and alive—before I needed to know how you work. I have never been so amazed by my own need for creativity, or awed by the creativity of another, until I began to see you learning—learning to smile, to see, to sit, to crawl, to walk, to laugh, to communicate, to talk, to read, to feel. As you draw me into these dimensions of my self by your very being, I understand more clearly what Keller writes when she describes how, as subjects, we arise from our relationships.[22] My experience of motherhood has taught me a great deal about how the self develops. It is rooted, of course, in watching the selfhood of my children come into being in marvelous and astounding ways. But it is also about seeing a new self in myself come into being—the self that develops in relationship is necessarily stretched outside of individuality. As I experience the unavoidably permanent and ever-present relationality that is motherhood, I realize more clearly that all selves develop in relationship and we are all necessarily stretched out of our preconceptions of individuality.

At first glance, motherhood as metaphor has a dangerous shade of essentializing women's experience and reducing women's complexity to a single, socially determined role. But stepping into the subject-position of mother and bodily recognizing our relationality does not create that relationality. The primary reality of the human condition that the experience of motherhood illumines is that we are—all of us—embedded in relationality. We enter this world dependent on those who have preceded us, and we walk through this world in complex networks of care, dependence, and fragile solidarity. This was true of the mother even before she became mother, for she herself is embedded in relationship to her mother, to her father, to her partner, to her partner's family. As one steps into the subject-position of 'mother', one is not suddenly entering relationality; rather, the relationships with family, brothers and sisters, friends and the wider social networks continue to impact the subject. Yet in mothering one takes on a new pattern of relationality, learning new ways of being in the world, and realizing new dimensions of the self as one takes on responsibility for another.

That is to say, the relationality was there before I became a mother; motherhood simply helped me to experience it in a radical way. Further, since I did not begin to be relational when I became 'mother', my becoming 'mother' does not cancel out all of who I had been before stepping into that embodied experience. And so, far from being a single, reductive relationship, motherhood speaks of the many, diverse, intersecting, conflicting, and complicated relationships that characterize the experience of being human. When one is a mother, one is also necessarily in relation to many others: all those with whom one has shared one's life, the biological other of one's partner, the emotional others with whom one shares (however loosely) child-rearing responsibilities, the material other of one's child. All of these apply to women in child-rearing relationships as they do to men in child-rearing relationships. When one is a mother, one is irreducibly relational, and it is a relationality that is ever-present. So while mother is in relationship with her professional others, she is also concerned about her children. This concern draws me out further into relationship with others—caregivers, teachers, community members—who will share in the development of her children. This, again, can be applied to women as well as to men. This multiplicity of relationality embedded in motherhood allows motherhood to serve as metaphor for human embededdness in relational networks even for persons who are not biologically or socially mothers.

It is a form of mothering that is reflected in the care that adult children must render to their parents in Jewish practice. In the description of Sylvia Barack Fishman, these practices reflect the intergenerational responsibilities that our multiple subject-positions entail. "Elderly parents were the responsibility of their middle-aged children," Fishman writes, "even more extensively than young children were the responsibility of their parents, according to Jewish law."[23] The relationality of motherhood reminds us of the multiplicity of relationships and responsibilities that emerge in our networks of care. In pursuing theological anthropology through the lens of motherhood, a multi-relational and multi-generational point of view emerges. Our sacred lives as human beings before God are not focused on ourselves alone but extend out to those who nurtured us and to those we nurture.

Leila Ahmed, in her memoir of growing up in an Egyptian Muslim family, recounts this relationality as well. In *A Border Passage*, she reclaims the traditional segregation of the sexes under conditions of harem, to recall the richness of life intertwined among the women in her family. In this memoir, Ahmed illumines the way that motherhood represents a diverse set of human relationalities. She writes:

All the aunts came nearly daily to Zatoun, sometimes with their children. Going to Zatoun and spending a couple of hours with Grandmother and

with other women relatives was no doubt an enormous source of emotional and psychological support and pleasure. It was a way of sharing
and renewing connection, of figuring out how to deal with whatever was
going on in their lives with husbands, children, and the people who
worked in their homes. . . . Their meetings surely must have helped
them keep their homes and marriages running reasonably smoothly;
three of the five, including my mother, managed to have tranquil, happy
marriages. But there were many other lives to be overseen. There were
the other people of their community, as well as the women relatives
who gathered here with them occasionally and those women's menfolk;
everyone's issues and problems had to be analyzed, discussed and
resolved. And there were, too, the lives of the workers, the servants, who
were in some sense under their jurisdiction. Generally speaking, the
women of Zatoun knew intimately the personal details of the lives of
those who worked for them, particularly their women servants, all of
whom had been with the family, in one household or the other, for many
years and many of whose mothers also had. Discussing and resolving
these people's problems when they could, delegating this sister or that
relative to talk to her lawyer husband or doctor husband were intrinsic
parts not only of their conversations but, to them, of their responsibilities.[24]

Seeing relationality from the experience of Ahmed's Muslim Egyptian
family in the mid-twentieth century, we find an indication of the way
motherhood is embedded in a wider network that extends care beyond
the mother–child dyad. Rereading the constant current of personal conversation among the women on the varied aspects of family life, Ahmed
reclaims "women's talk" as essential to the family's well-being. For her
mother, relationality extended beyond the mother–child dyad in complex ways that intertwined with economic need and social expectations
and expanded out into the public sphere, even if the women themselves
were limited in their public engagement.

Mothering in Multiplicity

The actual experiences of 'mothers' around the globe helps keep in sight
the way motherhood is metaphor. That is, 'motherhood' is a linguistic
construction that transfers the word from one context to another by
analogy. As a linguistic construction it both reflects and shapes our perception of particular experiences. To say that 'motherhood' is metaphor

and that the actual experiences of 'mothers' help remind us of this linguistic transference and fluidity is to say that even with the 'data' of 'mothers' experiences' there is multiplicity in what counts and constitutes the 'mother'. 'Motherhood' is metaphor, even for 'mothers'. Ahmed's experience of being surrounded by mothers is both similar to and different from my own; Fishman's description of intergenerational responsibilities is both similar to and different from those informed by other faith traditions. Motherhood varies as it shifts across time and place, informed in distinctive ways by the religious traditions that infuse these locations.

In the United States, what it means to be 'mother' in the twenty-first century is different from what it meant in the twentieth century both before and during the women's movement of the 1970s. Feminist suffragette Elizabeth Cady Stanton, mother of seven, gives witness to the burdens of motherhood under conditions of inequality in the early years of the century; middle-class women of 1950s America wrestled with the subject-position of motherhood in a new way after having experienced a more public role in production during the war years; mothers of the 1970s juggled roles affected by women's liberation in the networks of traditional relationships; and mothers of the twenty-first century realize the new challenges that come to them as full participants in the workplace as their concern for the well-being of children in the home continues. The intersection of this changing history with the reality of race and class indicates to an even greater extent the shifting relationality of contextually conditioned motherhood. The former slaves with whom Cady Stanton shared social concerns for representation had a different understanding of the burdens of motherhood; poor women of the 1950s did not have the luxury of returning to the home but continued the tradition of working women before, during, and after the war years, often as domestic help; black women of the women's movement in the 1970s shared some of the juggling of their white colleagues but juggled also the liberation struggles of the black movement for civil rights; and race and class intersect again as mothers of the twenty-first century meet not only the expectations of the professional workplace but the stress of challenges in the form of single motherhood, transnational motherhood in a nation inhospitable to immigrants, and the motherhood of women struggling with inadequate wages and the high cost of child care, health care, and housing. 'Mother' in the United States is a category of internal diversity.

Mothers in Asia share some of the same struggles and juggling but under different cultural conditions diversely experienced in different social locations. Socialized to "feed others first, to eat last, and to eat less," mothers in India continue to sacrifice their well-being for the well-being of others in their familial network.[25] Under the pressure of severe poverty, many Filipino mothers leave their familial networks to serve as domestic help and in service capacities through globalized networks.[26] Like women in many contexts around the globe, many in Africa are impoverished by state systems that do not value their work at home and in the marketplace.[27] Motherhood is complicated by race, class, economic standing, education, national policy, culture, and more, even as it continues to represent the multiplicity of responsibilities and relationships that shape us.

It is important to see motherhood as metaphor for the human condition of relationality from a global and historical perspective, because it provides features of the human condition that recur but are far from constant. Far from being a unitary or universal experience, motherhood is a site of radical multiplicity. The subject-position 'mother' is a most hybrid one, always constituted by a variety of informing conditions at play for any particular person. First, this is seen in the way that motherhood varies across cultures, historical contexts, and social locations. Motherhood could be the constricting limitation of raising seven children that propels one into advocacy for women's greater social and political freedoms, as was the case with Elizabeth Cady Stanton, who, no doubt, had all kinds of help in the child-rearing duties such that she might be able to take on a variety of roles.[28] Motherhood could be the surrogate role forced on slave women made to be mammy to white households in the American South.[29] Egyptian mothers created women's space and women's culture separated from the male-ordered public sphere, fostering essential family networks and becoming the transmitters of a living Islam, as the memoir of Ahmed recounts.[30] The mother-role could be identified as that of the soccer mom who juggles multiple responsibilities in North American comfort, or it can be identified with the immigrant mother who has left her own children behind to care for someone else's family in the affluence of a North American suburb. Mothers have borne their babies on their backs as they have worked the fields of China; and mothers have borne the symbol of the nation on their bodies as they struggled for independence under the sign of 'Mother India'.[31] The subject-position 'mother' is not only a hybrid one in light of the cultural, geographic, and economic differences that infuse the experiences within 'motherhood' as a category, but any particular subject in the position of 'mother' is multiple, as mother is called into a variety of roles, responsibilities, and relationships, none of which quite captures the whole.

An important element overlaid on the sheer multiplicity of relationships communicated in the metaphor of motherhood is the diversity of the textures of these relationships. Motherhood as lens on our human condition allows us to conceive of the human condition as constituted not merely by 'others' but by different styles of love and relationality in relationship to different others. The textures of love that relating to children bring introduce new ways of loving and experiencing love, which do not cancel out the many other ways of loving: loving as a daughter and granddaughter, loving as a partner with another woman or man, loving as a sister, loving as a friend. Each of these has its own texture. In recognizing motherhood as *metaphor*, we make room for the diverse forms of love, diverse textures of familial, agapic, and erotic love, and diverse ways of loving. If motherhood remains the possession or requirement for women in heterosexual relationships partnered with a male father, then motherhood participates in a dangerous, compulsory heterosexuality. Yet if all human persons take on the role of mothering—as men and women, as lesbian, gay, and heterosexual persons, as single parents, celibate religious, or as partners in contractual and sacred partnerships—it is truly *metaphor* of the human condition in which we bring others interrelatedly to life and sustain them.

The insistence on motherhood as metaphor for our human condition, illuminated by the experience of mothering, is critical if this theological anthropology is not to reinscribe gendered inequalities and heteronormativity in its attempt to raise up experiences of women. At the same time, the actual experience of women in mothering roles does illumine new aspects of our humanity. Not least among these is that our relationality is structured by a 'calculus of concern.' When the subject-position of 'mother' provides a symbolic starting point for understanding our human relationality, we are encouraged to think further about the fundamental human condition witnessed through the mother's experience and to see that human beings are embedded in networks of relationality to which limited resources are distributed and at cost to oneself. This is the calculus of concern evident in the mother-experience and identifiable across humanity at large.

The Human Condition: Relationality
and the Calculus of Concern

I wake first in the family. Half asleep, I think of the essay to be written and push myself to emerge from the comfort of warm blankets to the cold of the study, recognizing the scholarly commitments I have made and the limits of time in fulfilling them. Before I can get my feet to the ground, I hear from the other room the sound of a child, my son. If I can shift my trajectory toward the study quickly enough to 'catch' him, I can soothe him back to sleep; thus, I suspend one responsibility to attend to another, with the intention of fulfilling the first as soon as possible. But if, in my haste, I move too noisily, I will wake my second child, my daughter, who has found the way from her bed to mine in the night for comfort. The entangled web of relationship and responsibility begins before dawn and does not end; relationality entails commitment. And with our embodied materiality, this means that there are limits to our ability to care. The calculus of concern captures the way relationality calls forth the distribution of these limited resources: of time, of energy, of material goods. With limited resources of time, money, energy and material goods, the subject-position of 'mother' requires an unceasing calculus of concern. From the negotiation of needs among members of a family, to the negotiation of relationships in the broader community of caregivers, teachers, friends, and the negotiation of energy between the public and private, 'mothers' are constantly required to determine a range of immediate and long-term needs and to calculate the costs toward creating lives of sufficiency and, with any luck, wholeness.

An individual mother's calculus of concern under conditions of globalization can be recognized as not only complicated by, but also complicit in, the global dynamics of social injustice. In North America, the middle-class mother becomes linked with the woman from elsewhere on the globe who is willing to stand as surrogate for the former while the former continues to work. The latter becomes employee, but is much more. She is surrogate mother, but she is even more than that. She is teacher, friend, advocate, companion to my children. As our lives are linked over the subject-position of 'mother', I am given the opportunity to recognize the multiplicity and complexity with which she stands in my biologically given space of relating to my children. She may have left her own children at home (in Brooklyn or Barbados) to care for mine. She may have suspended the trajectory of her education to earn money while, in the meantime, I leave to educate the children of others. She may be learning English while she teaches and loves my children in her native tongue. As I struggle to find a just wage to pay her from my salary and cover my bills, I recognize her struggle and that of undocumented women like her to fight for a fair wage, dignified working conditions, and social respect.[32] There is something we share in 'motherhood', but differences shade that experience in real diversity as well. The subject-position 'mother' nonetheless provides the site for recognizing our interrelatedness.

As metaphor, the calculus of concern in motherhood is representative of the human condition writ large. Under conditions of relationality and finitude, the human condition is precisely one colored always by a calculus of concern; and in this the global inequalities make their way to the local realities. In philosophical or social terms, this calculus might be rendered through the categories of 'individual' and 'collective'; but the exploration of this calculus through the metaphor of motherhood gives texture and personality to such abstract concepts. In the same way that I have a calculus of concern in attending to the needs of multiple children, our human community must address with a calculus of concern the needs of the many different persons in the global family. In the same way that I have a calculus of concern that splits between my own individual needs, the needs of others—my children, my husband, my students and my colleagues—and professional commitments, the subject-position of motherhood demonstrates that the human condition is one in which we cannot 'have it all' and, moreover, demonstrates that concern for another requires relinquishing some portion of concern for the self. In the same way that my calculus of concern impacts others whose situations intersect with my own, the human condition can be seen not as isolated or localized but rather reflective of our interconnections under the conditions of globalization. The balance of self-concern and other-centeredness is in the nature of what it means to be human. And if sociality precedes individuality, then the 'self' I am has been nourished by countless others and, in turn, is called to nurture others in the ever-widening network of relationships. That the calculus of concern structures all human lives provides a basis for solidarity in thinking about the human condition. That the balance of concerns disproportionately weighs on poor women around the globe requires that we press further into the underside of relationality and witness the human failings it reveals as well.

The Human Condition: Limits to Our Love?
The Shadow Side of Relationality

The calculus of concern inherent in the human condition as it emerges from the subject-position of 'mother' allows for a theological anthropology that does not ignore the shadow-side of what it means to be human. For, as the subject shifts through her varied responsibilities in multiple relationality, there are limits to her ability. In these limits, we find that our shortcomings also emerge. When a mother breastfeeds her newborn, her own energy is depleted and the chemical transitions mean her ability to positively respond may be depleted as well. Constantly faced with the never-ending calculus of meeting multiple needs—of one's children, of one's own and others' expectations—and then dealing also with the emotional outbursts or illness of a child pushes relationality to limits. And the self that emerges in this constant depletion of a mother's energy is not always pretty—she is angry, and hungry, and frustrated, and exhausted, she is scared and desperate. These too are part of the human condition and constitute the underside of relationality concomitant with the calculus of concern. There is a price to motherhood and a cost to relationality. As limited human beings, we necessarily split our psychic, emotional, relational, and material abilities across the diverse relationalities to which we are responsible. And this is done at a cost. The calculus of concern in motherhood is representative of a common human pattern that is experienced in diverse ways in countless lives of women and men in myriad contexts in history and around the globe. The calculus of concern is a feature of our relationality and indicates that the self is both individual and collective and conditioned by limited resources. It further reveals that the self is material but has the capacity of a broad resourcefulness in seeking to attend to the many calls in the calculus of concern.

But the framing of a calculus of concern also draws attention to the ways that we as human beings refuse the 'other'. That human beings are able to cut themselves off from relationships of responsibility—interpersonally and internationally—must be held out as evidence also of the shadow side of our human condition. In theological perspective, the concept of 'original sin' maps onto this self-centered pattern that refuses the multiple relationships and responsibilities of an interconnected humanity. Writ large in the public disparities, deceits, and refusals of care for the least, sin is reflected in discrete decisions and in the intersecting systems that fundamentally structure our societies of separations. No one is exempt from the shadow side of the calculus of concern. Given the limitations of our material embeddedness, the sinful reality of the calculus of concern is a living reality. And it is to this reality that our constructive theological visions must also attend.

Pursuing further the discussion of 'sin', Michele Saracino reflects on this component of theological anthropology as it can be seen in the breaking of relationality that fundamentally constitutes us. Saracino uses the term 'hybridity' to capture the multiplicity that characterizes each human being who has been formed in diverse relationships and by multiple stories. Saracino writes:

> Sin is an important piece in the discussion of anthropology because when one refuses to engage their freedom in a way that respects their social relationships with all of creation, one risks refusing the call to live in the image of God and honor the incarnation. In the midst of hybrid existence, sin occurs when we fail to attend to the needs, feelings, memories, and stories of another. We sin not necessarily because we are mean-spirited or even because we are consumed by hubris, but perhaps as Bernard Lonergan explains, because such sin is a result of scotoma, of being blinded to our hybrid existence. We experience this blindness as bias, which prevents us from having insights about ourselves that would reveal our negative feelings toward others. Fear, prejudice, and anger permeate our biased outlooks, prohibiting us from acknowledging how our individual and group stories are multiple and enmeshed with those of others.[33]

To recognize our 'enmeshed' stories and to move outside of our blindness requires a willingness to respond to the 'calculus of concern', recognizing that our lives are interdependent and our stories move forward only together.

The Human Condition: Sacrifice and Sustenance

A third aspect that motherhood reveals about our human condition (along with relationality and the calculus of concern) is the need for both sacrifice and sustenance. Clearly in a world of limited resources, as embodied human beings who rely on material, psychic and spiritual sustenance, the willingness to care for all those embedded in our networks

of relationality will require some sacrifice. What this sacrifice for sustenance might mean is illuminated by the experience of the mother who
has chosen to breastfeed her child. When at three o'clock in the morning,
for the one hundred eightieth night in a row, she stumbles from her sleep
to answer the call of her crying child, there is little romance in this sleep-
deprived selflessness; it is truly sacrifice. It is night after night after night
after night after night after night after night. Around the globe, in every
culture, at every moment in time, women emerge from their sleep—
interrupted and silent—and care for a crying child. And, to capture the
experience in a phrase, at times, it sucks. But the commitment of relationality from the perspective of the breastfeeding mother illuminates the
necessity for self-sacrifice as part of the nature of the human being. If I
did not place the needs of my child before my own desires, she would
literally die.

Relationality can be glamorized as a process of mutual self-giving within
romantic and religious images of reciprocity. The self-sacrifice patterned
on adult relationships suggests some level of reciprocity where sacrifice is
mutually beneficial or a reciprocal giving. Self-giving can be constructed as
a romantic ideal of mutual interdependence that is fruitful in its benefits to
both parties. Or it can be glamorized in ideas of self-sacrifice where actions
are satisfying in themselves. But, at times, the relationality of 'motherhood'
is none of these. It is plain sacrifice. The sacrifice of the promise-keeping
mother holds no guarantee of return for her sacrifice. The pattern of
breastfeeding mothers bringing children with them to field and sanctuary
witnesses this sacrifice as well. And sacrifice at three in the morning is not
romantic interdependence. It is a plain old exhausting pattern of being
depended upon. And to witness this self-sacrifice on the ground is to
recognize that it is not always done joyfully. The woman who has committed herself to nurturing her child in this way must follow through on the
giving. And she herself is the gift. All that sustains the child has been produced within her, and all that can satisfy the needs of the other must come
from within. There is no other real alternative. This is sacrifice. It is self-
giving that empties the self, with no necessary return.

The self-giving of breastfeeding women does not end when the sun
comes up. It requires commitment, all night and all day, to giving of the
self to the needs of the other. It is an impossible balance but one that the
breastfeeding mother finds herself pursuing. She stops what she is doing,
bares her breast, and gives of herself. Or, sometimes, she simultaneously
completes the tasks at hand with baby on breast. There are times,

however, when the needs of the child demand more than a woman can give. She has given all that she has and is literally emptied. Giving of herself when the child wants more, she continues to offer comfort and suckle as all that she has left to give.

In many parts of the world, the expectation of women as mothers exploits this relationality of care and self-sacrifice. Muriel Orevillo-Montenegro describes "the socialization of Indian women to feed others first, to eat last, and to eat less."[34] A culture of *machismo* can turn the mothering roles of into sources of dehumanization.[35] In the North American context, women, in greater proportion than men, continue to take on child-rearing responsibilities in addition to their increased participation in the workforce. As Valerie Saiving has perceptively shown, the theological tradition can perpetuate gender injustice by holding up selflessness as the ideal. Saiving's critique is that women are socialized to sacrifice to the detriment of their selfhood. Gendered expectations that women as mothers be self-sacrificing, and theological traditions that see 'sin' as the inability to be self-sacrificing, collude in depriving women of a sense of 'self' that might sustain the sacrifice.[36] Articulated in 1960, Saiving's concerns are still relevant today. I do not contest her insightful observation that patterns of self-sacrifice are closely embedded in the social construction of the subject-position 'woman' and even more so that of 'mother'. However, the reality of self-sacrifice as it emerges from the experience of mothering encourages us not to deny the necessity of self-sacrifice but to apply it more liberally. That is to say, self-sacrifice emerges from the experience of motherhood when we recognize that we are embedded in networks of relationality responding to diverse needs. Yet, equally important, the experience of motherhood should be shared by *all* human beings. I learn from caring for my child that if I do not place her needs before my desires she will die. I also learn in the embodied experience of 'motherhood' that if I do not consider also my needs I will not be in a position to care for her and we both may suffer. Thus, the mothers must be mothered. My husband mothers me, and in his co-mothering of our children, he sustains my 'self' that is entangled in other relationships of responsibility. I am mothered by my colleagues who support my work collaboratively, and by my friends who mother me in other ways. I am mothered by my children's caregiver, who shows me better ways to be a mother, and by my mother, whose deep impressions of mother-care find expression in my own caring. All those who 'mother', in the countless ways we are invited to nurture in our networks of care, must also be sustained by others, and those others who mother must be mothered in return. The metaphor and experience of 'motherhood' must be seen in all its multiple relationalities, and the many forms of mothering must be called forth to employ that metaphor for our common future.

Reflections of a Creative God

The process of a theological anthropology rooted in mothering experiences returns to scripture and tradition to bring theological terms to bear on these experiences. When Rahner includes the human capacity for 'love' as essential to his theological anthropology, he returns to the Christian tradition to name God as the infinite source of love. Rahner asserts that all humanity is the creative work of the one God, as God chooses to come into expression through the multiplicity of created realities. In describing Rahner's work elsewhere, I write:

> God's overabundant nature courses through the universe rendering all creation graced. Yet, in order for the communication to be complete, there must be a hearer who receives it. Human nature is the only created reality with the freedom to accept God's self-communication in grace. When humanity accepts this self-communication, God's purpose in creation is complete as God's fullest self-expression can be manifest in the world.[37]

It is for this reason that Rahner articulates that the human being "is accordingly in the most basic definition that which God becomes if he sets out to show himself in the region of the extra-divine."[38] God comes into expression relationally through humanity.

As Rahner's Christian theological perspective relates the human capacity for love as limitless to the limitlessness of God, the extension of his ideas suits us here. While Rahner's reflections on the human capacity for love tend to be painted in broad strokes that reduce that love to a single pattern in the God–self / self–others relationship, the diverse shades and shapes of love explored in human relational multiplicity provides a more vibrant sense of what God's reality might be. The multiplicity of relationality and the infinite possibility for human forms of love is, in a Rahnerian sense, made possible by the infinite horizon of love, which Christians name God.

If God is the "unimaginable livingness" which "generates the life of all creatures," and if it is relationality that calls us into being, God, as "the power of being within all being," courses through creation through our relationality.[39] In Elizabeth Johnson's vision, God's recreating presence in the world includes "the integrity of nature, the liberation of peoples, the flourishing of every person, and the shalom of the whole world in rescue from the powers of evil, which foster sin and destruction."[40] But how does this power of re-creation enter the world if not through the networks of care and concern, the relationships of sustenance and solidarity that are forged between us? Our relationality, in its potential and its possibilities, is the presence of the divine among us.

And this brings me back to the way Chinese women and Christian Maryknoll Sisters encountered one another and encountered God. In the everydayness of their relationship, in the intertwining of lives, in the multiplicity of responsibilities, new ways of understanding the divine shone forth. God meets us in and through the relationalities of the everyday. This brings me back also to Islam as it was found in the life of Leila Ahmed. It is from her mother that Ahmed remembers learning 'Islam'; but it was a different style of Islam than Ahmed would discover in commentaries and that she overheard in the mosques. Like the 'kitchen talk' that fed the heart of the home in traditional Chinese families, Ahmed's Islam was infused throughout the everydayness of life and permeated experience. In Ahmed's words:

> For although in those days it was only Grandmother who performed all the regular formal prayers, for all the women of the house, religion was an essential part of how they made sense of and understood their own lives. It was through religion that one pondered the things that happened, why they had happened, and what one should make of them, how one should take them.
>
> Islam, as I got it from them, was gentle, generous, pacifist, inclusive, somewhat mystical—just as they themselves were. . . . Religion was above all about inner things. . . . What was important was how you conducted yourself and how you were in yourself and in your attitude towards others and in your heart.
>
> . . . Islam . . . was a way of being in the world. A way of holding oneself in the world—in relation to God, to existence, to other human beings. This the women passed on to us most of all through how they were and by their being and presence, by the way *they* were in the world, conveying their beliefs, ways, thoughts, and how we should be in the world by a touch, a glance, a word—prohibiting, for instance, or approving. Their mere responses in this or that situation—a word, a shrug, even just their postures—passed on to us, in the way that women (and also men) have

forever passed on to their young, how we should be. And all of these ways of passing on attitudes, morals, beliefs, knowledge—through touch and the body and in words spoken in the living moment—are by their very nature subtle. They profoundly shape the next generation, but they do not leave a record in the way that someone writing leaves a text about how to live or what to believe leaves a record. Nevertheless, they leave a far more important, and literally, more vital, living record[41]

In Hindu practice as well, the mother's role in making sacred the space of the home and punctuating a child's life with ritual carries on unnoticed by so many of the textbook descriptions of Hindu thought and practice.[42] The everyday practice witnesses a belief that the divine extends beyond the bounds of male-organized religion and into the places where people find God. So too in the traditions of Judaism as seen from the perspective of women's experiences. In Judith Plaskow's description:

> The *tkhines* [or petitionary prayers of Eastern European Jewish women] make clear that at the same time women participated in the established cycle of the Jewish year, they also sought and discovered God in domestic routines and in the biological experiences unique to women. Women were obviously able to find great meaning in their limited number of commandments. They were deeply involved with their families, a sphere of connection that extended to the dead. They felt deeply connected to the matriarchs, whose experience and merit they invoked. The *tkhines* testify to the importance of relationship in women's spirituality.[43]

From out of women's relational experience across religious traditions we might witness the God who meets us in and through multiplicity, in and through relationality, in and through the everyday.

As evidenced in the Maryknoll Sisters' accounts, interfaith encounter was not just about the 'faith' or communicating doctrine. Getting to know the women of China as complex human beings meant that catechism and ritual practices included an interweaving with the various dimensions of their lives. Through the witness of these Chinese women, we are reminded that 'religion' is not a separate endeavor dissociated from the everyday practices of our lives. With the vision of Gustavo Gutierrez we see that the profane no longer exists.[44] We are invited to witness the intertwining of the sacred with the everyday.

In emphasizing the relationality of the self, this theological anthropology develops a crucial component of Rahner's own understanding. For while modern theological anthropologies emphasized the individual knower possessing free will (two of the fundamental characteristics Rahner will emphasize), Rahner also included the capacity for love as inherent in what it means to be human. Following Rahner, I have radicalized his idea in two ways. First, this capacity for love (that is, our relationality) is not secondary but primary to the human condition. It is not an outgrowth of who we are as 'self', but relationality and love constitute our very selves. Second, the capacity for love and relationality, recognized as primary, conditions the whole of our existence. Religion is thus transformed as the relationality at the heart of existence. The presence of the sacred is in and through the experience of love and relationality. The reflection of Pedro Arrupe illustrates this intertwining when he writes:

> Nothing is more practical than finding God, that is, than falling in love. In a quite absolute, final way, what you are in love with, what seizes your imagination, will affect everything. It will decide what will get you out of bed in the morning, what you do with your evenings, how you spend your weekends, what you read, who you know, what breaks your heart, and what amazes you with joy and gratitude. Fall in love, stay in love, and it will decide everything.[45]

If God is love, and love is activated in the relationships that structure human existence, then God is found in the everydayness of relationality.

Through the relationality of the everyday, we are reminded of the Christian tradition's insistence on the unending source of God as love, and in this living recollection we are provided visionary resources for the motherly care of our world. As a corrective to the shadow side of the calculus of concern, by which human beings are deceived into believing that there is a limit to our love and relational abilities, we might turn to Rahner's God of limitless love and to a mother's experience of her love for a second child. In these, we might identify the power within us to extend the networks of care beyond what we currently believe.

Ask any of my colleagues or friends, I was nervous about the second child. I loved the first with such vigor and expending of energy, I couldn't imagine loving a second. I was doubly nervous since she was female, and fell prey to what Luce Irigaray indicts of patriarchy: the devaluation of the mother–daughter relationship. (As if in defense of this devaluation, I can hear myself say, "You know how complicated the relationships are between mothers and daughters.") But Ella taught me, from the moment of her entering this world, that the heart is capable of expansion and that love can take many and diverse forms. For as soon as I saw her, I felt she was intimately related to me, and she elicited the strong bonds of caring others had predicted but about which I myself had been uncertain. She was then, and has always been, herself. She slept differently, learned differently, laughed differently than Owen. She grows day by day with her own personality, delighting and challenging in her particularity. She is, by all accounts, beautiful.

Ella helps me understand, a little bit better the theological conceptions of a God who has unlimited love for all creation. She also helps me understand a little bit better Jesus' call to pattern God's love by widening our circle of familial concern. For just as Ella taught me that my love could be expanded beyond Michael and Owen to include someone new, the gospel challenges Christians to expand beyond the nucleus of my family to a mother's care for all those who need. Knowing them and loving them makes me want to be kinder and gentler to all children and to all creation. Has God shown Godself through the relationality of this child? Is it not God who has called humanity to come out of solitude and into relationship, yet again?

A Christology of M/otherhood

In Christian tradition, theological anthropology emerges not only from considering our human experiences in their reflections of God; theological anthropology is also expressed in the writings on Christology. As fully human, the person of Christ in Christology reflects the expression of Christian insights into human nature. The words placed on Jesus' lips in Matthew's gospel (18:3) provide continuity for the foregoing theology: Unless we become like little children fundamentally aware of our dependence on relationality with others, we will not experience the kingdom of God. What would it mean to pursue a theological anthropology of multiplicity and motherhood in the key of Christology? Tina Beattie has already argued that such a project runs to the heart of the Christian tradition. She writes:

> Christianity is essentially relational both in its proclamation of a Trinitarian God and in its celebration of the incarnation as an event that continuously reveals itself in the space of creative symbolic encounter between God, Mary, Christ and the Church. So the story of Christ is the story of Mary is the story of the Church is the story of humanity is the story of God, and the prismatic vision thus revealed cannot be adequately

expressed by any one symbol in isolation from the rest. To recognize this means developing a theological perspective that goes beyond the narrow Christological focus, to a more encompassing vision of incarnation that incorporates all of creation, including the male and female bodies and the natural world.[46]

A Christology of relationality insists, with Michele Saracino, that "the Christian tradition demonstrates hybridity as a normative dimension of human existence."[47] In embracing the multiplicity of motherhood, this theological anthropology reflects back on a Christology that draws out the distinctive characteristics of hybridity, multiplicity, and relationality embedded in the Christian story. This particular Christology does so by continuing the foregoing discussion of theological anthropology from out of motherhood.

Considering Christ's person through this lens, we are reminded that, fundamentally, the human person learns the first patterns of relationality in relation to the one(s) who will serve as 'mother' (whether this is a bio-logical mother or another mother). The 'm/other' (whether mothers, the father or fathers, the caregiver or grandparent or sibling) calls the child forth into being through relationship. While the child's individuality emerges from the simultaneous identification with the other/mother and the recognition of a 'separate' self,[48] some psychoanalysts posit that the act of individuation is never complete separation. Instead separation includes the internalization of that first m/other-relationship as well: "The loss of the other whom one desires and loves is overcome through a specific act of identification that seeks to harbor the other within the very structure of the self."[49] In this visioning of human development, the self is never alone but internalizes the relationships that are formative. Such suggestions about the nature of human selfhood return Christians to the story of scripture to recognize a new importance to Mary of Nazareth. Far from being a mere conduit for bringing a savior into the world,[50] as the person enabling the first primary relationship for the one who will come to be identified as savior, she constitutes his very self. In the gospel accounts, she is the one who cradles and shelters the helpless newborn (Luke 2:7) and who soon after introduces him to Jewish sacred ritual through presentation of him in the Temple (Luke 2:21–39). Co-mothering with Joseph, she continues his religious education—for example, mark-ing together with them the feast of Passover by journeying to Jerusalem (Luke 2:41). While she plays important roles in the gospel accounts of

Jesus' early life, her role in helping to shape Jesus' self-understanding is implicit throughout his life in her continuing influence on his ministry. It is Mary who calls Jesus into public ministry in John's account of the wedding at Cana (John 2:1–11). Was it perhaps Mary who instilled in Jesus a love for the weakest, the child, as she had once, in her response to the annunciation, given her promise to dedicate her life to such care? Was it she who shaped him to experience outrage at the misuse of monies as they were exchanged at the Temple? Did he draw strength in his trust of God's promised reign when at the crucifixion he encountered his mother, who stood by her commitment to God throughout her life? A Christology built in relationality recognizes Jesus' self-giving pattern fostered by those closest to him, and in this, we see Mary his mother.

But, since the self is not a static entity moving through the world from childhood onward, this dynamic development of the self is constituted not through the primary relationship alone but through a wide variety of relationships. The ties we have with others "constitute a sense of self, compose who we are."[51] As feminist theologian Catherine Keller has observed, "For if 'I' am partially constituted by you even as you partially constitute me, for better or for worse, that is if I flow into, in-fluence you as you in-fluence me, then my subjectivity describes itself as radically open-ended in time as well as space."[52] If what it means to be human is to be constituted by relationships and we are in multiple relationships, a sense of the self in multiplicity emerges. In the words of Morwenna Griffiths, "Identity [is] constructed, reconstructed and negotiated in relationships of love, resistance, acceptance and rejection."[53] Using this lens to understand the narrative of the gospels, we see Jesus' self emerging in relation to friends, strangers, and even adversaries. For example, Jesus is called into a sense of self through his relationships with Martha and Mary of Bethany (Luke 10:38–42; Matthew 26:6–13; Mark 14:3–9; Luke 7:36–50; John 12:1–8; John 11:1–4). In an interreligious exchange with the Gentile woman of Syrophoenician origin, Jesus' mind is changed in the theological engagement through which she lays claim on him (Mark 7:24–30; Matthew 15:21–28). In looking at the stories of Jesus through the lens of dynamic identity, we can imagine the way that his own understanding of himself and his mission was constituted by his own "creative, agential negotiation of the intersecting currents and competing loyalties" that ran through him.[54] Even one's adversaries call forth the development of one's own identity as a self. For example, it is when a lawyer challenges

Jesus, interrogating him on the necessary requirements for a life of wholeness and eternal life, that Jesus indicates the heart of his teaching: Love God with all your heart, mind, and soul, and your neighbor as yourself (Luke 10:25–37). With the foregoing recognition that love of God is activated in relationship, these two foci (God and neighbor) are not at all separate sites. And yet, embedded in this gospel story is a move that pushes this love further. In this teaching moment Jesus indicates that we find what it means to love neighbor, self, and God by loving the 'religious other'. For Luke's gospel continues with the story of the 'good Samaritan'. From the standpoint of his hearers, the Samaritan would have appeared as one who was socially and religiously other, held suspect because he did not fit neatly as Jew or Gentile.[55] But it is precisely *this* 'other' who stands as representative of the neighbor whose pattern is to be followed. The entire persona, mission, and ministry of Jesus seems to embrace the communal nature of what it means to be human—embedded in relationships, called in care for the least, shaped across the divides of difference, and fulfilling a vision of human being and becoming *together*.

As those around him call Jesus forth into new enactments of himself and his mission, he simultaneously transforms and empowers those who follow him. The very calling of disciples to follow him indicates that his mission was not solitary but depended on relationality. His teachings engaged his hearers in creative revisioning that drew them into the parables he used as vehicles. Jesus' vision of a reign of God had in mind not the well-being of an individual before God but a holistic well-being for all. And he called his disciples into a relationality that empowered them as well: They were constituted and empowered by their encounter with him and with one another. In Jesus' presence the broken are made whole, and in the dynamic exchange of the community those who follow Jesus are empowered to do likewise, as the Acts of the Apostles is full of stories of those who carried on Jesus' mission, continuing to share in his life-restoring power. The salvation that is announced in Jesus of Nazareth is not a singular salvation resting on one individual. The salvific vision of Jesus of Nazareth is enacted in his life and in the lives of those who follow him. The transformation of the world toward its fullness in justice and relationship is a process that discipleship enables in the many and diverse human beings who seek it. As Elisabeth Schüssler Fiorenza has offered, "Sophia, the God of Jesus, wills the wholeness and humanity of everyone and therefore enables the Jesus movement to become a 'discipleship of equals.'"[56]

Portrayed as an adult in the gospel accounts, Jesus has longed for such a community embodying the vision of wholeness, response, and responsibility, and he sees himself in the role of mother: Informing and being mutually informed by the community in which he is embedded. In the gospel of Luke, the words put on Jesus' lips envision him in the role of mother-hen, longing to gather her children together, as "a hen gathers her brood under her wings" (Luke 13:34). Jesus is both shaped by those who mother him into being *and* he himself takes on the role of mother. As Jesus steps into the subject-position of 'mother', he is not suddenly entering relationality; rather, the relationships with family, friends, and the wider social networks continue to impact his subjectivity. Yet in mothering, one takes on a new pattern of relationality, learning new ways of being in the world and realizing new dimensions of the self as one takes on responsibility for another. Stepping into the mother-role, what did Jesus learn about himself from those to whom he extended care? Perhaps the most powerful experience he claimed in adopting the subject-position 'mother' is that he understood that what it means to be human is not, in fact, to be autonomous, self-directed, and free but rather to be willingly restrained by those relationships to which one has committed, to be willing to embrace one's own vulnerability in care for the vulnerable-other. In the ultimate act of vulnerability, Jesus responds with his very life, refusing to compromise his countercultural vision and being murdered at the hands of those who found such a vision threatening.

Continuing the pattern of mother-care, early Christian writings envision Jesus' self-giving modeled on a lactating mother where the "milk of Christ" is spiritual nourishment.[57] This symbolism was taken up with enthusiasm during the Middle Ages, as Caroline Walker Bynum introduces us to the little-known medieval devotion to Jesus our Mother. Anselm of Canterbury (d. 1109) points to the image Jesus as mother hen, confessing, "Truly, master, you are a mother."[58] And Bernard of Clairvaux (d. 1153) entreats his readers to seek in Christ's breasts the milk of healing when he writes, "If you feel the sting of temptation . . . suck not so much the wounds as the breasts of the Crucified. He will be your mother, and you will be his son."[59]

Aelred of Rievaulx (d. 1167) similarly draws on the lactating imagery when he writes:

> On your altar let it be enough for you to have a representation of our Savior hanging on the cross; that will bring before your mind his Passion

for you to imitate, his outspread arms will invite you to embrace him, his naked breasts will feed you with the milk of sweetness to console you.[60]

The image of Christ as breastfeeding mother invokes a bodily humanity that includes his own having been suckled (and painted images of Mary breastfeeding will become popular a few centuries later).[61] Popular imagery of Christ employed this physical nurturance as metaphor for the divine self-giving that sustains humanity. Humanity suckles at the breasts of Christ as Christ gives himself for the lives of many, and Christians are called to carry on that mother role for a world in need. While an increasingly androcentric Christian tradition wrests the image of nursing away from the embodied experience of women as breastfeeders, it is only with the help of actual women's experiences of breastfeeding that the insight into Christ's mother role can be illuminated.[62]

Self-giving love in the pattern of a breast-feeding mother can be understood at three o'clock in the morning, when, for the one hundred eightieth night in a row, a mother stumbles from her sleep to answer the call of her crying child. The theological language of self-sacrifice can glamorize the process of self-giving through an image of actions satisfying in themselves, or be glorified under the banner of the ultimacy of the giving in light of a suprahuman ideal, or be constructed romantically in a mutual interdependence that is of benefit even to the one who sacrifices. But self-giving at three in the morning is none of these: It is not glamorous, self-satisfying, suprahuman, or rooted in mutuality. It is a plain old exhausting pattern of being depended on. And in history, the self-giving of breastfeeding women does not end when the sun comes up. It requires commitment, all night and all day, to giving of the self to the needs of the other. It is an impossible balance but one that a woman who has chosen this (or economically is required to choose it) finds herself pursuing. She stops what she is doing, bares her breast, and gives of herself. Or, sometimes, she simultaneously completes the tasks at hand with baby on breast. There are times, however, when the needs of the child demand more than a woman can give. She has given all that she has and is literally emptied. Giving of herself when the child wants more, she continues to offer comfort and suckle even when she has nothing left to give. And when her breasts are broken from the constant sucking, the child takes from her both blood and milk at the same time. Having committed to this course of action, she continues . . . a life depends on it. The woman who has committed herself to nurturing her child in this way must follow through on the giving. And she herself is the gift. All that sustains the child has been produced within her, and all that can satisfy the needs of the other must come from within. There is no other real alternative. This is sacrifice. It is self-giving that empties the self with no necessary return.

This is the pattern of self-giving that is the choice of many women, but it is also a pattern that has enslaved women as wet nurses in countless contexts. Also, it is a pattern required for women in families where economic resources are scarce. Further, when women who can choose whether or not to breastfeed make the choice to do so, they can become trapped in a process of unequal caregiving when partners or others in the community relinquish responsibilities under the presumption that it is the breastfeeding woman's responsibility to care for the child. There is danger, clearly, in holding up breastfeeding as yet another ideal to which women must adhere. And yet my aim here is not to set up breastfeeding as the only option or the only manner of nurturing.[63] Rather, I'd like to use the experience of breastfeeding as one lens through which to understand the depth of theological meaning communicated in the images of Christ as nurturing mother. Day after day, when there is nothing left to give, every two or three hours—sometimes more frequently—being asked again to give, even when it hurts. If Christians desire a world reconciled to God that reflects ideals of justice, this restoration of creation requires this kind of sacrifice. It requires self-giving that is not easy, that is not glamorous, and that offers few immediate rewards and, at times, little satisfaction. When theologians describe Christians patterning their actions on Jesus' self-giving love, they sound the prophetic call of patterning ourselves with a view toward this restoration of justice. When coupled with the imagery of humanity feeding from the divine breasts, we are offered a physical experience of what that sacrificial pattern entails. It entails round-the-clock attentiveness to the needs of the other. It requires self-giving that is self-emptying in a real sense. It demands a pattern of self-denial that puts the needs of the other before one's own. But just as the lactating mother requires nourishment to produce milk, so too must care be taken for one's own well-being. The pattern of self-giving love that is *Christa lactans* consists of a lifestyle of giving, not in discrete acts of charity but in the self-giving that nurtures others to become fully human themselves. That's what Christians are called to in the pattern of Jesus' self-giving love.

Framing Christ in the role of breastfeeding mother must also be joined with the remembered rejection of a narrowly constituted motherly role. While breastfeeding may give insight into the motherly care necessary for healing a broken world, it is the healing that is important, with breasts as illuminative, although not exclusive, vehicles: "While he was saying this, a woman in the crowd raised her voice and said to him, 'Blessed is the womb that bore you and the breasts that nursed you!' But he said, "Blessed rather are those who hear the word of God and obey it!'" (Luke 11:27–28).

In contemplating the mother role of Jesus, the early communities also were critical of the socially constructed mother role in its limitations. For example, in the story of Jesus' response to the approach of his mother and his brothers, we see a concern for the narrow mother care that social constructions enable.

> Then his mother and his brothers came; and standing outside, they sent to him and called him. A crowd was sitting around him; and they said to him, "Your mother and your brothers and sisters are outside, asking for you." And he replied, "Who are my mother and my brothers?" And looking at those who sat around him, he said, "Here are my mother and my brothers! Whoever does the will of God is my brother and sister and mother."
>
> Mark 3:31–35; see also Luke 8:19–20

What appears to be an affront to the mother love of Jesus' own mother is a reminder that it is not mothers who bring about the healing of the world but *mothering*. And this mothering must extend beyond the bounds of familial care: "Whoever loves son or daughter more than me is not worthy of me" (Matthew 10:37). The transformative healing of the reign of God announced by Jesus is not available through the narrow confines of family-first relationships. Rather, the mother-love care for children and others must extend out into the community, the wider community, the global community.

The reclaiming of sacrifice for a world in need runs the danger long identified by feminist theology of patterns of a patriarchal outlook that demands the sacrifice of women to the detriment of self. Certainly, this remains a live concern. But the mother care to which we are called is not about biology—whether the biology of s/he who is mother or the biology of the one receiving the care. The mother-care of Christ expands beyond the bounds of biology to pour forth for a world in need. That is, it is not biological mothers who are called to sacrifice; we are all called to sacrifice. To operate as if the transformation of a world in need will come without cost is to ignore the material realities of an embodied condition in a globalized world. For Christians to be willing to participate in the sacrifice that hurts is to embrace the human condition of our own vulnerability. In the words of Judith Butler:

> We come into the world unknowing and dependent, and, to a certain degree, we remain that way . . . infancy constitutes a necessary dependency, one that we never fully leave behind. Bodies still must be apprehended as given over. Part of understanding the oppression of lives is precisely to understand that there is no way to argue away this condition of a primary vulnerability, of being given over to the touch of the other, even if, or precisely when, there is no other there, and no support for our lives. To counter oppression requires that one understand that lives are supported and maintained differentially, that there are radically different ways in which human physical vulnerability is distributed across the globe.[64]

The acceptance of the human condition of vulnerability and the recognition of the differential experience of this vulnerability calls forth a response of the Christian mother love across boundaries for a world in need.

In our global age, the mother love of Christians mothered by Christ must extend to the global community and be willing to cross religious borders. A story from a young Muslim woman engaged in interfaith solidarity resonates with the mother care of Jesus and the necessity for envisioning affinities that arise from our human condition despite cultural and religious difference. This young Muslim was a resident of Jerusalem, and her outlook had been structured by the media's portrayal of Jews in the conflict of the Middle East, which grew to a hatred of Jews and a general distrust of any non-Muslims in her community. Although she lived and worked side by side with Jews, Christians, and people of the Druze faith, she described these working relationships as distant and filled with distrust. It was not until she found herself in the common nursery of the maternity ward shortly after having given birth to her daughter that her experience of her neighbors of other faiths shifted from her seeing them as 'the enemy' to her recognizing their common humanity. For around the room were new mothers of every religion represented in the region; women whose backgrounds placed them on opposing sides of the conflict; women from families who were enemies divided by their faiths. But as she sat in this nursery, exhausted from the pains of childbirth, holding her daughter in her arms while her daughter nursed at empty breasts, she had an insight.

She had just lived through months of physical transformation and physical sacrifice, through sickness and change in her public persona. After months of anticipation and preparation, and after hours of agony and pushing and pain, somehow she had brought a small new life into the world. This new life was utterly dependent on her, completely vulnerable. And the young mother was vulnerable too, dependent on some reality beyond herself as she waited for her milk to come in. Having chosen to breastfeed her newborn, in the first days of the baby's life she was helpless until the milk began to flow. She waited, as her child sometimes wailed, as her daughter lost ounces that felt like pounds. The new mother was exhausted, helpless, and vulnerable as she could do nothing but wait.

For this young Muslim mother, this experience of her own vulnerable humanity—dependent on a force, a reality greater than herself—provided a foundation for recognizing the humanity of the other. And this young woman had the powerful realization that she shared with every single mother who surrounded her—the Christian, the Jew, the Druze—the desperate experience of waiting for her milk to come in. It was at this moment of profound realization of what connected this group as new mothers, a connection that was physical and embodied, that she recognized the common humanity of her neighbors of other faiths. This experience of connection with other new mothers transcended the boundaries of religion that had so long distanced her from her coworkers and neighbors in the conflict. It was this recognition of shared humanity through the particularity of being vulnerable as a new mother that led her to take part in an interreligious dialogue circle of women concerned for peacemaking in their city.

The subsequent dialogue among this young mother and her neighbors was not focused on "how rationally to convince someone from another tradition that yours is true."[65] Rather, their conversations developed out of a keen sense of the necessity to work together to protect the bodies of their sons and daughters, their husbands and parents. They talked about how each of them was vulnerable and how neighbors of diverse religious backgrounds might share the same physical space in a way that allowed for the fullest human flourishing. In the process, they drew on their religions to envision a way forward, but their primary focus was not to compare and contrast the diverse details of doctrine but rather to preserve the integrity of vulnerable bodies in a location where human well-being was threatened daily.

In telling her story, the young woman provided a metaphor for the desperate search for a common foundation for peace refracted through the lens of motherhood. She closed her reflection with the following words:

> We feed them milk, we feed them love
> We feed them hatred,
> Whatever we feed them they will eat
> And they will become.[66]

In these words, we are broadened out from the circumscribed experience of women in the nursing ward to a symbolic representation of how each of us feeds the other, with motherhood as a metaphor for the countless relationships and the ongoing actions of women and men as we relationally bring one another into being. We are all waiting for our milk to come in. We are all seeking the resources and the strength to sustain our world, our children, and future generations, in contexts divided by religious differences. Desperation arises from the sense of urgency that the earth and its inhabitants face in our times of limited resources, corporate greed, and national distrust. The metaphor of waiting for our milk to come in derives from one woman's embodied experience and is offered as a powerful metaphor through which women and men might share the experience of desperately wanting to be agents of sustenance and change in our religiously plural world.

If the Christian is fashioned on Christ as breastfeeding mother, s/he too is waiting for her milk to come in. As Aelred of Rievaulx in the twelfth century held, "Nothing is better fitted to serve as our mother than charity. These cherish and make us advance, feed us and nourish us, and refresh us with the milk of twofold affection: love, that is, for God and for neighbor."[67] And in our interreligious and globalized world, the neighbor to whom our care extends stands in need across religious boundaries. A Christology sufficient for a globalized world increasingly interconnected with religious difference and increasingly aware of the pervasiveness of injustice is a Christology that must stand on behalf of those in need. I am thinking with a hybridized Christ, a Christ-Christa who, having been nurtured by her mother emerges from out of embodied experiences of sacrifice and relationship to nurture the other. Such a Christ/a stands on behalf of a broken world. But standing on behalf of the other must not be a patronizing gesture. Rather, it must be understood instead in the way that Homi Bhabha envisions, where speaking on behalf means being willing to 'half' oneself, to restructure one's interests and privileges in solidarity with the other.[68] As a mother, I act on behalf all the time. And while I first feared that this meant the loss of me, it is an invitation to a dynamic evolvement of myself. In the parallel language of Christian theology, God was not fearful of becoming less in the person of Jesus but lives in and through Jesus of Nazareth as a way of dynamically involving Godself in the world, because behalfing/half-ing does not diminish but calls something particular into being.

In this age of interreligious awareness, I am also willing to share the divinity of God with other persons, figures, and events that emerge from a wide variety of religious realities. In a sense, I am willing to half Christ, because God is infinite.

"'The *Divine Mother* exists in everything, animate and inanimate, in the form of power or energy. It is that power that sustains us through our lives and ultimately guides us to our respective destination,' quotes Swarupa Ghose, a housewife with a newborn baby in her lap."[69] As this mother, Swarupa Ghose, reminds us, the visions of God and the experiences of being human as they are illumined in various religions are multiple. And her vision invites us further to a renewed care for creation— to attend to relationship with God through relationship with 'everything'. The practice of mothering must be a metaphor for the ongoing commitment we might make to sustaining one another in relationship and sustaining the earth in reciprocity. This is a task we can share across religious boundaries, an idea that Chung Ok Lee promotes from a Buddhist point of view:

Today human-centered materialism increases suffering of other forms of life such as animals and plants. We are destroying our own future. The elimination of suffering is the ultimate concern of conscious people. Human behavior can be evaluated in terms of its capacity to promote or reduce suffering of all forms. Human beings create suffering because of greed, anger and ignorance. It is apparent that greed, hatred and ignorance in their various manifestations are also the factors that generate insecurity among people. We must seek to improve our earth community by improving ourselves as individuals first and then trying to change social structures to reverse our trends. The path to enlightenment includes overcoming these forces through spiritual practice. Such practice will deepen human relationships with other forms of life.[70]

The nature of the human condition from the perspective of lactating mothers is that although we are stretched, it is the condition of humanity that we are capable (physiologically, materially, spiritually) of producing the necessary nutrients to support the life of our children. We are able to sustain our future generations through the powers embodied within us.

And here, once again, it is key that motherhood be understood as metaphor for the human condition. If motherhood and sacrifice are taken as literal directions for how we are to participate in the salvation of the planet, women's self-sacrifice is reinscribed in unhelpful ways. Yet the response is not that mothers should cease their necessary sacrifices inherent in the calculus of concern that is part and parcel of the human condition of relationality but that motherhood is shared more broadly across subject-positions. By invitation, all human beings are called into the self-giving of motherhood for the future of the planet.

A theological anthropology rooted in the experience of 'mothering' affirms the human condition as one constituted by relationships of care and responsibility. We are not isolated subjects making our way through the world. We are dependent and depended on. And, further, we thrive and survive together. At the same time, the multiplicity inherent in the subject-position 'mother' indicates that 'we' are not all reducible to the 'same'. Our internal multiplicity reminds us of the dynamic and shifting ways we are constituted in a wide variety of networks of care. The metaphor of motherhood, finally, brings us back to a particularity that reminds us that the 'human condition' is that we are irreducibly particular even while inextricably relational. In our multiple and shifting relations, we find a new sense of 'self' and new possibilities for our common future.

In thinking about a theological anthropology rooted in this sense of 'self', we might be guided by Aimee Carrillo Rowe, who shifts the thinking from 'identity' to a distinctive form of 'multiplicity' when she writes:

> I seek an alternative to a notion of identity that begins with "I"—as does the inscription "I-identity," which announces itself through its fixity: "I am . . ."—to a sense of "self" that is radically inclined toward others, toward the communities to which we belong, with whom we long to be, and to whom we feel accountable. Perhaps "positionality," with its

multiply placed "*i*'s," is a more appropriate signifier. . . . I think of it as *differential belonging*—shifting the terms of interpellation from the individual subject to the spaces between them. These belongings may be multiple, shifting, and even contradictory (in terms of the norms they produce, the politics that drive them, the conditions for loving they request, or demand): family, neighborhood, friends, allies, colleagues, social groups, lovers, nations, transnations. These sites of belonging are political as they operate in relation to power: with and through, as well as against, in resistance to, and possibly in directions that redefine and redistribute it.[71]

Rowe invites us to see this radical relationality of our human condition as it is constructed in community and through which solidiarities for action might be forged. It is just such an 'interreligious' action of solidarity to which we now turn in the investigation of the global women's movement. Just as the investigation of women in mission through the metaphor of motherhood brought out new dimensions of a theological anthropology of relationality, so too will this examination suggest a revision of traditional theological anthropologies in their construction of 'freedom / free will', seeing freedom as both a divine gift and as a human problem.

PART II

In the Sacred Secular

3 Encounter in Global Feminist Movements

ENACTING TRANS-RELIGIOUS ALLIANCES

You can see them in the brown and white photos.[1] Mothers marching for freedom. With their children in tow, women publicly demonstrated for greater political rights in the suffrage movement of early twentieth-century America. That they did so as women is obvious. That they did so as mothers gets lost in memory, except for the visual traces from long-forgotten photos. That they did so out of complex multiplicity—as black women, as educated women, as poor women, as teachers or doctors, as lesbian or heterosexual—gets lost as well. And that this multiplicity included a religious identity is further obscured. The first wave of the feminist movement in the United States is the story of the way social movements provide a space for interreligious awareness and global solidarity. In investigating this history we see possibilities for the future.

A Trans-religious Movement of Women

In the preceding chapter, the exploration followed Catholic Christian women religious of the Maryknoll order to China and witnessed their encounter with women of Chinese traditional religions. Through this encounter, there emerged an opportunity to consider what it means to be human not as isolated individuals but as formed through relationality. From the women encountered in mission who balanced multiple identities through the subject-position 'mother' to contemporary reflections on motherhood, I suggested motherhood as metaphor for our radically relational human condition. In this chapter, I will continue these themes—of motherhood, relationality, and interreligious encounter—and follow the trajectory that has been begun into contexts where Christian women met across religious lines.

The preceding analysis took as a point of departure the explicit task of meeting religious others in the mission context, and yet it brought us to the affirmation that a theological anthropology cannot be reduced to what is found under the banner of 'religion'. Indeed, the sacred and the everyday are found intertwined in human lives; thus the consideration of theological anthropology must also follow the experience of humanity 'out in the world'. In trying to raise to the surface examples of women's interfaith engagement as a site for reflecting on what it means to be human, this chapter extends the arenas for exploration to the so-called nonreligious sphere of secular activity, remembering always that the secular cannot be untangled from the sacred. But, since in the secular women's movement faith perspectives were often not explicitly articulated, the term 'interfaith' to describe these exchanges may be a bit of a misnomer. As 'interfaith' or 'interreligious' connotes the meeting of persons of different traditions for the explicit aim of interreligious exchange, we might hold those terms for the investigation in chapter 5. Perhaps it is best to describe the solidarities that emerged in the secular women's movement as 'trans-religious' encounters and alliances. Following the work of Aimee Carrillo Rowe, the 'trans-' indicates "deep connections across lines of difference [that] are a transformative source."[2] Or in the words of Lieve Troch, "dialogue of committed women across ethnicity, culture, religion and class is always a multireligious dialogue even if religion is not the issue."[3]

This chapter will also carry our conversation forward through the metaphor of motherhood as we follow mothers in their struggles for a better, future humanity. But, when 'motherhood' is claimed as metaphor for configuring our relationality, 'mother' must also be addressed directly for its configuration as a social role. As such, it has related women to the domestic space, in effect erasing them from the public sphere of politics. 'Motherhood' has thus served as a social and political category (often by exclusion), materially impacting actual lives. The limiting link between 'mother' and 'woman' created the context for the modern women's movement, to which this chapter turns.

Finally, because the preceding chapter positively reclaimed a Christian theology of motherhood as necessary for the future of the planet and promoted a synergy between women's experience and the Christian faith, this chapter must address the way religion itself serves a negative function in the struggle for women's well-being.

Elizabeth Cady Stanton, mother of the modern feminist movement, allows us to enter the secular women's movement in all of these dimensions: as a place for seeing the social and political roles of women as 'mother', as a location for witnessing trans-religious alliances, and as a voice willing to critically engage the role of religion within the social and political landscape.

Cady Stanton was born in 1815, in an America suffering under slavery, and she emerged as a voice crying out against the many systems and situations that would compromise human flourishing. Deeply concerned about the nature of the human condition, Cady Stanton worked as an antislavery activist in the mid-nineteenth century. She intuited that the subject-position 'mother' might be a nodal point in a network of care that extended beyond one's own kin, reflecting, "I know the care of one child made me thoughtful of all."[4] At the same time, as a mother of seven herself, she was not naïve to the negative impact motherhood held for many. As she recounted in her diary:

Tenafly, February 22, 1881

Doctor Channing brought me a little poem on motherhood, which, however, I do not like as it expresses the old idea of maternity being a curse. I have come to the conclusion that the first great work to be accomplished for woman is to revolutionize the dogma that sex is a crime, marriage a defilement and maternity a bane.[5]

While the "little poem" she received at the height of her work as leader of the modern women's movement is lost to history, her reflection on it may bring to mind resistance to 'motherhood' both in her day and our own. Concerned for the full humanity of women, Cady Stanton spent her life's work struggling not only for her own well-being but for the well-being of women, men, families, and society as they were intimately intertwined, organizing with Susan B. Anthony the first women's rights convention in Seneca Falls, New York, in 1848.

Cady Stanton's recognition of women's unequal social place saw the part religion played in policing women's roles. As Kathi Kern describes:

During the nineteenth century, women rooted their claims to public power in their natural piety and the moral authority it inspired. Under the broad banner of women's moral authority, many women united, identified for the first time as women, and experienced their first potent dose of political agency. Unlike most reformers of the period, who absorbed this rhetoric and frequently subverted it to more radical ends, Stanton by the 1880s had rejected it outright. A platform for women's political liberation could never be built upon the faulty foundation of religious faith because it would not bear weight. The corrosive principle of women's subordination was sealed into every plank: the church, the clergy, and the Bible.[6]

Witnessing the degradation of women through Christian thought, preaching, and practice, Cady Stanton unflinchingly drew back the curtain on a system that perpetuated women's inferiority and compromised human well-being. Openly critical of the negative influence of Christian thought and practice, she also held faith in a spiritual presence in the world that might empower humanity toward a more humane future.

> Toulouse, June 15, 1882
> I have been into many of the ancient cathedrals—grand, wonderful, mysterious. But I always leave them with a feeling of indignation because of the generations of human beings who have struggled in poverty to build these altars to the unknown god. In a chapel of one of these churches, before the altar to one of the saints, lies a large open book in which you are invited to write your name, pay a franc and then make a wish, which you are assured will be granted. I put down my name and the coin, and then asked that American women be enfranchised.[7]

Elizabeth Cady Stanton was willing to call for the transformation of religion, and she was ready to do this in a very public and interreligious way. For Cady Stanton raised her critique of religion not merely internal to a Christian audience, but in the setting of the 1893 World's Parliament of Religions, she simultaneously raised the critique for other traditions as well.

> "Equal rights for all" is the lesson this hour. "That cannot be," says some faithless conservative: "if you should distribute all things equally to-day they would be in the hands of the few to-morrow." Not if the religious conscience of the people were educated to believe that the way to salvation was not in creed and greed, but in doing justice to their fellow men.[8]

Leader of the secular women's movement, and critical of religion in its damaging strains, nevertheless, Cady Stanton used the language of religion to frame her cause envisioning 'salvation': "not in creed and greed, but in doing justice." The secular becomes sacred in the pursuit of justice, and the sacred is mobilized for the task.

That Cady Stanton was outspoken for women's rights is evident. That she raised her concerns in the interreligious context of the World's Parliament of Religions is documented. But she is not often held up as representative of the budding 'interfaith' movement, although, as we will see, she was in contact and conversation across multiple religious lines. In thinking about women's interfaith encounter, we might recognize that just as they have been erased from malestream religious histories, they have similarly been erased from the interreligious histories that are being written. A closer look at the Parliament may provide tools for reclaiming her heritage as our power.

"Sisterhood Is Superfluous": The 1893 World's Parliament of Religions

The World's Parliament of Religions was an assembly of religious leaders from around the globe—one of the many congresses held to coincide with the 1893 World's Fair. Evidence that participants came from around the world leads historian Richard Seager to suggest that "the global and inclusive composition of the Parliament, however limited by today's standards, made the assembly a first-of-its-kind event in the history of the world."[9] Branching out from the Columbian Exposition designed to celebrate the four-hundredth anniversary of the so-called discovery of the New World, the 1893 Parliament seemed to be celebrating the West's recent 'discovery' of the 'New Worlds' of the religious traditions of the globe. It was, after all, only recently that colonial enterprises in India and Africa had paved the way for missionaries and explorers to recognize the great variety of religious patterns in diverse cultures; and even more recently that this information had been organized for scholarly study. In the late nineteenth century, information about the diverse religions of the world had overflowed from colonial and mission enterprises into the academy and out to the wider public. In 1893, these newly discovered 'religions' were showcased among the other representative examples of innovation characteristic of a World's Fair.

The sense of wonder and discovery of new cultural and religious forms was seized upon by the media, which capitalized on the exotic that stirred the imagination. The *Daily Inter Ocean* announced the opening of the Parliament with vivid fanfare:

> About 10 o'clock strangers from every clime began to arrive, and for the next half hour President Bonney's office was turned into a reception room, where Chinese in the mandarin's robes and pigtails; Japanese in picturesque garb of chaste colors and varicolored head-dresses, Indians in their gaudy gowns of red, orange, and green; Germans, Russians, and Scandinavians; natives of Britain and her dependencies; and half a dozen interpreters mingled and mixed in a medley of universal brotherhood. The fair sex were there, too, and they were not neglected. But sisterhood in such a gathering was superfluous. The air was full of brotherhood, and it was of the generic kind, such as fits both sexes.[10]

In the *Daily Inter Ocean* account, attention once devoted to the "fair sex"—so named, it underscores women as the object of the masculine gaze—had now turned to the exotic foreigner dressed in "mandarin's robes and pigtails," "chaste colors," and the "gaudy gowns" of the "stranger" (note that the dress of European delegates remains unmentioned). Apparently, the masculinist gaze of mainstream religion in the late nineteenth century could hold its attention on only one 'other'. The non-Western, non-Christian brother had been identified as 'other', shifting attention and creating the perception that the Western, Christian 'sister' was no longer 'other'.

This newspaper account provides a transparent example of the androcentric construction that regularly frames the writing of history.[11] When brotherhood is the norm, women are included in the generic masculine. In the words of this one reporter, the male-centered focus of brotherhood makes "sisterhood" superfluous. This androcentric bias creates historical sources that omit the presence and experience of women, leading readers of such histories to assume that women were not present unless they are explicitly mentioned. But as this account so enthusiastically shows, the erasure of women's particular voices and experiences was intentional, the intent being to underscore the spirit of camaraderie that extended to women and men. Sisterhood in this account is superfluous in its redundancy, since the brotherhood already present extended to all. Even some of the prominent women at the Parliament spoke in language that participated in this erasure. For example, the chair of the Woman's Committee of the Parliament, the Reverend Augusta J. Chapin, reflected poetically on the event in her closing statement with the words "We have heard of the Fatherhood of God, the Brotherhood of Man, and the solidarity of the human race. . . . We are glad you came, O wise men of the East."[12]

Despite this rhetorical erasure of women's presence at the 1893 Parliament, historical evidence of women's high-profile addresses to the assembly allows us to see that women indeed had a voice in the first World's Parliament of Religions. This is reflected in even a cursory glance at the list of presenters reproduced in Seager's *The Dawn of Religious Pluralism: Voices from the World's Parliament of Religions, 1893*. While not equal to the number of men who participated, of the 186 individuals who presented papers at the Parliament, about 25 of them were women.[13] Further, Seager's list does not include the additional women who made statements at the opening and closing of the Parliament, such as the vice president of the Woman's Branch of the World's Congress Auxiliary (a parallel congress to the Parliament of Religions) and the chair of the Woman's Committee of the Parliament itself.[14] In fact, from Seager's 1993 collection of 1893 Parliament addresses and introductory notes—the most widely accessible scholarly collection on the Parliament—one would not know that there was a "Woman's Committee" at the Parliament. None of the historical records account for the exact number of women present in the audience gathered in the newly constructed Memorial Art Palace (today Chicago's Art Institute), further suggesting that women's participation in this groundbreaking interreligious dialogue was greater than it might appear. We are wise, then, to take up the suggestion of Ellen Martin Henrotin (or Mrs. Charles H. Henrotin, as she is named in the papers of the proceedings), vice president of the Woman's Branch of the World's Congress Auxiliary. Reflecting on women's participation in the Parliament, she recalls to the assembly that "the place which woman has taken in the Parliament of Religions and in the denominational con-gresses is one of such great importance that it is entitled to your careful attention."[15]

Heeding Henrotin's advice, we can hear the prophetic voices of Christian women in interreligious dialogue from the 1893 Parliament, not only Cady Stanton but suffragist Julia Ward Howe as well.[16]

Often in their addresses to the assembly, these leaders of the nine-teenth-century women's movement drew on the Parliament's shared sense of camaraderie to capitalize on the common endeavors facing the worldwide community of religions. They integrated women's concerns into the 'spirit of brotherhood' in a way that did not render 'women's concerns' the concerns of women only but rather emphasized the responsibility of all members of the religious communities to keep these issues in mind. In her address, Ward Howe extolled the virtue of the religions as noble voyages "into the unknown infinite of thought, into the deep questions of the soul between men [sic] and God." But in positively evaluating the project of religion in the persons of the great founders, Ward Howe broadcasts a critique of the way in which the principles of religion can no longer be found in the practices of the people. In her words,

> these great founders of religion have made the true sacrifice. They have taken a noble human life, full of every human longing and passion and power and aspiration, and they have taken it all to try and find out something about this question of what God meant man to be and does mean him to be. But while they have made this great sacrifice, how is it with the multitude of us? Are we making any sacrifice at all? We think it was very well that those heroic spirits should study, should agonize and bleed for us. But what do we do?[17]

Extending this critique, she levels a charge that resonates still through all the religious traditions of the world when she announces:

> I think nothing is religion which puts one individual absolutely above others, and surely nothing is religion which puts one sex above another. . . . And any religion which will sacrifice a certain set of human beings for the enjoyment or aggrandizement or advantage of another is no religion. . . . Any religion which sacrifices women to the brutality of men is no religion.[18]

Deliberately raising a feminist critique in a mainstream interreligious venue, Ward Howe demands that the representatives of the world's religions look critically at their own practices through the lens of women's experience and that they transform these practices to match the noble cause of their founders. She calls for agreement that all go forth from the Parliament ready to sustain a courageous influence within each faith to ensure that religions be for the glory of God and the sake of humanity.

Echoing the feminist concerns of Ward Howe, Cady Stanton raises them in the broader context of the well-being of all people. Cady Stanton envisions a future of the religions:

> As I read the signs of the times, I think the next form of religion will be the 'religion of humanity,' in which men and women will worship what they see of the divine in each other; the virtues, the beatitudes, the

possibilities ascribed to Deity, reflected in mortal beings. . . . The new religion will teach the dignity of human nature and its infinite possibilities for development. It will teach the solidarity of the race that all must rise or fall as one. Its creed will be Justice, Liberty, Equality for all children of earth.[19]

A liberationist reading of Christian scripture follows as Cady Stanton highlights the words of Jesus and the prophets and calls for their application to her own late nineteenth-century world. As Elisabeth Schüssler Fiorenza remarks on Cady Stanton's 1895 *The Woman's Bible,* "Elizabeth Cady Stanton conceived of biblical interpretation as a political act."[20] This is clearly the case in Cady Stanton's Parliament address, as she uses the Bible to challenge structures of domination and exclusion in the wider society. Far from being a disengaged, scholarly discourse on religion, what Cady Stanton urges is that all the delegates understand their religions in their political context and work for the transformation of the world. She announces:

To build a substantial house, we begin with the cellar and lay the foundations strong and deep, for on it depends the safety of the whole superstructure. So in race building, for noble specimens of humanity, for peace and prosperity in their conditions we must begin with the lowest stratum of society and see that the masses are well fed, clothed, sheltered, educated, elevated and enfranchised. Social morality, clean, pleasant environments, must precede a spiritual religion that enables man to understand the mysteries binding him to the seen and unseen universe.

This radical work cannot be done by what is called charity, but by teaching sound principles of domestic economy to our educated classes, showing that by law, custom and false theories of natural rights, they are responsible for the poverty, ignorance and vice of the masses. Those who train the religious conscience of the people must teach the lesson that all these artificial distinctions in society must be obliterated by securing equal conditions and opportunities for all.[21]

Speaking to a group of religious leaders and persons interested in 'religion', Cady Stanton argues that it is in the everyday that we succeed or fail as a human community. Hers is a political call for social change, and she suggests that it is in the secular that the sacred compels us to work. At the 1893 Parliament, Cady Stanton applied her concern for the disenfranchised in two distinctive ways, which become characteristic of later feminist thought in religion. First is the concern for women's well-being as reflected in equal representation and participation in the religions; second is the wider concern for the well-being of all the marginalized and disenfranchised as reflected in the above address to the Parliament representatives. Cady Stanton conceived the context of interreligious dialogue not as a neutral ground for comparison and contrast, nor a contest of which religion was 'true'. Rather, as indicated in her powerful words, interreligious dialogue was a forum for mutual struggles for justice and equality.

Ward Howe, Cady Stanton, and others brought to the 1893 Parliament feminist concerns that critiqued the structures of domination identifiable in patriarchal religions and societies organized in oppressive patterns. Annis F. F. Eastman spoke on "the influence of religion on women," bringing to light the negative assessment of women's nature that runs through many of the religious texts of the globe.[22] Yet others highlighted the positive roles religion can take in the material lives of women, as Henrietta Szold addressed the question "What has Judaism done for woman?"[23] and Fannie Barrier Williams asked, "What can religion further do to advance the condition of the American Negro?"[24] Demonstrating their status as experts in the traditions of the world, women's voices rang through the Parliament halls, for example, in "The Outlook of Judaism," by Josephine Lazarus.[25] Note was taken of the landmark quality of women's participation in the event. The Reverend Augusta J. Chapin remarked:

> Woman could not have had a part in [a Parliament of Religions if it had been convened prior to this age] for two reasons: one that her presence would not have been thought of or tolerated, and the other was that she herself was still too weak, too timid and too unschooled to avail herself of such an opportunity had it been offered. . . . Now the doors are thrown open in our own and many other lands. Women are becoming masters of the languages in which the great sacred literatures of the world are written. They are winning the highest honors that the great universities have to bestow, and already in the field of Religion hundreds have been ordained and thousands are freely speaking and teaching this new gospel of freedom and gentleness that has come to bless mankind.[26]

Chapin's reflection on the landmark quality of women's participation in the 1893 World's Parliament of Religions points to the wider social changes afoot that prepared women for such public engagement. Importantly, she identifies that it is not only in the American context that women's public and political engagement has seen them take on more social roles; as she notes that "now the doors are thrown open in our own and many other lands." Empowered by new social roles, the American Christian women at this Parliament had the opportunity to publicly share their voice and experience of religion. They also had the opportunity to hear about the experiences of women in other parts of the world, as delegates had traveled to Chicago from the various parts of the globe. Jeanne Sorabji of Bombay, for example, brought with her a perspective on women of India that challenged the perception of her audience. She illumined the advances in women's education, introducing to her audience the "schools and colleges for women in Bombay, Poona and Guzerat; also in Calcutta, Allahabad, Missoorie and Madras."[27] Identifying Indian women poets, physicians, and artists, she stirred the imagination of Western women to recognize the lead that women of other countries had taken and were continuing to take. "My countrywomen have been at the head of battles, guiding their men with word and look of command. My countrywomen will soon be spoken of as the greatest scientists, artists, mathematicians and preachers of the world."[28] The 1893 Parliament of Religions gives evidence of a global feminist movement emerging in its first wave around the globe and across religious lines.

That the first wave of feminism was a movement with the potential for interreligious contact and solidarity is borne out also at other sessions of the 1893 World Congress. Although the Parliament of Religions was explicitly focused on 'religion', it was not the only place where women of diverse religious backgrounds gathered and where religion intersected with their struggles. Another session of the World Congress (of which the Parliament was a part) gathered women from around the globe under the heading of the World's Congress of Representative Women. Focused to a great degree on the social issues facing women (education, social reform, civic participation, and suffrage) and on women's contributions to their culture (in science, literature, industry and the arts), the international forum provided the opportunity to introduce also a religious perspective to the feminist movement. As the editor of the published papers describes it, "The World's Congress of Representative Women anticipated the World's Parliament of Religions in bringing together, on the plane of mutual respect and sympathy, representatives of rival sects, nay, of antagonistic faiths."[29] Throughout the discussions of this 'secular' Congress, the individuals of the women's movement called out a religious perspective that demonstrated that they experienced the two as intimately intertwined. No speech said it more clearly than that of the president of the International Kindergarten Union, Sarah B. Cooper, when she proclaimed:

> There is no greater hindrance to the training of workers than the distinction which is drawn, even by professing Christians, between secular and religious work. Just as if one must go apart from his secular tasks to get at his religion. A religion that has everything for a future world and nothing for this world has nothing for either. . . . Genuine religion is not alone a preparation for some future world, but a grand instrument for the improvement of this.[30]

Here again we see a common feminist theme: Genuine religion is for the improvement of the world—the sacred and the secular meet.

Admittedly, representatives to the Congress were heavily dominated (almost exclusively) by countries of the West, with insights from the global feminist movement in Sweden, Canada, Iceland, Poland, Italy, Spain, England, Germany, France, Denmark, Finland, Greece, and the United States. This meant that the religious outlooks communicated through the conversations were largely Christian. Nevertheless, the experience of Jewish women was heard, as were a few voices that represented perspectives from South America, Syria, and Siam. So, the global feminist movement provided a space to witness the experience of women interreligiously, directly challenged preconceived assumptions about women in other parts of the globe, and indicates the changes that were afoot globally in the areas of women's education and legal, social, and economic rights.[31] Given voice through distinctive cultural and religious settings, the overabundance of women's experiences was in evidence at these international meetings.

While there was sparse representation of non-Western women at these landmark events, the story of the women's movement as it intersects with religion is incomplete without the recognition of a global character of the first wave. Describing the emergence of the Indian women's movement, Manisha Desai wrote:

> Although the reform movement was led by men who viewed women merely as objects of reform, it resulted in creating a small group of upper caste, educated women who, along with some English and Irish women, initiated the first wave of the women's movement in India. They did so by forming autonomous women's organizations. The first such organization, the Indian Women's Conference was formed in 1904. The most important one, the All India Women's Conference (AIWC), was formed in 1927.[32]

Among the women of India who emerged as leaders, Sarojini Naidu is remembered. Born in India, Naidu was educated at Girton, Cambridge, and returned to her native land as the champion of women's rights as early as 1898, campaigning for women's education, suffrage, and the rights of widows. She worked alongside Mohandas Gandhi in the nonviolent social movement for India's independence from colonial rule, a movement infused with the religious symbolisms of Hinduism yet interreligiously concerned. Asked at an international peace conference about her work in politics, Naidu framed her response interreligiously: "I think it is inevitable that one should become interested in politics if one is a true Indian. I lived in a Muhammadan city, and you see, I had so many Muhammadan friends. . . . I have taken part in all their political and educational meetings. I have presided over their meetings and spoken at mosques."[33] Religion, politics, and the social intertwine in the sacred secular in such a way as to cross sectarian lines. Traveling to international congresses, in South Africa and the United States, Naidu had the opportunity to shape the interreligious imagination of persons around the globe in the early part of the twentieth century and to impact her local context as the first woman president (elected in 1925) of the Indian National Congress.

Just as Naidu and other women took part in the nationalist movements of their home countries, so too the women's movements in other parts of the globe took root in similar struggles. As Geraldine Heng reports, "It is a truism that nationalist movements have historically supported women's issues as part of a process of social inclusion, in order to yoke the mass energy of as many community groups as possible to the nationalist cause (Anderson 1983)."[34] This nationalist-feminist characteristic is evidenced in women's activism in China broadly collectable under the banner of the first-wave feminism. As Sharon Hom reports:

> When feudal China began to crumble in the last half of the nineteenth century from the pressures of internal corruption and the impact of the Western influences and imperialism, the voices and participation of women were crucial in the political and military struggles to modernize and build a new China. Beginning with the May Fourth Movement in 1917, Chinese women and progressive men condemned the bankrupt social system and institutions of feudal China and demanded the recognition of rights for women: equal participation in politics and government, the abolition of arranged marriages, and equal rights with men in employment and educational opportunities.[35]

History shows Chinese women and Indian women finding space within nationalist movements to raise feminist concerns, as women of Egypt in the early twentieth century did likewise. Here, Huda Sha'rawi is remembered (1896–1947). As early as 1917, Sha'rawi was organizing public forums for women on their condition in Egypt, and in 1919 she organized an anti-British demonstration. As Leila Ahmed describes it: "In 1922 Huda Sha'rawi formed, with her friends, the Egyptian Feminist Union and was from then on throughout the 20s and 30s to be a central figure in the women's movement. In 1923 she led the Egyptian women's delegation to an international women's conference in Rome. It was at this time that she cast off her veil."[36] To Sha'rawi, the veil symbolized the repressive elements of religion and social expectations that compromised women's full humanity.[37] An advocate for women's rights, like her sisters around the globe, Sha'rawi intersected her activism with attention to the religious dimension.

In all these cases of 'representative women' we are best served not to see them as 'the remarkable few', but to recognize these few names as evidence of the yet-to-be named countless others whose collective work set to transforming societies. Ahmed, for example, shows the many outlets that any number of women engaged at this time:

> Women wrote in the numerous women's journals published then, such as *anis al-jalis* (1898–1908), *Fatat al-sharq* (1906–1939), *Al-jins al-latif* (1908–24), *Al-'afaf* (1910–22), and *Fatat al-Nil* (1913–1915), as well as, in some cases, in the mainstream press. They founded organizations for the intellectual improvement of women, the Society for the Advancement of Woman, established in 1908, being among the earliest; it took a conservative Islamic line. Another, the Intellectual Association of Egyptian Women, founded in 1914, included among its founders Huda Sha'rawi, the preeminent feminist leader of the 1920s and 1930s, and Mai Ziyada, a feminist intellectual and writer.[38]

Malak Hifni Nassef also struggled alongside Sha'rawi for women's rights in Egypt, and turned her attention to include also women's religious rights.

> In 1911, when the first Egyptian congress met to deliberate and issue recommendations on the needs of the country, Nassef, noting that the points presented for the congress to consider addressed every issue of importance except women's issues, hastily drew up a list, which she

presented to the congress. It included the demand that all fields of higher education be opened to women and that space be made available in mosques for women to attend public prayer.[39]

Just as Sha'rawi and Nassef represent the many more women who contributed to the movement, Cady Stanton, Ward Howe, and Susan B. Anthony were but the most public figures in the North American context where we must recall also the countless women who picketed, demonstrated, and gathered in the many congresses for women's rights. In the context of India, Naidu's name is among the many, many more whose collective work impacted their society.[40]

In many of these locations, the struggle for dignity was one that crossed religious lines: Cady Stanton not only spoke publicly at the World's Parliament of Religions, in her diary she recounted her being visited by a delegation of Jewish women seeking a more intimate inter-religious exchange.[41] Cady Stanton cites Rabbi Felix Adler as someone who informed her thinking on religion and life,[42] and in her diary she recalled meetings with Annie Besant, who brought to the table the influence of Hinduism and Buddhism.[43] Sha'rawi's education at Cambridge and her participation in global congresses saw her work crossing religious lines, just as Naidu had already reflected that to be Indian was to engage Hindu, Muslim, and Christian communities.

Infusing nationalist and peace movements with women's perspectives, the women in these international movements had the opportunity to learn from one another—for example, at the international congresses of the varied organizations of which they were part. Under conditions of a globalizing world, where the interconnectedness of colonialism, travel and economics rendered the world 'a single place', feminist ideas flowed across geographical and religious lines for a transnational social movement that impacted also religion, just as people flowed through these systems bringing with them (and seeking) change. In Chava Frankfort-Nachmias's description, "Israel is considered among the 'first wave countries' where women gained political rights, including the right to vote, early in the twentieth century. . . . The struggle for gender equality was led by a minority of revolutionary Jewish women who emigrated from Russia to form a new egalitarian society in Palestine."[44]

While an appropriate dose of suspicion asks us to interrogate whether the global feminist movement consisted in the westernization of the world, feminist historians insist that there is evidence that these global, universalizing ideas met with native ideas to find unique and full flourishing. Ahmed writes:

> Arguably [Sha'rawi's] most daring and authoritative act—the act of leaving a marriage in defiance of husband and family—occurred when she was thirteen and when her exposure to Western ideas had been minimal. Evidently, therefore, there were sources within her background prior to her exposure to Western ideas that endowed her with a sense of her right to autonomy and her right to follow her own sense of what was morally correct in defiance of elders.[45]

The creativity of countless women of the first wave has seen the transformation of societies and social practices around the globe, challenging not only traditional social roles and expectations but at times traditional religious expectations as well.

Standing in Solidarity: Women of the Second Wave and the Emergence of Feminist Theology

The interweaving of religion, the social and the political, in the various movements of the late nineteenth and early twentieth centuries, created sites where religion was interrogated in critique and employed as transformative resource. But, as yet, women's training as religious leaders remained minimal around the globe. Without access to theological education in the various traditions, the level of theologizing around the issues remained underdeveloped. While the theologizing of women in the first wave is evidenced in their own reflections, the development of a feminist theological voice developed only after women gained access to education as part of the broader movements of social change. Thus, what scholars describe as 'feminist theology' has its origin within the 'second wave' of feminism.

In the West, the trans-religious social movement therefore had an implicit impact on the way Christian feminist theology would be voiced. As Peggy Antrobus describes the emergence of feminism's 'second wave': "The women's rights movement [of the late twentieth century] was largely an upshot of the movement for women's suffrage that blossomed in the latter part of the 19th century, and women from different countries had already formed alliances to advance their common cause."[46] In the North American context, the continued struggle for racial equality of the civil rights era (1960s–1970s) coincided with women's struggle for gender equality. Although many factors coalesced to form a women's movement in the 1960s with public and political influence, a key moment to include is the publication of *The Feminine Mystique* by Betty Friedan, a journalist and a Jew, in which she chronicled the emptiness and traumatic paralysis of the 'modern woman' confined to mothering roles of domestic home-making. A trip to Washington, D.C., in June 1966 to speak before a commission on the status of women brought Friedan into the center of a group of female politicians concerned to secure women's rights under Title VII (of the U.S. Equal Employment Opportunity Commission). The twenty-eight original members of the National Organization for Women (NOW), which sprang from that meeting, soon grew to three hundred charter members, electing Friedan its president in October 1966. Within one year, membership rose to one thousand.[47]

Remembered as being at the heart of a secular movement, the National Organization for Women was in actuality a coalition across religious lines, as the women of NOW came together in their complexity, which included varying degrees of religious affiliation. As Ann Braude describes it: "An often reprinted early photograph of the founders of NOW begins to tell the story. It shows a nun in full habit standing next to the Methodist lay leader Anna Arnold Hedgeman, coordinator of the Commission on Religion and Race of the National Council of Churches, standing next to [Jewish] Betty Friedan."[48] Indeed, the founders of NOW represented the faith traditions of a diverse American society, with its varied Christian denominations and Jewish faith communities. Some of the founding members of NOW were leaders in both the secular movement for women's rights and the emergent movements in feminist theology. Elizabeth Farians, for example, was already actively involved in the writing of feminist theology. "Farians attended the first graduate program in theology for women at Saint Mary's College–Notre Dame"[49] and earned a doctorate in theology.[50] Another founding member of NOW, Pauli Murray, a lawyer, went on to become the first black woman ordained as an Episcopal priest. Murray's preaching suggests that the collaborative efforts experienced interreligiously in the women's movement called forth a particular theological vision. "When I truly believe that God is my Father and Mother, in short, my Creator," Murray proclaimed in her 1975 Father's Day Sermon, "I am bound also to believe that all men, women, and children of whatever race, color, creed, or ethnic origin, are my sisters-and-brothers-in-Christ, whether they are Anglicans, Roman Catholics, Methodists, Black Muslims, members of the Judaic faith, Russian Orthodox, Buddhists, or atheists."[51]

Participation in the social movements for women's rights in North America transformed not only the faith of Christian women but their Jewish sisters as well. As Deborah Lipstadt describes,

American Jewish feminism began to take shape in the late 1960s in direct response to the second wave of American feminism. . . . Propelled by the wider challenges of American feminism, Jewish women began examining critically both their own status within Jewish tradition and the political and social structure of the American Jewish community. Some Jewish women, particularly those already active in the broad-based feminist movement, who often lacked strong Jewish communal and religious attachments, attacked the cultural and social norms that they believed had shaped them. But those who called for reevaluation were not only women estranged from the community or at the periphery of Jewish life. Among women actively committed to Judaism and their Jewish communities, a similar feeling that all was not right developed. Some, as a result, began to focus their energies on winning women greater roles in Jewish religious and communal life.[52]

An interreligious solidarity in the secular movement of women's rights propelled women of diverse social locations to transform their religious traditions.[53]

Despite their efforts on many fronts, and a variety of political gains, the U.S. constitutional amendment for women's equal rights was never ratified.[54] Nevertheless, the cross alliances of women as scholars and activists propelled the emergence of a distinctive feminist theological movement in the American context from out of the energies of this political movement. Ruth Rosen describes it:

Fragmented and wounded, the movement remained immensely alive. In religion, for instance, women scholars in theological schools and seminaries challenged orthodoxy, reexamined translations, and reinterpreted religious texts. . . . Meanwhile, feminists challenged all kinds of religious orthodoxy. The scholar Mary Daly, a member of NOW's task force on women and religion, launched what would soon become a widespread assault on the identity of God "as an old man with a beard." Merlin Stone imagined life "When God was a Woman"; Rosemary Radford Ruether, a longtime activist and well-respected theological scholar, critiqued the Judeo-Christian duality between mind and body and its ecological impact on humans and the planet; and Judith Plaskow resurrected the feisty Lilith, whose insubordinate behavior had resulted in God's creation of the more deferential Eve. Carol Christ extolled the psychic importance of rediscovering prehistoric female goddesses, and Marija Gimbutas excavated goddess cultures of the ancient world. Charlene Spretnak analyzed the politics of women's spirituality, Paula Gunn Allen explored the place of the spiritual in Native American cultures, Delores S. Williams, Audre Lorde, and Alice Walker explored what kind of 'womanist theology' would nourish African-American women; and Gloria Anzaldua examined the impact of Catholicism on the lives of Chicanas.[55]

In Rosen's description, the momentum of the women's movement in North America, as a movement that crossed religious and social divisions, propelled transformations within these varied groups. And, as she underscores, the impact was felt profoundly within the religions. Developing out of an interreligious secular movement, feminist theology itself carried with it a new way of thinking interreligiously. As Carol Christ recounts, "I vividly remember the days when the women in religion section [of the American Academy of Religion] was a place where feminists in religion engaged in dialogue across religious boundaries. I believed that we were working together to transform and recreate religious traditions."[56]

The second wave of feminism gave rise to a feminist theology with strength and staying power precisely because of the social advances women had gained. Women were now pursuing theological training in areas formerly reserved for men. For example, Mary Daly's doctorate in theology from the University of Fribourg saw her trained in "the most traditional Thomistic education from Dominican priest professors lecturing in Latin."[57] And in the early 1960s Elisabeth Schüssler Fiorenza "became the first woman [at the University of Würzburg] to complete the full range of theological and pastoral options previously reserved for male candidates for the priesthood."[58] Women were ordained in the Lutheran tradition in 1965 and as Episcopal priests in 1975. The first female rabbi in America was seen in 1972. Engaged in the study of religion or theological training, women impacted by the second wave of the women's movement carried with them a sense of solidarity across religious boundaries. Many of them applied this to their collaborative work, as can be traced through a series of texts that brought together women of varied faith traditions. In many ways, feminist theology continued to cross religious boundaries, just as the feminist movement in many parts of the world had done. This is evidenced, for example, in the collection, *Womanspirit Rising: A Feminist Reader in Religion* (1979), which included writings from Christian, Jewish, post-Christian, and pagan feminists, reflecting well the range of women engaged together in the North American women's movement. *Weaving the Visions: New Patterns in Feminist Spirituality* (1989) continued the interreligious coop- eration, expanding to include Native American spirituality and reflec- tions from the perspective of African traditional religion. The practice of thinking theologically with other faiths continued in the volume *After Patriarchy: Feminist Transformations of the World Religions* (1991), in which feminists from Christianity, Hinduism, Islam, Buddhism, Judaism, and Native American traditions applied shared methods to their specific faith traditions. The interreligious cooperation of the women's movement encouraged the fruitful exchange of methods and strategies so that femi- nist theology emerged in many places as an interreligious approach.

In these texts we have evidence that feminist theologians across the religious traditions are reading one another's work. That is to say, when Christian feminist theologians reflect systematically on their tradition, they draw on non-Christian sources. For example, in her theological con- sideration of the doctrine of God in *Sexism and God-Talk*, Rosemary Radford Ruether draws also on the pre-Christian conceptions of God as resources for challenging Christian hegemony in the form of a male- symbolized God. In her many works of biblical scholarship and christol- ogy, Elisabeth Schüssler Fiorenza consults the works of Jewish feminist theologians and so is sensitive to the ways Christian theology might neg- atively reinscribe anti-Jewish attitudes. And the conversation works in reverse as well. Judith Plaskow, a Jewish feminist theologian, draws on the work of Elisabeth Schüssler Fiorenza, Mary Daly, and other Christian feminist theologians;[59] and Riffat Hassan, a Muslim feminist theologian, reads Jewish and Christian resources on the Genesis account, among other texts.[60] In the representative texts of feminist theology of the second wave, there is already an interreligious methodology at work. That this methodology is trained toward the social and the political is reflected in the perspective of one of these early texts envisioning the feminist theological project across religious lines: "We are engaged in a common project of working toward more just and humane religious and social institutions."[61]

While the movements of feminist theology emerged out of the inter- religious secular women's movement in a radical way in the United States, by no means was the second wave of feminism limited to the boundaries of North America. It was a worldwide movement. A book entitled *Sisterhood Is Global* (1984) gives witness to the similar changes taking place around the globe. Its editor writes, "The book you hold in your hands reflects the intense network of contacts and interlocking activities the world's women have built over the past two decades."[62] With contributors from over 72 countries, the text captures the sense of a collaborative movement that transgressed boundaries of national, religious, and social identities.[63] In the words of Robin Morgan, "Just as *Sisterhood Is Global* is a cross-cultural, cross-age-group, cross-occupation/class, cross-racial, cross-sexual-preference, and cross-ideological assemblage of women's voices, so is the movement itself."[64] Morgan echoes Rosen's affirmation that the so-called 'secular' women's movement was populated by women who were eager, then, to apply the insights of the movements to their religious traditions. Morgan asserts that in *Sisterhood Is Global* "no patriarchal religion is left unconfronted."[65] But simultaneously revealed in the pages of the volume is that, while women challenged their traditions of origin, they nevertheless often found within them constructive resources for a feminist theological future.[66] We see here both a challenge to the patriarchal constraints of religion and, nevertheless, a willingness to creatively employ religious communities as sites for change. Morgan writes:

> Arungu-Olende of Kenya and Griffen of the Pacific Islands are only two of many contributors who write about the activism of women's church groups in their respective regions. Women's constructive use of the churches—as meeting places, bases of female friendship and solidarity, for social and political activity and such progressive community services as childcare, credit unions, and shelters—points to women's use of religion as a code for political organization, or at least for the expression of rebellion and individualism with a modicum of safety.[67]

Morgan names a theme we see throughout the secular women's movement: Religion is political just as the secular is sacred. From China to the Middle East, Africa, and South America, the second wave of the women's movement was global. It intersected with religion regularly, and it brings to light the deep intertwining of religion and politics. In so many examples, women in the trans-religious movement both critiqued their religious traditions and employed them to further the cause of a fuller human flourishing.

The Superfluity of Sisterhood: Overflowing 'Woman' in the Third Wave

If the first and second waves of feminism encouraged women from across religious traditions to see themselves sharing in a struggle 'as women', a third wave emerged from this historical moment that began to see the collective of 'women' as internally diverse and the identity of 'woman' as necessarily hybrid. Concerned that only some 'women' were being represented under the category 'woman', black feminists challenged the women's movement of the 1970s to see the racism internal to the movement itself. It may not have been the outright racism of the first wave's Elizabeth Cady Stanton, who came to see the causes of women's suffrage and black enfranchisement as fundamentally in competition, but racism persisted when white women's experience counted as data for explaining women's condition while black women's experiences were simply ignored. By privileging sexism over other forms of oppression, second-wave feminists participated in a movement that sought gains for white women of some economic standing while ignoring the privileges they enjoyed.[68]

The undertow from the second wave in the United States brought about the third wave here and can be identified in the unrest of black feminists who challenged the second wave as a white woman's movement. The struggle, they said, was not just against patriarchal injustices but against the very fabric of white supremacy. Such a fabric of existence fundamentally impacted what it meant to be 'woman' under the triple threat of sexism, racism, and economic disparity. The constraints for black women meant a creativity played out within conditions that denied their very humanity: The white supremacy of the slave economy and lynch culture, and its insidious pervasiveness in the Jim Crow South and the segregated North, created the conditions for a very different experience of 'being human' for black folks in the United States.[69]

While the bane of motherhood and the boredom of domestic life may have propelled white women to seek equality of rights and opportunity, black women in the United States had long experienced motherhood and the domestic life in ways very different from those in which their white counterparts did. Under conditions of slavery, motherhood was an economic institution that benefitted the white slaveholder both in terms of future labor for production and in terms of sexual slavery under which black women were made available to their masters. The domestic life of mammies to white children was an institution both before and after emancipation, an institution that benefitted white women as well as white men. As surrogate 'wives' and 'mothers', black women in white racist culture experienced being 'woman' in a way very different from that in which their white counterparts did. 'Woman' and 'mother' are social and political categories and highly racialized.

Womanist perspectives give voice to the different experiences of black women in the United States and demonstrate how their dehumanization was caused by white racist ideologies and white culture. Womanist literature provides a rich tapestry and vivid texture for the ways white culture dehumanized black women. In Zora Neale Hurston's *Their Eyes Were Watching God* (1937), three generations live out their womanhood in white racist social systems. The enslaved Nanny Crawford gives birth to a daughter by her white master and is expelled by her white owner's wife. The daughter, raised by this fiercely determined woman, is raped by a white schoolteacher, giving birth to Nanny's light-skinned granddaughter, Janie. Janie enjoys some benefits from the light skin that was hers, but at the cost of the dehumanization of her mother and grandmother, as she moves in a world where whiteness is a form of privilege and situates her uneasily in her own community. In Toni Morrison's *The Bluest Eye* (1970), whiteness/blackness forms the matrix of dehumanization for Pecola Breedlove, who is mothered into ugliness by her own mother, who had internalized white racist ideologies. Through womanist literature we are reminded of a world where white women, as well as white men, form the fabric of a culture of white supremacy, which devalues black and brown bodies. But womanist literature also attends to the persistence of a spirited creativity despite the death-dealing of racism. Hurston's novel, as well as Alice Walker's *The Color Purple* (1982), amply demonstrate this. In writing and activism, the third wave of feminism spoke forth the multiplicity of women's experience under racism and economic disparity conditioned by the history of slavery and white supremacist ideologies in the United States, demonstrating 'women's' diversity, the unequal distribution of social and material well-being, and our human creativity.

At the same time, so-called Third World women spoke forth conditioned by and resistant to the Western colonial programs that had impacted the conditions of their humanity, challenging again any universal notions of 'woman' and further challenging women to see their complicity in damaging other women. Gayatri Chakravorty Spivak offers a rendering of 'woman' in postcolonial perspective that brings us face-to-face with the mutually damaging and internationally entangled experience of woman. Like womanist writers, Spivak claims literature as source for revealing the conditions of our humanity, reading Bengali novelist Mahasweta Devi's *Breast Stories* to complexify 'woman' in post-colonial India. Devi's "Breast-Giver" tells the story of Jashoda, an Indian woman caught in a professional 'mothering' as wet nurse to the extended family of her employer. While motherhood is her familial subject-position, it is also Jashoda's economic contribution to the sustenance of her family. "She never had time to calculate if she could or could not bear motherhood. Motherhood was always her way of living and keeping alive her world of countless beings."[70] In a nexus of relationships where the part of 'woman' as 'mother' is valorized in many strands of Hindu and Indian thought, Spivak reads Jashoda's professionalization to move "mothering in its materiality beyond its socialization as affect, beyond psychologiza-tion as abjection, or yet transcendentalization as the vehicle of the divine."[71] For Spivak, 'mothering' is not merely a social, psychological, and religious category; it is also an economic one. Jashoda, however, does not stand for all 'women' but rather reveals 'motherhood' as a conflictual category in modern times. With the 'modernizing' of a new generation of women who are claiming, "I'm a woman! Not a mother, not a sister, not a wife,"[72] 'woman' is both exploiter and exploited as Jashoda tends, nurses, and raises the children of these 'new women'. In the end, however, she is alone and exploited, a cancer in her breast taking her life from Jashoda as she wonders, "You grew so big on my milk, and now you're hurting me so? . . . she had suckled the world, could she then die alone?"[73]

Spivak reads this story on the many levels of a postcolonial India, seeing Jashoda as India in an exploitative neocolonial global landscape; but also seeing her exploited by her own daughters and daughters-in-law and foster daughters who employ her services while renouncing their own position of mother; and also seeing Jashoda as "complicit victim" who materially benefits for a time while employed as wet nurse and "professional mother." Spivak writes, "The critical deployment of liberal-feminist thematics in Mahasweta's text obliges us to remember that 'we' in this passage might be parasitical not only upon imperialism (Haldar) but upon the gendered subaltern (Jashoda) as well."[74] The rights denied to Jashoda are denied not only by men but also by elite women.[75] Reading the story on many levels, Spivak also resists packaging the story for transparent consumption. Devi and Jashoda, and Spivak herself, stand as witness to the way 'woman' and 'mother' in the complex context of a postcolonial world do not rest simply with one narrative telling and, at times, exceed understanding.

In superfluity, women of the third wave insist on multiplicity within the category of 'woman', as gender alone does not capture who we are. The experience of 'women' is intersected with race, class, culture, religion, sexual orientation, and more. The flow of multiplicity in recognizing women's diverse embodiment enables the reclamation of "sisterhood as superfluous" in the embrace of women's superfluity, not in its negative connotation but derived from the original meaning of the Latinate word, 'overflowing'. In the 1893 account of the World's Parliament of Religions, 'sisterhood' was deemed superfluous in its redundancy, since the many brothers present flowed sufficiently with camaraderie as to encompass women as well. With mimicry, the term might be reclaimed to embrace not redundancy, but overabundance. Sisterhood is indeed superfluous, as multiplicity overflows in generative diversity, where 'women' are unable to be captured by 'brotherhood' or even by 'sisterhood' alone.

As women around the globe proliferated the discourse of feminist thought in the third wave, the overflowing of women's voices and experiences rendered 'woman' irreducibly diverse. In the flow of globalization, as ideas and peoples move rapidly and regularly, the global women's movement created a 'transnational discourse' whereby conversations and struggles in solidarity transgressed national boundaries.[76] Following Arjun Appadurai's tracing of such discourses, the feminist movement in each part of the world has both a history and a genealogy: There is the impact of Western feminist movements whose history spreads out from itself and influences other forms of feminist movement around the globe, but in each location the feminist movement has a genealogy that is indigenous to events, movements, realities, and discourses that impact the movement's taking root.[77] Thus, in the process, the key terms of the discourse 'feminism', 'women's rights', and even 'woman' take on different shades of meaning. Whereas Appadurai describes this multiplicity within the discourse of 'democracy', a similar pattern is evident in the global discourse of feminism. Appadurai writes:

> As a result of the differential diaspora of these keywords, the political narratives that govern communication between elites and followers in different parts of the world involve problems of both a semantic and pragmatic nature: semantic to the extent that words (and their lexical equivalents) require careful translation from context to context in their global movements, and pragmatic to the extent that the use of these

words by political actors and their audiences may be subject to very different sets of contextual conventions that mediate their translation into public politics.[78]

Thus the term 'feminist' or 'woman' or 'mother' may convey different meanings in different cultural and religious contexts; 'sisterhood' is superfluous in its overflow of meaning.

The superfluity of sisterhood suggests that the experience of 'woman' is always more than what can be contained in a category or description. It suggests further, as an insight for theological anthropology, that humanity is infinitely internally diverse. Women of 'third wave' feminism and the feminist theology that emerges from it reflect this in vivid particularity and detail. The insights of womanists and postcolonial feminists point persuasively to the constitution of 'woman' with both internal difference *and* differential privileges, locally and globally.

As third-wave feminists have demonstrated, not all women bear the burden of inequality equally, and some enjoy privileges rooted in racial and global exploitations of their sisters. Thus, while the third wave of feminism is characterized by 'difference' as a constitutive dimension of what the category 'woman' is, nevertheless the feminist movement continues to aim at creating bonds of solidarity across these differences for the well-being of women and men and for their liberation from the multiple oppressions that characterize human existence around the globe. The diversity of what it means to 'be woman' (as a social category) is acknowledged while nevertheless the struggle for the well-being of women (as a political category) continues. As Judith Plaskow describes it:

> Feminism begins in resistance and vision, a resistance and vision that are not simply personal but that are rooted in "communities of resistance and solidarity" that are challenging specific forms of oppression out of concrete experiences of alternative ways of being in the world. . . . Out of participation in a community of resistance and transformation, one then looks for and consciously claims the resistive elements in a particular tradition, in order to mobilize them toward a different future.[79]

Since we are constituted relationally by our networks of relationships, for better and for worse, the feminist vision of being human includes joining together in networks of solidarity and communities of resistance.

In their work for justice, women in the feminist movements have continued to find their religious traditions as sites from which and in which to bring about holistic healing. For even as women marched and demonstrated, wrote and legislated for greater social and political rights, and even as they may have experienced their traditions as constraining in their assignment of gendered spheres, women have still, at times, found sources for wholeness in the practices of their faith.

In the context of India, gendered expectations often kept women in the private space of the home, but their religiosity found meaning-making practices within the domestic ritual space.

> In India, religion is not predominantly a male enterprise. Women play active and conspicuous roles in the religious life in the domestic sphere, although they are invisible socially. Most Hindu women across India have some kind of religious life of their own, even where they conform to male ideas of womanhood. In both the domestic and public sphere, a man's and a woman's religious life are distinguishable. There are innumerable domestic rituals for the attainment of fortune and prosperity that are exclusive to women. The religious world of women is rich, vital and diverse. These women may not fit into the category of religious leaders in the public domains, but they wield the power of auspiciousness (*mangala*) and beneficence, valued dearly in Hindu society.[80]

In India, distinctive spaces and communal rituals are also carved out to celebrate the religious calendar as it intersects with the life cycle of women.[81] In these settings, women develop relationships and affirm aspects of themselves in their particular life situation in deep relationship with the Divine. Lynn Teskey Denton notes that "most available accounts demonstrate that childbirth rituals, family and household rites, and a large range of vows and fasts constitute the core of women's religious practice (stri-acar), and that this practice is concerned almost exclusively with the welfare of others, particularly male kin."[82]

Vashudha Narayanan chronicles, in addition to domestic rituals, the diverse ways that women found outlets in religious practices despite the complex contexts of caste, class, age, gender, and religious exclusion. Women wrote as bhakti poets, they have been patrons of temples; women can be educated as reciters of the Vedas and be recognized as the embodiment of the divine.[83]

There is creativity within the constraints of traditions, and there is creativity transcending those constraints.

Similarly, as Judith Plaskow has reminded us, "[Jewish] women were obviously able to find great meaning in their limited number of commandments. They were deeply involved with their families, a sphere of connection that extended to the dead. They felt deeply connected to the matriarchs, whose experience and merit they invoked. The *tkhines* testify to the importance of relationship in women's spirituality."[84]

In the writing of Jewish women who observe the constraints of the Sabbath, for example, a more positive understanding of bounded time and space emerges. The limitations placed on persons within the ritual observation of the Holy Day allows for a freedom of reconstituting the space in relationships. As Adele Reinhartz describes it, "traditional Sabbath observance entails not only synagogue worship but also ritual meals, abstention from work, driving, writing, cooking and other activities that we engage in throughout the week. In practical terms, Sabbath observance also entails living in proximity to the synagogue and to other people who observe a similar lifestyle. Living within such a community is simply wonderful from a social point of view, and allows the Sabbath truly to be a day that is different from the rest of the week."[85]

The superfluity of women's experiences means that diverse expressions within faith traditions have been sources for women across the three waves of the feminist movement. As Leila Gal Berner reflects:

> As a Jewish feminist, I take one particular kind of feminist journey. I am a Jew who honors but does not consider herself bound by traditional *halakha* (Jewish law). Other Jewish feminists have elected to carve out a place for feminism in the ritual realm while remaining with the boundaries of traditional halakha. Our approaches are quite different, but we share a commitment to giving voice to Jewish women's spiritual concerns, and shaping a Judaism for the future that incorporates women's voices and life experiences as part of the legitimate Jewish Tradition (with a capital "T").[86]

Within each of the traditions, women's engagement has taken diverse forms of meaning-making within proscribed constraints and transformative resistance to those constraints. The result is diversity within *and* among women's experience of religion, revealing a further fluidity to women's religious identities. As Miriam Cooke describes it:

> Islamic feminism is not a coherent identity, but rather a contingent, contextually determined strategic self-positioning. Actions, behaviors, pieces of writing that bridge religious and gender issues in order to create conditions in which justice and freedom may prevail do not translate into a

seamless identity. . . . The term "Islamic feminist" invites us to consider what it means to have a difficult double commitment: on the one hand, to a faith position, and on the other hand, to women's rights both inside the home and outside. The label Islamic feminist brings together two epithets whose juxtaposition describes the emergence of a new, complex self-positioning that celebrates multiple belonging. To call oneself an Islamic feminist is *not to describe a fixed identity but to create a new, contingent subject position.* This location confirms belonging in a religious community while allowing for activism on behalf of and with other women.[87]

The investigation of women in the three waves of the women's movement *and* in the accompanying changes within their religious lives demonstrates that there are a diversity of subject-positions that women and feminists inhabit. The tracing of women's religiosity through the three waves of the feminist movement has shown that religious traditions are *both* the site of constraint and the site of meaning-making creativity. The question raised by womanist and postcolonial feminists continues to be, as we find sites of meaning and wholeness within our communities: How do we maintain an awareness of those beyond our particular community?

In the preceding pages, we have seen examples of human becoming in which representatives of the women's movement cross religious boundaries to create solidarities and alliances. In this, I see what Aimee Carrillo Rowe identifies as alliances across difference: trans-religious alliances that witness to the powerful potential for human solidarity.[88] Throughout, there have been witnesses to the idea that what religion is has to do with the well-being of the world, and that our sacred concerns are enmeshed within a secular world. Thus, the project of finding sites of wholeness in our religious traditions leaks out into the secular and necessarily inter-religious space, where differences of religion, race, class, culture, and gender meet. The witness to the sacred secular is witness to an interreligious future for humanity.

The Project of Human Becoming: Theophanies and Religion Transformed

The point of investigating the global feminist movement in its many forms is, in light of the aims of this book, ultimately theological. That is to say, I am in search of witnesses to fundamental insights about what it means to be human and, subsequently, to read these insights within a theological anthropology that closely situates the human person in relation to the mystery that Christians call 'God'. Read theologically, this witness to solidarity then opens up to the very mystery of God glimpsed in the struggle. In her foundational work of feminist theology, *Beyond God the Father: Toward a Philosophy of Women's Liberation*, Mary Daly saw in the women's movement the very being and becoming of God. Fundamentally, Daly challenges the image of God as patriarch controlling and securing the status quo; but even further, she challenges any conception of God that would construct God as one more 'thing' alongside others. Classically, she writes:

> Why indeed must 'God' be a noun? Why not a verb—the most active and dynamic of all? . . . . The anthropomorphic symbols for God may be intended to convey personality, but they fail to convey that God is Be-ing. Women now who are experiencing the shock of nonbeing and the surge of self-affirmation against this are inclined to perceive transcendence as the Verb in which we participate—live, move, and have our being. . . .
>
> When this kind of sororal community-consciousness is present—this 'us versus nonbeing'—there are clues and intimations of the God who is without an over-against—who is Be-ing. The unfolding of the woman-consciousness is an intimation of the endless unfolding of God.[89]

If God is Being-Itself, the Power of Being that courses through creation bringing newness and novelty, then the women's movement is evidence of that Power of Being activated in and activating human lives. Once again, a feminist theological method invites us to witness the power of the divine not as some transcendent reality 'out there' but as one that empowers and enlivens us 'in here'. Or, in the words of Leila Ahmed, we find religion and our human meaning "always only here and now, in this body, for this person. Truth only here and now, for this body, this person. Not something transcendent, overarching, larger, bigger, more important than life—but here and now and in this body and in this small and ordinary life."[90] This small and ordinary life witnesses the Power of Being as women across the globe are sustained in their process of becoming in and through the trans-religious alliances of the global women's movements.

But, unlike Being Itself as unlimited source and resource, the being and becoming evidenced in the global women's movement is necessarily a power under constraint. This reality offers theological insight into the nature of the human condition and revisions classic approaches to theological anthropology with a critical edge. Whereas classic theological anthropologies argue for a fundamental principle of human freedom, this trajectory of feminist tracings indicates that any freedom we may have is first and always under constraint. Coupling this reality with the theoretical investigation of chapter 2, we recognize that this constraint is not ultimately to be subverted but that our human condition of radical relationality is one in which we must recognize constraint as constitutive of our human existence. As persons, we are brought into 'selves' in complex relationships, and it is within constraints, then, that we find courage to employ our human creativity. This challenges the theological anthropology that has been our inheritance from modernity.

4 Creativity Under Constraint

FREEDOM IN THEOLOGICAL
ANTHROPOLOGY

Modern Theological Anthropology Privileges Freedom

It may be a peculiarly 'modern' understanding of the human person as one in which freedom is pressed to the fore. In *Sources of the Self: The Making of Modern Identity*, Charles Taylor traces this sense of freedom back to René Descartes and the Enlightenment trajectory that linked disengaged reason to "a sense of self-responsible autonomy."[1] Indeed, in Taylor's view the culture of modernity distinctively embraced the principle of autonomy as fundamental to its understanding of the nature of the human person. Taylor writes of 'Enlightenment' culture: "It is a culture which is individualist in the three senses I invoked earlier: it prizes autonomy; it gives an important place to self-exploration, in particular of feeling; and its visions of the good life generally involve personal commitment."[2]

Framing this through the work of Immanuel Kant, Taylor highlights the modern self in the notion of the radical autonomy of rational agents, writing that "the fully significant life is the one which is self-chosen."[3]

It is clear that many dimensions of the women's movement have capitalized on an understanding of the human person as self-directed, as it has claimed this for women themselves. Indeed, if we trace the first wave of the women's movement back to one of its earliest roots, we hear Mary Wollstonecraft articulate such a strategy in *A Vindication of the Rights of Woman* (1792, written in response to Enlightenment philosopher Jean-Jacques Rousseau). She enjoins women to

> cultivate their minds, give them the salutary, sublime curb of principle, and let them attain conscious dignity by feeling themselves only dependent on God. . . . These may be Utopian dreams. Thanks to the Being who

impressed them on my soul, and gave me sufficient strength of mind to dare to exert my own reason, till, becoming dependent only on him for the support of my virtue, I view, with indignation, the mistaken notions that enslave my sex.[4]

Wollstonecraft identifies with the Enlightenment value of the use of self-sufficiency in reason and claims it to subvert those Enlightenment thinkers who would restrict such human ability to men. Indeed, Taylor offers a similar assessment of some feminist strategies, insofar as "the rebellion against the patriarchal family involves an assertion of personal autonomy."[5] In thought and practice, the women's movement was fostered on Enlightenment principles, adopting to a great extent the modern emphasis on freedom and extending its application to women.

Modern Christian thought has also insisted on human freedom as constitutive of the human person, and in Karl Rahner's view, human freedom demonstrates universally the presence of God to humanity. For Rahner, each and every time the human person goes beyond him/herself in growth or love, or pursues a life path not bound by convention, or recognizes the incomprehensible in the process of learning, that individual extends beyond the limits of what s/he presently is and creates something new. As the individual self-directs him/herself to press beyond the boundaries that define the present self, he or she has the experience of reaching into what is not the self and of encountering the boundless range of possibilities contained in the ever-receding horizon of transcendence. S/he is opened up to the absolute fullness of being. When the individual realizes that the self's extension is limitless and that the ultimate term toward which we reach can never be grasped or even understood, s/he has the opportunity to recognize the infinite mystery that is God. Reflecting on the connection between the inexhaustibility of human growth and what makes this endless growth possible, Rahner names God as "precisely that mystery of the incomprehensible, the inexpressible, toward which at every moment of my life I am always tending."[6] Rahner's theological exploration of 'transcendence' as human growth toward God rests unmistakably on the notion of human freedom. It is precisely freedom that makes transcendence possible. Persons have the freedom to make choices that encourage their growth, to choose a path not bound by the gains of the material world, and to pursue the possibilities for knowledge that constitutes us as human beings. In Rahner's words, "When freedom is really understood, it is not the power to be able to do this or that, but the power to decide about oneself and to actualize oneself."[7]

But the witness of women who struggled for social change across the globe in the three waves of the feminist movement indicates clearly and repeatedly that women have not been provided the power to decide about themselves and to actualize themselves. One has to ask whether, under Rahner's conceptualizations, women, constrained by social expectations, barred from political action, excluded from education and the possibilities for knowledge, would have been considered fully human at all. Freedom may be an illusion, given the pervasive reality of constraints.

New York, May 20, 1896

I am being constantly asked by reporters to talk and write on every imaginable subject. I have just finished for *The Wheelman* a little article touching on these points: Should women ride the bicycle? What should they wear when riding the bicycle? Should they ride on Sunday? My answers to these three questions are as follows: No. 1. If women can ride, God intended they should do so. No. 2. They should wear what they find most convenient and comfortable. No. 3. This is the most serious question of the three, and interests me the most. I believe that if women prefer a run in the open air on Sunday to a prosy sermon in a closed church, they should ride by all means. With the soft changing clouds before their eyes, and the balmy air in their lungs, moving among hills, rivers, trees, and flowers, singing with the birds the praises of the Lord in that temple not built with human hands, but standing eternal under the blue heavens—this worship is far preferable to playing the role of "miserable sinners" in the church service, and listening to that sanctimonious human wail, "Good Lord deliver us."[8]

Elizabeth Cady Stanton stands as powerful witness to claiming self-determination and freedom, but she also witnesses to the reality of constraint. As ridiculous as it sounds today, Cady Stanton, champion of women's freedoms, was seriously being asked—in a very public manner—whether women should ride the bicycle. And this is not much more than one hundred years ago. As powerful as the witnesses to claiming freedoms as the examples from the global women's movement are—and they are innumerable—nevertheless the claiming of freedoms demonstrates by contrast the social condition that had limited those freedoms. Given that the women's movement shows that women have not had the freedoms to decide about themselves and actualize themselves in making free choices about their lives, their education and their proximate and ultimate futures, this emphasis on freedom must be critically reconceived.

The Reality of Constraint

The rethinking of freedom has its seeds already in modern theological anthropologies such as Rahner's that propose that freedom is lived out in material conditions and historical situations that limit our choices. Rahner writes that "freedom is always mediated by the concrete reality of time and space, of man's materiality and his history."[9] Freedom is always and necessarily multiple and diverse as it is lived out in distinct contexts. Within these contexts, there may be constraints placed on the actualization of human freedom. "Actions are always a synthesis of original freedom and imposed necessity," in Rahner's formulation.[10] Given the limitations pressed on us by distinct contexts, freedom will always be manifest within limits.

And yet in Rahner's conceptualization there is a constitutive freedom that is primary and fundamental to our humanity and that takes priority over limitations, however real those may be. For Rahner, "freedom is not just characteristic of the human, but is fundamentally part of what the human *is*."[11] Freedom is existentially prior to constraint and privileged as a transcendental of humanity. In the words of Kathryn Reklis, "Freedom is the experience by which we realize that we are responsible for ourselves, for what we make of the concrete realities of our lives, the givens beyond our control."[12] But theology and theory emerging from women's experiences around the globe and in virtually every religious tradition shed a different light on the relationship between freedom and limitation. That is to say, the history of women around the globe seems to suggest that limitations or constraints precede freedom and that transcending previously imposed limitations is not the most basic way we constitute ourselves. It is not only our transcending of limitations that creates who we are as human beings; the limitations shape who we are in particular contexts and precede (predetermine) our freedom. As the stories of women around the globe affirm, while these limitations of context may precede and predetermine our freedom, these limits of context simultaneously call forth the courage that humans exhibit as characteristic of who we are. It is not that we are free to make of our context whatever we choose and thus 'become' in the transcending of limitations placed on us. Rather, as human beings we are thrown into particular contexts that constitute us by the limits imposed therein. Our primary quality of being human is not freedom to transcend and choose and determine our own lives; rather, it is creativity within the particular contexts in which we find ourselves, and it is the courage to employ creativity that marks our fundamental human reality.

The Human Condition: Constituted by Our Constraints

CONSTRAINED BY OUR BODIES

The most basic recognition that we are limited in our freedoms is rooted in the insistence that we are found in bodies. There is no doubt that the category 'woman' has been conceived as one linked to a particular type of body and has thus been a category through which bodies have been seen to serve as a source of constraint. Some strands of feminist thought have resisted this association of woman to a body with mothering capacity to bring forth new life, while others have identified the unique configuration of the female body as grounding for a celebration of 'woman' as a mothering body.

As embodied beings, our bodies constitute a real something of who we are. Our limbs and flesh and the blood that courses through us are fundamental components that shape our experience of being human in the world. This experience itself is relationally determined by the biological configurations that brought us into being. That a childhood photo of my mother looks remarkably like my daughter indicates some element of our relational biology that comprises in a very intimate way our bodily selves. My three sisters and I share in varied modifications of a similar body type and of facial features so that we are easily recognizable as sisters. But the shared heritage is more than skin deep, as our mother regularly reminds us of the medical issues that have been part of her own history may be part of ours. That our maternal aunts had breast cancer substantively increases my risks and recalls the frailty of the bodies we actually inhabit; that this cancer has been found in our father's family as well expands the networks of biological relationships that constrain our experience of being human. These networks of biological shaping, passed through mothers and fathers, constitute who I am not in some abstract way but in my very physicality. I experience this physical body as site of distress at the limitations of who I am as a human being but also as the very medium for being human and encountering Being Itself. As intimate as my body is to me, I am not fundamentally free to determine and self-direct my biological life; a course has been set for me by those who have gone before. It was a course that was ultimately not theirs to choose either.

CONSTRAINED BY SEX, GENDER, AND POLITICAL ORGANIZATIONS OF SEXUAL DIFFERENCE

As bodiliness indicates a certain givennenss in our physical existence, it is also simultaneously witness to the malleability of our most basic selves. It is not only our biological networks but our social networks that name and constrain our bodies in particular ways. In feminist perspective, the conditioning of bodies under the social constraints of gender has been a crucial witness to the way the distinctiveness of our bodies has put constraints on who we are and who we will become. This is, perhaps, both the very heart of the women's movement in all its waves and the grounding assertion of feminist theology: that the designator 'female' when placed on bodies results in very specific expectations, identifications, and limitations because our social world has been structured to make 'gender' a constitutive feature for determining roles.

Feminist theory, like theology, has debated at length whether 'gender' is given in nature or primarily constituted by our social networks—and so has wrestled with the relationship between the biological and the social construction of our embodied selves. On the one hand, social constructivists embrace the idea that what we think of as a 'female' sex and identify with 'women' are characteristics utterly socially determined as indicated in their variability across cultures. On the other hand, there are strands of feminist theory and theology which lean toward the embrace of a distinctiveness to the embodied experience of being 'female' that is the ground of the gendered designation of 'woman'. Without resolving the debate, I want to make a broader point. Whether 'woman' is something inherently connected with characteristics that are 'female' or not, those who have been designated 'female' move through the world in a particular way because of the way the designation 'female' has currency in our socially constituted worlds. The global women's movement has been founded on an advocacy position that resists the constraints of gender when they have limited human becoming of those categorized as 'female'.

Feminist perspectives have sought to secure well-being for those who have been categorized 'female' as well as for those who have been categorized 'male' within a world where the latter regularly gains access to freedoms denied to the former. This essential thrust of a feminist approach is one that this theological anthropology seeks to uphold. And yet the very categorization 'woman'/'female' within the dualism male/female has created conditions that privilege those who benefit from the heteronormativity accompanying this dualism. For Judith Plaskow, a 'compulsory heterosexuality' is communicated through human social and religious systems. In her words:

> The phrase refers to the complex political and social processes through which a polymorphous human sexuality comes to be channeled and expressed in certain narrow and definite ways. It names the complex web of ideologies and institutions through which people learn how and are made to be heterosexual. Over the course of the last twenty-five years, feminists have shown how gender roles are communicated from birth and enforced by social and ideological structures as diverse as family, peer group, school, medicine, religion and workplace. Still much less visible are the ways in which expectations of heterosexuality are imparted and maintained through all the same mechanisms. The romantic fairy tales told to children; the grade school readers, even in their multicultural versions; the obsessions of the media; the constant questions, "Do you have a boyfriend/girlfriend yet?" all convey the assumption of heterosexuality, at the same time that social ostracism, beatings, military discharges, psychiatric incarceration, job firing, and the like enforce the boundaries of acceptable behavior, punishing those who fail to get the message and trying to force them back into line. So pervasive is this network of stories, expectations, rewards, and punishments that it is as invisible and taken for granted as the air we breathe.[13]

The binary 'male' and 'female' itself privileges some and disadvantages others. The categorization 'male'/'female' not only privileges male over female but also privileges those whose sexual orientation fits this gendered dualism.

Under conditions of compulsory heterosexuality and patriarchy, the male/female dualism constrains relationalities; but it also constrains bodies. Following Judith Butler, we might recognize that not only is 'gender' socially constructed as ways for groups of humans to be in the world but that 'sex' also, in its limited designation of 'male' and 'female', constrains actual bodies in the world.[14] Virginia Ramey Mollenkott has powerfully investigated the way 'gender' and 'sex' serve as socially constructed dualisms that do not match the reality of bodies as they are born into the world. The number of babies born 'intersexed'—that is, with ambiguous chromosomal or genital features of 'male' or 'female' (estimates range from 1 to 4 percent of all births)—suggests that our human nature regularly exceeds the sex dualisms into which we constrain bodies.[15] Such intersexuality undermines any stability to the constraint of 'female' and 'male', even though these are the 'givens' of our biological categorizations.

What feminist theorists insist is that 'gender' is not simply biological, nor merely social, either, but that it is 'political'—that is, gendered identifications structure the social networks of relationality that are infused with power and material consequences.[16] The construction of gender is therefore a political categorization that keeps power and material control in the hands of some identified by one category of the gender dualism and out of the hands of the other. Power and material advantages are assigned to those who fit the gender-normative coupling, with 'male' retaining privileges over 'female' in many social and political contexts. Gender is among those mechanisms by which power is "manifested and maintained."[17] Just as gender is a political category, so too 'motherhood' as a social category has kept a subset of those gendered 'female' in certain positions of power and powerlessness. Further, in the United States, gender, 'woman', and 'mother' are all embedded in a heterosexist nexus where those inhabiting subject-positions of a heterosexual union enjoy certain privileges that others do not. In the words of Adrienne Rich, "I am suggesting that heterosexuality, like motherhood, needs to be recognized and studied as a *political institution*."[18] In our present U.S. context, nowhere is this clearer than in the debate over same-sex marriage. As a social and political institution, 'marriage' provides economic and material securities to those who abide by the dualism 'male' and 'female', keeping these same securities from those who do not. Our naturalized social categories have political and material ends.

The women's movement has wrestled with the way 'female' and 'woman' have designated social and political categories of lesser power and compromised material well-being. The usefulness of 'woman' as a naturalized category and/or a category of resistance has been debated. Feminists must continue to wrestle with the hidden and overt privileges ordained by compulsory heterosexuality as LGBTQ issues assume a more central role in our social, religious, and political landscapes.

CONSTRAINED BY RACE

As LGBTQ issues play an increased role in our social, political, and religious discourse, they do not eclipse but rather complicate the continued gender injustice that distinctly adheres to bodies marked as 'woman' and 'female'. Similarly, the constraints of sexual difference do not eclipse the continued racial injustice in our world. In 1870, Elizabeth Cady Stanton felt she needed to choose between black enfranchisement and women's rights. She chose to champion the latter while maligning the former. At the 1893 Parliament of the World's Religions, the gaze locked on the religious other erased the 'sisters' present. White feminists of the twentieth-century women's movement often retained the category 'woman' so intensely as to simply ignore the difference of race. But a feminist theological anthropology attendant to our creativity and constraint must squarely face race, while not losing site of the multiplicity of features that impact us.

The same bodies that are physically constraining and socially determined (as sexed/gendered) are also racialized, again by our social systems that name and constrain bodies. Womanist voices and postcolonial perspectives arising from the secular women's movements make us keenly aware of this. Camara Phyllis Jones proffers that "the variable 'race' is not a biological construct that reflects innate differences, but a social construct that precisely captures the impacts of racism."[19] On this view, the globally orchestrated designations of race primarily are constituted by a social attempt to name and constrain variegated bodies. The naming of bodies through these constructed categories conditions lives of all who live in the society so constructed. Importantly for our theological anthropology, race has figured significantly in our Christian theological heritage.[20] The material reality of lives differently impacted by the designations of race constitute again a recognition of the way context creates and constrains us. This was the essential insight of the womanist movement that so fundamentally altered feminism's second wave. Race constrains human flourishing as a socially orchestrated categorization with material outcomes that postcolonial perspectives demonstrate are at work in a globally orchestrated dynamic.

Recognizing the superfluity of sisterhood and the myriad ways humanity can be constituted, I must also wrestle with the different way we experience this multiplicity. I walk through a world knowing that we are 'gendered' and 'raced' by our social constructs, but I nevertheless must face squarely that these constructions have material outcomes. How do I come to terms with the reality that my path of education and privilege was laid not only by the forward-looking concerns of my parents (and theirs before them) but also by the economic stability they enjoyed, a stability from which their black counterparts were restricted systematically and politically? How do I come to terms with the reality, in this country, that while I enjoy the privileges of a university education along with 50 percent of my age and race cohort, only 20 percent of those of African-American and Latino/a categorizations do? To recognize and embrace the reality of multiplicity also requires addressing the material differences that accompany diversity.

CONSTRAINED BY MATERIALITY

Considering the various modes through which we are constrained, we might roughly group them into those material limitations to our freedoms (emerging from our bodiliness) and the socially imagined categories that constrain us. But lived experience of the women's movements across its three waves demonstrates that these two groupings are not separable. Social imaginaries impact real bodies, serving as tools for withholding or granting material vehicles for human becoming. Black and brown bodies constitute a far higher percentage of those in material want around our globe than do white bodies. Women's bodies constitute a greater percentage of those in material need around our globe than do male bodies. Gay and lesbian bodies are under threat in a way that heterosexual bodies are not; and the bodies of our religious 'others' may not be granted the same political, social, or material well-being as are our religious 'selves'.

The material and the social are coextensive where social constructs impact material well-being. Religion, as a dimension of the social, is a source of imaginings that have direct and relevant impact on the social and its material distribution of well-being. When visioning 'the social' in its large scale and public forum, we are necessarily brought into the realm of the political. Religion is a dimension, also, of the political. Religion serves as a source of imaginings that have direct and relevant impact on the political and on its systemic distribution of material well-being. Because of the intertwining of the sources of our constraint, the religious is necessarily embedded in the social, which is necessarily political. Even the religious that spiritualizes *away* from our material conditions impacts those conditions with its imaginings that leave the status quo intact.

The multiple and diverse ways persons and communities have constructed their religious, social, and political lives is a piece of the recognition of our multiplicity by the feminist third wave. While this diversity is upheld as constitutive of our very human being, in feminist perspective it is important to recognize also the human relations that place limits on our freedoms both within relationships that are life-giving and those that are life-destroying. Thus, in the theological anthropology of this chapter, it is not simply 'freedom' that is a quality of human beings. The freedom we intuit in our ability to make choices about how we might live is always already constituted by constraint. The calculus of concern courses through the multiple constraints that create and constitute our very selves. As distinctive from a focus on mere bodiliness that constraints our 'selves', materiality draws attention to the way our social mechanisms differently impact our bodily selves.

CONSTRAINED BY SOCIAL AND RELIGIOUS NORMS

Underlying the many socially constructed ways we are constituted by our constraints, the religions of the world have served as raw material for envisioning and policing our creativity. That is to say, when we think about what it means to be embodied, sexed/gendered, racialized, and materially constituted, we are guided in our thinking by the classic articulation of these categories in our sacred texts and theological authorities. Caste constitution in India finds imaginative explanation in the Gita; woman's place is reflected in the teachings of the Buddha; racial discrimination defended by Christian theological treatises; and the distribution of material well-being described in our sacred texts.

Among the many sources from which the constraining assignments of gender might emerge (biological, medical, social, material/economic), there is ample evidence that religion plays a key part in assigning and securing gender roles.[21] It is never 'religion' alone that constructs these roles, but religion plays a significant part, subtly or explicitly informing social and political decisions. In Israel, for example, Chava Frankfort-Nachmias reports that "the combined influence of the Jewish religion and the institutionalization of security issues [that is, military practices] has served as a significant mechanism sustaining the traditional family, the gendered division of labor within the family, and consequently, gender inequality."[22] Riffat Hassan draws attention to how religion and politics functions in a particular way for women in Muslim countries. She writes:

> Since the nineteen-seventies, largely due to the pressure of antiwomen laws which have been promulgated under the guise of 'Islamization' in a number of Muslim countries, women with some degree of education and awareness have begun to realize that religion is being used as an instrument of oppression rather than as a means of liberation from unjust social structures and systems of thought and conduct. This realization has stemmed from the fact that women have been the primary targets of the 'Islamization' process.[23]

Given that we can see very clearly how religion is mobilized for social and political ends, the question that feminist theorists and theologians have asked is whether and how religions can be mobilized for social and political transformation. Women across the traditions and across the three waves have debated among themselves (and within their own persons) whether or not the master's tools of religion can sufficiently dismantle the master's house of sexist and androcentric religious and social practices. On questions at the intersection of religion, gender, politics, and material well-being, it is not always clear whether religion is a help or a hindrance.

Sacred Stories: Models or Idols?

From the first-wave feminist encounter with religion, it has been made clear that religious resources are *both* a site of creativity and of constraint. The religious norms that create us as human persons at times create us toward human flourishing, and at others have recognizably restricted us on the basis of class, gender, race, sexual orientation, and more. In the creative matrix of feminist theological thinking across the three waves, this back-and-forth movement between witnessing the divine within secular sacred spaces (rejecting, ignoring, or expanding the religious sacred space) and witnessing the sacred possibilities within the resources of religious traditions (allowing them to infuse the secular as well) has been the pattern from Elizabeth Cady Stanton to Mahasveta Devi, from Sojourner Truth to Judith Plaskow, from Huda Sha'rawi to Mary Daly.

This simultaneous and dynamic acceptance and rejection of religious resources as sources of human becoming brings us to the question of whether our sacred traditions provide models or idols for our own human becoming. The answer is, of course, both.

Mary Daly, in her *Beyond God the Father*, warned of the dangers of too easily accepting external models as sources for our own becoming. The deeply patriarchal trajectory through which Christianity has developed has traded in symbolisms of God, Jesus, and Mary that have confirmed sexual hierarchy and contributed to the dehumanization of women.[24] In Daly's view, therefore, "no adequate models can be taken from the past" as sources of contemporary self-actualization.[25] "Women have the option," Daly writes, "of giving priority to what we find valid in our own experience without needing to look to the past for justification."[26] Daly's cautions are necessary. As a Catholic Christian theologian embedded in what continues to be a patriarchal church, concerned for the dehumanization of myself and my daughters, I often feel as though I am complicit in the patriarchy I detest. Placing my son and daughters in contemporary Christian contexts that have learned nothing from feminist revisioning runs the real danger of reinscribing with misogynistic acceptance the dehumanizing models of the past. We find ourselves constrained by sets of relationships under which we are shaped and over which our control may be limited. Such is the case with so many persons in relationship to their religious traditions. The community is at once locally constituted and shaping of our selves, and beyond our control. At times, this means we are shaped negatively by the communities that constitute us. The words voiced by a sister in the struggle more than thirty years ago still hold true: "So many times I've tried to decide whether I should just drop out and forget the church or whether I should hang in there."[27] At the same time, in the intervening years the emergence of a vibrant textual and living feminist theology means that I myself have been shaped in the Catholic Christian tradition by a sisterhood of feminist theologians who see in the stories of the Christian past viable models for authentic human living as women and as men, but also as persons who trouble these binaries of 'woman' and 'man'. Feminist theologians like Elisabeth Schüssler Fiorenza retell the Christian story with a purpose. She writes:

> Thus to reclaim early Christian history as women's own past and to insist that women's history is an integral part of early Christian historiography imply the search for roots, for solidarity with our foresisters, and finally

for the memory of their sufferings, struggles, and powers as women. . . . . Therefore, a feminist reconstruction of early Christian history has not only a theoretical but also a practical goal: it aims at both cultural-religious critique and at reconstruction of women's history as women's story within Christianity. It seeks not just to undermine the legitimization of patriarchal religious structures but also to empower women in their struggle against such oppressive structures. In other words, a feminist reconstruction of early Christian beginnings seeks to recover the Christian heritage of women because, in the words of Judy Chicago, "our heritage is our power."[28]

In constructing a Christian theological anthropology that witnesses to the fundamental condition of creativity and constraint, the tension between 'models' and 'idols' is the heart of the matter. If we should seek to offer a *Christian* theological anthropology, then the sources of Christian scripture and history would seem to be necessary. And yet it is precisely these sources that too often offer the stone of idols that compromise women's flourishing with patriarchal values rather than the living bread and life of models to follow. With characteristic creativity under constraint, the feminist theologian attempts to navigate a theological anthropology from out of the resources of the Christian tradition. In the words of Judith Butler:

> In a sense, all signification takes place within the orbit of the compulsion to repeat; 'agency' then is to be located within the possibility of a variation on that repetition. If the rules governing signification not only restrict, but enable the assertion of alternative domains of cultural intelligibility, i.e., new possibilities for gender that contest the rigid codes of hierarchical binarisms, then it is only within the practice of repetitive signifying that a subversion of identity becomes possible.[29]

A feminist theological anthropology that learns from women's interfaith encounter in the secular women's movement also has a new set of tools with which to navigate the Christian tradition. The interreligious engagement of women across the three waves of the feminist movement recognizes the way that awareness of the strategies of women from other faith traditions can be theologically inspiring and politically motivating. As we turn to the biblical resources of the Christian tradition, we are encouraged by the creative strategies and comparative possibilities of our sisters of other faiths.

Troubling Eve

Although the biblical figure of Eve is not historical in the method that Schüssler Fiorenza enjoins on us, she does figure historically as a potent symbol within diverse Christian contexts. She is central to theological anthropologies that attend to 'women'. Understanding Genesis as a myth that conveys "archetypal anthropology," Eve has figured the form of 'woman' from her origin in the sixth to fifth century BCE to our own time.[30] Thinking through a Christian theological anthropology attendant to the experiences of women, Eve is necessarily confronted and questioned as idol and as model.

There is no doubt Eve has functioned as idol for far too long in Christian theological history. Blamed as the source of human evil, she has swept 'woman' into her orbit of damnation from the earliest Christian writers to their male medieval heirs, with residual effects deep in the Western psyche of modernity.[31] As mother of all the living, the new idol of Eve is presented in a compulsory complementarity to her male counterpart.[32] But she is far too influential to simply be discarded; Genesis serves too fundamentally as a constraint on Christian theological anthropology for her to be ignored. As Deborah Rooke explains, the story of Genesis continues to have an imaginative hold on cultural outlooks in many parts of the globe. Rooke writes:

> One part of the Old Testament that has been enormously influential within the Western world's Christian-based culture, and which even now in post-Christian society has a disproportionate amount of currency among the biblically literate and illiterate alike, is the narrative of Adam and Eve in Genesis 2–3, a narrative which is widely understood to show women as being intrinsically inferior to men, weak, susceptible to temptation, a bad influence, and therefore both by right and by necessity under male authority.[33]

How often have Christians heard the story of God's creation of the paradisal garden, of God's having given the first humans everything they need but directing them not to eat of the fruit of one tree? How often have they heard or read of the serpent's arrival on the scene and of Eve's being tempted to eat of the fruit of that one tree? How often has the story been interpreted so that Eve is blamed for the transgression, and Adam for participation in the 'sin', which sees them banished from the garden? No wonder one malestream archetype of 'woman' is as temptress and originator of 'the Fall', so much so that her influence is beyond the bounds of professed Jewish and Christian communities. Eve is, indeed, a troubling idol.

But, could we also trouble Eve with alternative tellings of her story? How is Eve a model of the human being as witnessing power and agency under conditions of constraint? Could she be proclaimed to demonstrate the fundamental characteristics of humanity, as Eve is one who strives after knowledge, transgresses boundaries, stands in relationality, and seeks the fullness of her human becoming 'in the image of God'? Rooke resists the constraining interpretations that are our heritage and rethinks instead Eve's creativity when she writes that "although the conditions for a 'fall' are set up before the woman arrives, she is not just a victim of circumstances. Rather, her depiction has a number of surprisingly positive elements in it. Having weighed what the snake says and evaluated the tree, she is prepared to take and eat, in the hope of gaining knowledge and becoming like God (Gen 3.5)."[34]

The witness here is to creativity and self-development, an interpretation that has been sustained through many feminist rereadings. Of Eve's eating from the fruit of knowledge, the nineteenth-century commentators of Elizabeth Cady Stanton's *The Woman's Bible* wrote: "The unprejudiced reader must be impressed with the courage, the dignity, and the lofty ambition of the woman. The tempter evidently had found a profound knowledge of human nature, and saw at a glance the high character of the person."[35] As Kathi Kern explains, in their reading, "Eve had 'fallen' as a result of woman's 'natural' instinct for knowledge. . . . Knowledge for Stanton was a positive good; it was the key to woman's self-development and power."[36]

Feminist theological anthropology continues to wrestle with Eve as model, desiring to reclaim her and restore 'woman' in God's image:

> Eve found a tree
> With beautiful fruits
> Legended to give knowledge
> Of good and evil
> Of God and the Omni-scient
>
> I want to be wise
> I want to be a person of myself
> Knowing all and being empowered
> Nor being ordered neither dependent
> Not even on God, the Controlling Almighty

I want to use good sense of mine
And pursue the infinite realm
Of knowing to have access
To the governance
Of life of mine and my people
Expanding our world to the boundless bountiful
And to the horizons of eternity

Eve took the fruits and ate
And she gave some to her husband
Without reasoning Adam ate
And he became knowledgeable
As much as Eve

But ever since it is Adam
Who monopolizes the power of knowing
For his reasoning has become
More radically capacitated than his wife
Who was wiser than he in the beginning

But Eve, even in her forced subjugation
Still holds Godly pride and self-esteem
Fit to be the image of the Creator

And human history
Unfolds into modernity.[37]

In feminist reclamation, Eve becomes a model as seeker of knowledge
and transgressor of boundaries. She brings about a new creation, one in
which humans hold the knowledge of good and evil and must, necessarily, make a decision between them.

Eve has served as archetypal 'woman', but precisely what is 'woman'
according to the Genesis account? When 'woman' in relation to 'man' is
mapped onto the sex differences of 'female' and 'male', the relation
between them in the biblical text remains unclear. 'In the beginning' (of
Genesis 1:27), 'male' and 'female' are made simultaneously. Sexual difference, in this telling, is constitutive of human being in an equal duality,
with neither male nor female prioritized. Both are created 'in the image
of God'. Yet in the account of Genesis 2:22, man is created from dust, and
"the rib that the Lord God had taken from the man he made into a
woman." This becomes the source for many interpretations of women's
unequal status and a heteronormative explanation of why 'man' "clings to

his wife and they become one flesh" (Genesis 2:24). Yet holding the two narrative strands together, we see clear contradictions. In the first chapter of the story, humanity is made male and female; in the second, man and woman are relational categories that become man and wife. Readers of one text at a time see stable categories; but in concert they do not line up easily. In Genesis 1, male and female simply 'are' in the image of God created, each named independently and as such. Genesis 2 has man formed from the dust of the ground, expressly other than God, although vivified by God's breath; here, man is first, woman second as helper and partner and wife, and man seems to need woman. Reading the text straightforwardly, we're left feeling as though 'man' and 'woman' in precise relationship with God and one another remain a mystery.

The first two chapters of the biblical text have narrated an ambiguous relationship of sexual difference. And yet, Eve has been used to order persons who are identified as 'woman' into unequal relationships with 'man'. Eve has served as the marker of sexual difference in a way that demonstrates how gender is used as a social and political category of control. Although her biblical character is short-lived in Genesis, her persona lives on in the Christian testament as archetype of 'woman' and category of control for a community's women. A brief but potent flash survives in the letters from the early Christian community. In feminist perspective, we can see with great clarity what the idol Eve has become for the writer of 1 Timothy: "I permit no woman to teach or to have authority over a man; she is to keep silent. For Adam was formed first, then Eve; and Adam was not deceived, but the woman was deceived and became a transgressor. Yet she will be saved through childbearing, provided they continue in faith and love and holiness, with modesty" (1 Timothy 2:13).[38]

But even here, idol gives way to model not in the figure the author of this letter holds out for women but in the women whose witness lies 'behind the text'. For if the author of the letter is refusing women the right to teach and requiring that they keep silent, there is no reason for this rhetoric and strongly worded directive unless actual women in the community *were* teaching with authority and in fact *not* keeping silent.[39] The evidence here is that 'Eve' as 'woman' is a category employed for social and spiritual control, even while a community's women demonstrate resistance.

Evidenced as source of social control, Eve never resolves the question of what 'woman' is or where 'she' fits in relation to 'man'. This much is clear in early Christian writings such as Paul's, where some of his letters seem to abolish the distinctions of gender (in Galatians, "there is no longer male and female"), while other letters (e.g., to the Corinthians) exhibit both "deeply hierarchical" and "profoundly patriarchal" perspectives.[40] This ambiguity is transferred through to the early Christian writers whose study indicates that "within an Adam-Christ typology such as that deployed by the early Christians, the figure of the paradigmatic woman cannot be grasped, located, pinned down (or eradicated) in any totally stable way—but at the same time, she is not *absolutely* other (and hence not totally unrecognizable)."[41]

Interpretively the relationship of 'male' and 'female' or 'woman' and 'man' is found to be unstable and unsettling. They are unable to be finally pinned down in their essence and relationship. Nevertheless, the categories have been used as if they were self-evident in their relationship; they have become stable givens, rigid in the application and recognizable as sources of social control.

In Christian history, Eve has been employed to naturalize the category of 'woman' and secure her unequal place. But the naturalized category of gender must be recognized clearly as a social category (one by which we organize our public relationships) and more pressingly as a *political* category. As a political category, the designation of 'female' and 'woman' is recognized as a tool by which social organization provides material well-being and differential access to some persons and not others. Where the political and the religious are part of the same fabric, the religious mobilizations of these categories must be interrogated. What is at stake in religious designations of 'male' and 'female', of 'woman' and 'man'? Who among those so categorized benefits, and who loses a say, a voice, decision-making abilities, and, ultimately, material well-being?

It was activist women in Pakistan who propelled Riffat Hassan to reinvestigate what the Qur'an had to say about Eve. "I was urged by those spirited women who were mobilizing and leading women's protests in the streets to help them refute the arguments [based on quranic interpretation] that were being used to make them less than fully human."[42] In pursuing this task, Hassan was struck by "the extent to which the Muslim psyche bears the imprint of the collective body of Jewish and Christian ideas and attitudes pertaining to women" and links these with the figure of Eve, imagining her to be secondarily created from the rib of Adam. But, as Hassan's study shows, although the story of creation in the Qur'an is similar to the Jewish and Christian story of Eden, "there is no mention of Eve at all in the Qur'an."[43] Hassan concludes that "the Qur'an even-handedly used both feminine and masculine terms and imagery to describe the creation of humanity from a single source."[44]

Similarly, Hassan charts a frequent commentarial practice of assigning blame to Eve (and woman) for the Fall, even though "there is, strictly speaking, no Fall in the Qur'an"[45] and "the Qur'an regards the act of disobedience by the human pair in *al-jannah* (the Garden) as a collective rather than an individual act."[46] While traditions of Muslim interpretation have been infused by Jewish and Christian readings of Eve, feminist interpreters of the Qur'an find clear and compelling resources within the Qur'an to establish "women's equality with men and their fundamental right to actualize the human potential that they share equally with men."[47] A Muslim feminist strategy toward Eve reclaims the qur'anic portrait of a fully human, fully equal woman. But this also shows how text and traditions are wielded to yield diverse interpretations with distinct material, social, and political outcomes.

Given the interpretive variability and textual inconsistencies recognizable in Christian traditions of encountering Eve, we might learn a strategy form our Jewish sisters. Judith Plaskow offers a Jewish feminist strategy toward Eve in the pattern of her tradition's midrash. In an interpretive practice of filling in the gaps of scriptural accounts, Plaskow follows medieval predecessors who envision Eve not alone as Adam's mate, but 'woman' first takes form in Lilith. In feminist midrash, Plaskow revives the first woman (Lilith) as an 'uppity woman' refusing Adam's domineering and his ordering her around. In response to Adam's orders, "Lilith wasn't one to take any nonsense; she picked herself up, uttered God's holy name, and flew away."[48] The patriarchal God sides with Adam and rather than insist on equality between them, creates a second female in her stead—Eve. Content for a time to serve Adam, Eve also jumps the garden walls and joins Lilith in a sisterly struggle for creating a more humane and just living environment.

In interreligious perspective, we are reminded that our sacred stories are *stories* with a great deal of variability and insight into the nature of our human condition. Accepting them as stories, we open up to a more malleable framework for rethinking the sacred narratives and how they shape us. But we also now are empowered with a solid hermeneutic of suspicion when it comes to the enactment of these stories on the social constitution of our material and political world. If we recognize them as stories, *why* does Eve continue to function as a negative constraint on women? If we can see them as one story among many, toward what end are they employed to guarantee material well-being and political rights for those who fit the gender binary in heteronormative coupling? How are our sacred texts *supplemented* by material desires for socially organizing some to the disadvantage of others? Simply put, why do we *allow* the story to shape us—personally, socially, and politically—in some ways and not in others? Whose interests are being served when we tell the story in the way that we do? How does our storytelling 'touch down' in the real world of our social, material, political embodiment? In what ways does our storytelling encourage a flight from our embodied experience in such a way that maintains an unjust status quo? How might we mobilize our stories toward more just personal, social, and political relationships?

In contemporary feminist reinterpretation of the Genesis myth, the desire to elevate Eve from the damaging interpretations of her is recognizable. Such elevation, at times, comes at a cost to Adam, seen as the bedrock figure of patriarchy. Feminist interpretations of Eve have identified her as actively making a choice and authentically owning her decision, while Adam is cast as passive bystander and one unable to take responsibility for his own mistakes.[49] The turning of tables that might precipitate a turning of tides in gender relations is certainly under-standable, but for a reinterpretation to holistically guide the Christian community—male and female, gay and lesbian, transgendered and intersexed—the food for thought must be offered that navigates a vision of ourselves as human beings before God and one another, a vision that does not "place one sex above the other" (as Julia Ward Howe cautioned) and that also does not place other forms of sexual difference (hetero-sexual or homosexual) against or above each other. What sort of reread-ing can the text yield toward a theological anthropology that resists placing sexual difference in a hierarchy of its many and diverse forms?

We see feminist theology reclaiming an active Eve, restoring to women (as well as men) the activities of free will that have come to define being human, aligning seamlessly with the modern emphasis on human beings as self-directing subjects. But Eve is also entangled in relationships. In the narrative unfolding of Genesis, Eve is not actually present (having not even been created yet) when God commands Adam not to eat of the tree. Only midrash can fill in the gap of how Eve received the directive not to eat; and for the sake of our story, let's imagine she hears it only through Adam (a logical filling-in of the story, since Eve even adds to the directive given by God, indicating to the snake that not only are they not to eat of the tree but that they should not even touch it [Genesis 3:4]. Has Adam added this embellishment to protect Eve from transgression?) Embedded in a set of relationships, Eve's constraints take their form. Being born into the primary relationship by which Adam is constrained, Eve finds herself with a particular kind of freedom: one that is always, already under constraint, and one that holds within it consequences. We are constituted as human persons in the constraints of our relationality.

There is also a system of knowledge that flows through these networks of relationship. In the Genesis account, God has proclaimed knowledge of what will happen when the humans eat from the tree of good and evil: "For in the day that you eat of it you shall die" (Genesis 2:17). But, the serpent comes with a different knowledge system: "You will not die" (Genesis 3:5). And, in fact, in the day Eve and Adam eat of the tree, they do *not* die, except for the metaphorical death of being banished from the garden.[50] It is only after their taking leave of Eden that God is heard conversing among Godself, "See, the man has become like one of us, knowing good and evil; and now, he might reach out his hand and take also from the tree of life, and eat, and live forever" (Genesis 3:23). There does not appear to have ever been an ontological or causal link between eating of the tree of good and evil and the death that humans inevitably will encounter. God's 'knowledge' of what will happen when humanity eats of the tree of good and evil is derived simply from God's power to banish, because the death that is humanity's future is logically (and narratively) unrelated to the tree of good and evil and related instead to the tree of life. From this perspective, woman and man are both subject to a power and a knowledge system that is rooted in their relationships, and both are constrained by the power that courses through those relationships. Together they demonstrate the human condition of relationality and creativity under the constraint of a knowledge system imbued with differentials of power.

On considering theological anthropology from the perspective of agency and relationality, the Genesis account yields a retelling wherein woman and man are equally formed in relationality (to God and to one another) and equally spend their lives under conditions of constraint, in which they exercise their creativity. The systems within which they exercise their creativity, and under which they experience constraint, are not 'ontologically' so, nor are they 'objectively' true and universally the case; the constraints are both the function of the relationship itself and the power dynamics within the relationships at hand.

But, the Genesis account and the figure of Eve have also functioned within theological anthropology as a discourse on sexual difference—that is, they tell us what it means to be 'man' and 'woman'. The history of biblical interpretation shows that the text(s) as we have them yield radically different interpretations down through the centuries; interpretations that are egalitarian or hierarchical, depending on what is emphasized and drawn out.[51] Such consistent ambiguity of interpretation reflects a text that is ambiguous—so ambiguous, in fact, that perhaps the biblical theological anthropology of our sexed and gendered human condition is precisely that it is unstable and open to interpretation. This narrative ambiguity of what constituted 'man' and 'woman' and their relationship vis-à-vis God and one another becomes less ambiguous as a heteronormative coupling emerges: "A man leaves his father and his mother and clings to his wife, and they become one flesh" (Genesis 2:24). To the woman, God says, "In pain you will bring forth children, yet your desire shall be for your husband" (Genesis 3:16). The heteronormative coupling of Genesis has produced distinctive gender roles, where Eve as 'woman' is 'mother' of all the living. What options does the tradition yield for troubling the heteronormativity and its concomitant assignment of motherhood to woman?

One note for unsettling the heteronormativity that haunts Eve is her proclamation "I have produced a man with the help of the Lord" (Genesis 4:1). The mother of all the living does not credit her heterosexual partner for the children she will bear; she credits the divine power. In order to destabilize Eve from Christian heteronormativity, we need to enlist the help of Eve's advocate and the woman through whom Eve herself is recapitulated: Mary. For Christians, the trajectory of Eve-woman-mother finds its final fruits in the figure of Mary, who rights the wrong of Eve's transgression by bringing forth a savior to recapitulate the original creation with a new creation; but Mary, similarly, brings forth this child (doctrinally) emphatically *not* with the help of a man, in heterosexual coupling. "How can this be, since I am a virgin?" (Luke 1:34). Once again, the power to bring forth children from the womb is not the power of heterosexual biology, it is the power of God, the Holy Spirit, the Most High. (Luke 1:35). Or, in the words of Sojourner Truth, "Where did your Christ come from? From God and a woman! Man had nothing to do with Him!"[52]

Monique Wittig has incite-fully argued that 'woman' is a constructed category that necessarily stands in relation to 'man'. "For what makes a woman is a specific social relation to a man, a relation that we have previously called servitude, a relation which implies personal and physical obligations as well as economic obligations."[53] In the fully human flourishing of woman in Mary, man had nothing to do with the bringing forth of divinity within humanity, the bringing forth that is the story of incarnation so central to Christian understanding. Woman alone with God's power coursing through her queers our notions of heterosexual union as the creative power of woman. Mary's sexuality so celebrated as celibate should disturb our gendered reinscription of her role as female, as mother, as nurturer. The twofold saying and unsaying necessary here is that Mary both *is* woman with a power to bring forth new life and divinity through the very darkness of her womb and that she *is not* woman in the very queerness of her sexuality—a sexuality that needs no man to complete it. But Adam also then is 'woman' with the power to bring a separate life from a singular body. With Eve springing from his rib, our midrash might have Adam generatively exclaiming: "I have produced a woman with the help of the Lord."

The interglossing symbol system that constitutes Christian theological anthropology has gaps and inconsistencies, queer orientations of 'man' and 'woman' as categories that are slippery in their relation to one another, but it also presents 'man' and 'woman' in archetypal persona who can generate offspring without a biological relation to another. It is this unsettled account of sexual difference and the generation of children that is most helpful in this theological anthropology. In chapter 2, I proffered a christology of m/otherhood to argue that all Christians should be modeling themselves on Christ's self-giving love and sacrifice for the future of the planet. All Christians should show forth Christ's mother love. In concert with the troubled notions of generativity springing forth from non-heterosexual unions (in the persons of Adam and Mary), this showing forth of Christ's mother love is not limited to women, is not bound by the designation 'male' or 'female', and is not restricted to heterosexual coupling. It is a giving of mother love from out of relationships that take many and diverse forms. It is 'with the help of the Lord' that we bring forth new life and lives within our care.

Mothering is not about biology. If the generative persona of Adam, Eve, Mary, and Christ call each of us to bring forth our 'others' with a creativity rooted in divinity, we most certainly recognize that generation is not the only mother role but that Christ's own mother role is one that consists in the ongoing care and self-giving of the breastfeeding Jesus.

Relationally constituted, Jesus learns from the mothers in his midst the patterns of care for humanity. Returning once again to Jesus and his followers, we might see in the women of the Jesus movement models for a feminist Christian theological anthropology and for our future human becoming.[54]

A MOVEMENT OF MOTHERS: CREATIVITY
AND CONSTRAINT IN ACTION

With Jesus, the sacred was not confined to sacred spaces but happened in what we might think of as secular places. Of course, concepts of 'sacred' and 'secular' would be configured differently in first-century Palestine than they are today, but the point is that the encounter with the holy in the person of Jesus (as we have remembrance of it in the New Testament) happened only infrequently in the sacred spaces of the Temple or syna-gogue; rather, they usually happened in Jesus' street preaching. He was, scholars of the historical Jesus argue, a teacher who wandered the countryside demonstrating for a new social vision under the banner of the 'kingdom of God'. With such a phrase, Jesus' hearers would have been ready to expect military overthrow of Roman occupiers (as the Zealots rallied) or pious retreat to the sacred (as the Pharisees may have done).[55] But as Jesus' allies, people gathered to hear the vision of a new way of being in the middle of things, in the world, in relation to one another, a new way of being that transformed expectations.[56] His was a vision of social transformation.[57] The secular becomes sacred not through ritual purity but through the realignment of relationality in a wholeness that brings holiness.

With people gathered to hear him rally toward this new vision, we might envision something like a modern-day demonstration of grass-roots organizing toward a more just society. Word got around about the new program Jesus announced, and 'the people' came to hear about it. As happens today, perhaps 'the people' came regularly to hear Jesus when-ever he came through their part of town, gathering to show their support for this new way of being in the world. That's how 'movements' work: a vision repeated, mass gatherings witness support, and a wave goes out in hope and commitment to change.

Just as women were part of the twentieth-century movements for social change, we have witness that women of the first century were part of the Jesus movement. As Amy-Jill Levine reminds readers: "It is certainly possible that, in the Q community, women were among the interants. In antiquity, women traveled for various reasons: trade, pilgrimages, visiting relatives, even engaging in political protest. Women likely followed Jesus from the Galilee to Judea."[58] Women also were present in the Jesus movement, as benefactors to it.[59]

> Soon afterwards he went on through cities and villages, proclaiming and bringing the good news of the kingdom of God. The twelve were with him, as well as some women who had been cured of evil spirits and infirmities: Mary, called Magdalene, from whom seven demons had gone out, and Joanna, the wife of Herod's steward Chuza, and Suzanna, and many others, who provided for them out of their resources.
>
> Luke 8:13

Constituting an itinerant movement finding home bases within peoples' homes, women played central roles in the Jesus movement, as remembered in the close companionship of Mary and Martha, who welcomed Jesus and others into their home for meals and teachings. Culling from other gospel witnesses, we see women among the followers up to and through Jesus' death: "At the death scene, the three women [Mary Magdalene, Mary the mother of James and Joses, and Salome— named as disciples following Jesus and ministering to him] are accompanied by many others who had come up with him from Galilee (Mark 15:41). While this is the first explicit mention of these women, it implies that women were on the road with Jesus throughout his preaching career."[60] "Many women were also there, looking on from a distance; they had followed Jesus from Galilee and had provided for him. Among them were Mary Magdalene, and Mary the mother of James and Joseph, and the mother of the sons of Zebedee" (Matthew 27:55–56).

We might remember not only those of means who supported Jesus' ministry, or those whose lives could afford the challenges that itinerant preaching had in store, but average women, countless, nameless women among 'the people' who came out to hear him as he preached his vision, demonstrating with their presence their commitment to his vision. Androcentric readings of the tradition simply lead us to believe that 'the people' were primarily male, but, as Schüssler Fiorenza reminds us, there is no reason for us not to read the generic terms for those gathered to *include* women, unless expressly excluded. Moreover, the narrative remembrances of the Jesus movement in the gospel stories invite such readings, for, like the women of the twentieth century, women were likely among 'the people' who had their children in tow when they went to Jesus' 'kingdom of God' tour, rally, and demonstration.

> People were bringing little children to him in order that he might touch them; and the disciples spoke sternly to them. But when Jesus saw this, he was indignant and said to them, "Let the little children come to me; do not stop them; for it is to such as these that the kingdom of God truly belongs. Truly I tell you, whoever does not receive the kingdom of God as a little child will never enter it." And he took them up in his arms, laid his hands on them, and blessed them.
>
> Mark 10:13–15

These mothers were close enough to the inner circle of Jesus' teaching that they were present among the disciples when Jesus passed through Galilee and stayed in Capernaum (as Mark's gospel recounts). They were at the center of the debate among the disciples about *who is the greatest*. For when the disciples had argued on the road to Capernaum among themselves, Jesus reminds them, when they arrive 'in the house' where they will sit, by taking a little child and putting it among them. (Mark 9:36). On the historical evidence, Elizabeth Johnson writes of women in this first-century context that "a mother was primarily in charge of the care of small children. Rather than compete with her other workday obligations, this care was subsumed into the routine of daily tasks, the children being present where the mother was working."[61] We remember the mothers who may have anxiously awaited the arrival of the traveling demonstration to the home. We remember these mothers who, in their multiplicity, followed Jesus while simultaneously fulfilling their expected child-care responsibilities.

Like the women of the twentieth century in those brown and white photos demonstrating for rights with their babies in tow, we might envision the women of the Jesus movement struggling and juggling but demonstrating their commitment to the kingdom vision with its inclusive well-being for themselves, their families, their children. What did these women gain by being present among the crowds who followed Jesus, witnessing their commitment to his vision in their following? What did they risk in pursuing this commitment? Many of them were likely not juggling work and family in the same mode that twenty-first-century mothers do, for these mothers were quite young, especially those who would be accompanying a small child. As Aram Tropper reports, "For many girls, adolescence was not a time for fun, education, experimentation or professional training, rather it was a time when one was already expected to assume the full responsibilities of a mature woman, as wife and mother."[62]

In searching the scriptures for models to guide contemporary creativity from within the constraints of the Christian tradition, these adolescent young women in their commitment and courage might be raised up as models of our own human becoming. To be fully human is to be embedded in relationships of responsibility as these mothers were to their children when Jesus took a little child and put it among them (Matthew 18:2), when he took a child up in his arms (Mark 9:36; Mark 10:15) or placed a child by his side (Luke 9:47). When reminding those who would keep them away he said, "Let the little children come to me," surely their mothers were not far behind (Luke 18:16). But in the witness of the Jesus movement, to be fully human is also to extend these networks of care beyond family alone. "Blessed are the breasts that nursed you," someone in the crowd shouts out, but Jesus replied, "Blessed are all those who hear the word of God and heed it" (Luke 11:27–28). As Amy-Jill Levine notes, "Q . . . insists that the biological family is not the locus of self-identity or loyalty."[63] Yet while androcentric traditions have often valorized the breaking of ties in the spiritual quest—from Buddha to monks and mendicants, and Jesus himself insisting that the dead bury the dead—the women who brought their children along with them in the hearing of Jesus resist the breaking of relationality by being committed both to those in their care *and* to Jesus' vision of extending that care to all.

Schüssler Fiorenza visions the concern for child care in the Jesus movement as arising from the communities of the gospels as they write this memory to life in their narrative account. As the first Christians were struggling to affirm that care for the least, the child, was the responsibility of the entire community, they narrated a remembered Jesus modeling this care—let them come to me, he said. In fostering the multiplicity of simultaneous roles within the community, the earliest Christians drew on their own received tradition as structured through the narrative of the Hebrew scriptures and the patterns of relationality it fostered. "Hebrew Scripture . . . takes for granted that women did and should serve, inter alia, as judges (Judg. 4:4–5), officiating clergy at funerals (Jer. 9:16–19), slaughterers of animals for both human and divine consumption, sages (2 Sam 14; 20:16–22) and prophetesses, and that provision was made for women to combine child-rearing with participation in the divine service of periodic public reading of Scripture."[64] Our foremothers are not mothers only but guide us in a mother-care that is practical, spiritual and political.

These mothers show what it is to follow Jesus, to be Christian. And if 'mother' signifies a social position charged with responsibility for 'the least', and Jesus calls all to a responsibility for the least, then the Jesus movement is a 'movement of mothers' where women and men together, straight, gay, lesbian, bisexual, transgendered, and intersexed, assume the subject-position of caring for the least. Perhaps when Jesus pulled the child into the center of the discussion, it was with a nod to the child's mother—unless you become like these—a nod that swept the mother into the orbit of Jesus' teaching example. Jesus' teaching also required his hearers who would be his followers to push the boundaries of their circle of concern beyond their families and kin to neighbors, 'others', even enemies. "Blessed are the breasts that nursed you." "Blessed are all who do God's will." This extension of care widens the network of relationship to those who are other than us culturally, racially, religiously.

Here, what stand as witness to the humanity that Christians are called to become are not only Jesus' life and teaching that but also the conditions of his death. Unwilling to relinquish his mother-care vision, even in the face of pain to himself, Jesus' mother-care for the least reminds us that solidarity comes at a cost. As M. Shawn Copeland writes: "[The] shouldering of responsibility obliges us in the here-and-now to stand between poor women of color and the powers of oppression in society, to do all that we can to end their marginalization, exploitation, abuse and murder. In memory of the cross of Jesus, we accept this obligation, even if it means we must endure rejection or loss."[65]

As a movement of mothers, followers of Jesus are enjoined to look beyond biology to the shared responsibility for the future of the world, seeking especially those who have been made into the least among us. "Your mother and your brothers and your sisters are here." "All who do the will of God are my brothers and sisters." Repeatedly, and in various ways, Jesus called his followers to extend the circle of care beyond biology, beyond family, beyond community, to the neighbor who is 'other'. As a movement of mothers, the followers of Jesus are enjoined also to look beyond family to the responsibility for others, a responsibility that is personal, social, and political. As a movement of mothers, the followers of Jesus must bear children beyond their own.

Which brings us back to Genesis, where God pronounces that "in pain you shall bring forth children" (Genesis 3:16). The pangs of childbearing are not physical alone. They are the markers of the more long-term costs of mothering in the world. Tzvi Novick rereads the text to see God "telling Eve that he will lengthen the gestational period, so that she will have to endure prolonged pregnancy (an onerous if not quite a painful condition) in addition to birth pangs."[66] While the idyllic scene of Eden may have promised an effortless childbearing, the human reality is not so. It is in pain that we bring forth children—constrained bodily by the stretching of our relationality. But pushing Novick's extension even further, we see that the pain of bringing forth children extends into the future far beyond the birthing pains. With Eve, as archetype of this pain, we might imagine a mother whose pain in childbearing reached its height when her firstborn, son Cain, killed her second-born, Abel, a pain undiminished when Eve bears a third child. Eve's witness is that our mothering will not always be fulfilling and that our relationality may bring us real pain.

The human person cannot simultaneously exist fundamentally concerned about him- or herself as 'self' *and* other without experiencing some dimensions of pain. It is in pain that we care for one another, negotiating that calculus of concern that balances the well-being of many persons as I constitute my freedom, not simply making choices that are primarily self-interested. Further, the 'children' we bring forth are not singular but are multiple in their callings to us as well, and 'children' here must be imaginatively expanded, from the audience of one's scholarly work, to one's patients or clients, to one's elderly neighbors, to another's children who are in your care, to the exploited worker, the undocumented, those excluded from education, the maligned immigrant, the religious other, and beyond.

A Christian theological anthropology that recognizes our creativity invites human persons to pattern themselves on the mother-love of Jesus even while it means accepting the mother-pain of Eve. The textual tradition has yielded a troubling of 'man' and 'woman' so as to recognize that this patterning is not the call of 'men' and 'women' in heterosexual union but a patterning enjoined on all. Recognizing both creativity and constraint, this theological anthropology insists that we willingly constrain ourselves within the pattern put forth by the person of Jesus, knowing that this is not 'ontologically' the case of who we are as human beings, nor 'universally' true as the only way of being human, but accepting the constraining pattern of Jesus as one in which to enact our creativity toward a more just and humane world, brought about by our own willingness to conform to the mother-love pattern and accepting the mother-pain it may bring.

The Christian textual tradition with its gaps and inconsistencies has brought about building blocks for a rereading of the tradition with Eve and the mothers of the Jesus movement at the center, and with Mary and Jesus as symbolic allies. But in this rereading of the tradition, even the serpent yields important insights. Like Eve, the serpent has regularly been appointed the 'bad guy' of the Genesis account. Challenging God, the serpent informs a listening Eve: "You will not die; for God knows that when you eat of it your eyes will be opened, and you will be like God, knowing good and evil" (Genesis 3:5). The serpent offers a lens of suspicion for the Lord God's words, since Adam and Eve do not die in the day they eat the fruit. The serpent's speech holds some truth in the Christian affirmation that humans are like God: having been created in God's image and knowing good and evil. Further, the serpent's truth reminds us of the ways we, as human beings having knowledge of good and evil, continue to choose evil—in the choices that privilege one sex above another; in the choices that privilege heterosexual persons over our queer brothers and sisters; in the choices that privilege whiteness to the many hues of our being human.

It is also the serpent who reveals that there is not a singular logic and ontology for which God alone has knowledge. In contradicting the knowledge that God has put forth, the serpent reveals that there are other worlds, other ways of being, other readings, and other frameworks for being human in the world. Christians have constrained themselves in the knowledge-world of the symbol system of which Jesus, Mary, Eve, Adam, and their God are a part. But the serpent reminds us that other worlds are possible.

Interreligious Alternatives

In interreligious perspective, we can see that the serpent is right. As patterned on women's religious lives across traditions, there stand potent and positive examples of other options for modeling our humanity. The possibilities for who we are to become, reflected likewise in the diversity of the many waves of feminist struggle, give witness again to the overflowing forms that sisterhood might take. Where the Christian story offers the divine model on which to pattern our mother-love despite the mother-pain it will bring, in these examples drawn from other religious traditions, the model—and the divine—is found within.

A modern Indian guru, Anandamayi Ma (1896–1982), was a woman who drew to her crowds of devotees who experienced her as the face of God. 'Mother' to those who know her, Anandamayi Ma had one simple message as she traveled throughout India and to those who would visit her ashrams: find the Divine within. As Lisa Lassell Hallstrom describes her message:

> Anandamayi Ma's teachings can be reduced to one statement, "God alone exists." The Divine Absolute veils him/herself in order to enjoy the divine play of life in the world of form, the world of duality in which everything is impermanent and illusory. The person who has forgotten that he or she is God suffers as things change and eventually turns within to find that which is permanent, the Self of All. Ma recommended that people begin the process of turning within at whatever point they are.... Ma was tireless in stating her conviction that anyone can know God, indeed can become God, if only they possess the desire.[67]

To her devotees, Ma's teaching of God's intimate presence within was realized in their experience of Ma as God, God to whom they could relate personally, spiritually, physically, God who invited them to see their own divinity, realizing this in their spiritual growth, experiencing themselves as "sitting in the lap of the divine Mother."[68] How might our imaginings be shaped differently with this concept of the divine nearness to humanity?

In a similar way, Anne Klein offers an alternative site for considering sacred resources for contemporary modeling when she thinks from a feminist perspective on the insights of Buddhism. The Great Bliss Queen, as she identifies her, is the form of the Buddha in everyday access in many parts of Tibet. She is the site of devotion and source of wisdom. Through this mother figure, the fundamental value of Buddhist compassion radiates. Fundamental to this posture of relating to her is the orientation that the Great Bliss Queen witnesses back to the devotee what the devotee already is, like a mirror allowing her to see what she already possesses. Taking refuge in the Great Bliss Queen, Klein writes, is with a sense that her mind is no different from one's own.[69] As Chung Ok Lee explains:

> Buddhists believe that all humans have a light within, the divine Buddha Nature that can lead to attainment of enlightenment. Therefore we must

spend part of our life in silence and meditation to discover this Inner Light. Then this light must be translated into our daily life. Through mind-cultivation, we can channel our positive energy, and bring forth our inherent goodness and universal compassion. Through meditation we reduce our own suffering, and also reduce others' suffering. Mind-cultivation leads us to self-discipline and self-transformation and enables us to practice love and compassion for all.[70]

From a deep place, then, one accesses the infinite source of compassion which the Bliss Queen and the Buddha represent. "One moves from the position of a child, grateful for a mother's kindness, to that of an adult, who now cultivates a mother's care for all living beings. A practitioner imagines that her own love and compassion take the form of light, emanating from her heart in all directions."[71]

In meeting the models of the Great Bliss Queen and Anandamayi Ma, we are reminded of Mary Daly's important caution against privileging external models to the detriment of our actual selves. In Anne Klein's invitation, the meeting of the Great Bliss Queen is an essential posture toward the is-ness of our present humanity. "Engagement with ideals can distract us from self-understanding, directing attention to what is wished for rather than what is. Being present is the antithesis of being overwhelmed by ideals of what one should become. Letting go of ideals provides the space for letting be in acceptance of the self."[72]

This theological anthropology stands tentatively, then, as an offer to one way of being human in the world: a way modeled on a particular reading of Jesus and the symbol system of the Christian tradition. Aware of other systems of knowledge, the Christian willingly extends her creativity within the constraints of the vision of mother-care and mother-pain for the well-being of the world. The truth of an active Eve and of a slippery 'man' and 'woman' joins up with a non-biological bringing forth of divinity and humanity with 'the help of the Lord'. With the witness of a movement of mothers, we are all called to be mothers to the world, bringing forth the Christic pattern in our own self-giving.[73] There is a truth to this story of self-giving and a full humanity that might emerge in its practice. And the serpent's truth reminds us that there are other stories to be told.

PART III

In Lives Intertwined

5 Encounter in Philadelphia

ENGENDERED DIALOGUE TODAY

"I actually want to start with the group and go backwards, if that's okay, because currently this is also my spiritual home in huge, huge ways."[1] When asked about the community that shapes her sense of self and purpose, her spiritual orientation in the world, Anne thought first about the interfaith group of women who have shaped her story and her life. They gather each month in the living-room area of a small Quaker meetinghouse outside of Philadelphia. Leaving workplaces in the city and surrounding neighborhoods a few hours early, they make time for one another and commit to this interfaith meeting. On ancient acres with a newly built thoroughfare humming nearby, they share their experiences, their faith journeys, and, by now, their lives. The Philadelphia Area Women's Multifaith Group provides a living example of the power of the interfaith movement for building bridges, solidarities, friendships, and more. "We are busy women yet somehow we all make it there once a month—so we are [talking about] something that is fulfilling a need in our lives . . . that is sustaining for us."[2] Their home traditions range from a variety of Christian denominations (Episcopal, Catholic, Methodist, and more) to Judaism, Islam, and Baha'i. While their commitment to interfaith work began as a way of getting to know neighbors of other faiths, and picked up steam in response to the divisions experienced after 9/11, their primary aim when they gather is fellowship. They are in a dynamic conversation and relationship; they are the best of friends. And in the vision of the participant whose words opened this chapter, their gathering functions as a spiritual home for many of them.

While the reality of women's interreligious encounters have undoubtedly spanned history in ways that are buried from access, it is distinctive in our contemporary period that we can frame them under the banner of 'interfaith work'. Certainly, in the context of mission, Christian women were directed toward engagement across religious lines, but the binding across those lines was far more tentative.[3] The Christian women were primarily interested in binding their non-Christian counterparts to Christ, although in the process they may have found their lives woven into the lives of the women they met—converted or not. Shifting to more recent encounters, we can move outside the strictly 'religious' framework to recognize encounter in the secular women's movement. But here the binding across religious lines was secondary to the primary work of shared concerns for women's rights. In the contemporary period, we can investigate a more concerted effort to cross religious boundaries in solidarity through the various grassroots efforts of women in the interfaith movement. But even with this shift to the 'explicitly religious', we are perhaps moving into new territories in recognizing interreligious space *as* religious.

'Interfaith'—a word that expresses the positive status of the distinctive traditions and the commitment to relationships across them—broadly encompasses an innumerable variety of projects: from interreligious dialogues, to learning about a faith other than one's own, to common civic projects and peace efforts, and more.[4] In a world broken by conflicts that press 'religion' into the service of violence and division, 'interfaith' characterizes the attempt to mend the world of this brokenness by consciously claiming one's religious identity and pressing religious identities into the service of peace. Whether this peace is interpersonal or international, the interfaith movements around the globe witness women and men committed to their religious traditions and to peaceful coexistence with others. Because the interfaith movement is characterized by a wide variety of activities, women's participation in this movement is widespread. While women may not be at the center of the most high-profile interreligious dialogues, owing to the persistent exclusion of women from leadership in so many traditions, the commitment to peace has enabled countless women and men to be part of the transformation of interfaith relationships 'on the ground.'[5]

The Need for Dialogue: The Philadelphia Area Multifaith Women's Group

> When people say, "All Islam is about terrorism." I think of Homara, I immediately go to Homara. Always. . . . When people say one bad thing about Islam, I go to Homara. Viscerally she is with me, you know?
>
> Ava[6]

The Philadelphia Area Multifaith Women's Group had its original impulse out of an annual Thanksgiving citywide interfaith prayer service. In this forum, leaders from the many living traditions of Philadelphia and members of various congregations came together in public prayer. As part of that tradition, a few regular participants felt the desire and calling to extend their interfaith participation beyond the yearly meeting and began to seek ways to engage more ongoingly with their neighbors of other faiths. In 2000, a small group began to brainstorm and vision together what such a regular meeting might look like, and in the summer of 2001 planning was underway for a community event of interfaith learning and exchange. As for many in the United States, September 11, 2001, changed the way dialogue was done. The event raised into consciousness the need to address the way religion is pressed into the service of dividing our world. And yet, in the memory of one of the women of Philadelphia, the trauma of interreligious fear and violence was interrupted by the possibilities of interfaith solidarity and healing. As she recounts:

> On 9/11 I was in a Jewish building . . . working for the Jewish community relations council. . . . When we found out what happened everybody gathered in the auditorium in the building and I walked downstairs and there was a look of . . . a look of terror, you know. . . . And not everybody's Jewish, you know, you have people working in business offices—all ethnicities and races, but there is just this sense of terror. This is a Tuesday, Rosh Hashanah was that weekend . . . since 9/11 *every* synagogue in the Philadelphia area has a police car on Rosh Hashanah and Yom Kippur. People have no idea that this . . . I mean, the vulnerability. And we think it's insane—I mean me, in my generation.
>
> Ava[7]

The terror of Tuesday, September 11, instilled fear and shaped preparations for the upcoming celebration of Rosh Hashanah, wrapped up as it was now in the terror and brokenness of the world. Ava continues: "Friday night I am going to synagogue for Rosh Hashanah. Literally walking out the door, the phone rings. It's Homara. And she said, 'I just called to wish you happy new year.' I just, like, melted, and I thought, 'That's it. I am back! . . . Yes! The world can make sense. We can do it. We are not all insane.' And I was back."[8]

Reflecting on the way her Muslim friend was able to reconnect her to the world she wanted to live in, Ava says, "We can choose to be a community of hope, we can choose to be a community of people who are living our lives the way that we want to live them, and this is our world. Or we can go into the world that is kind of crazy and insane and we can live in that world."⁹ Creating the world that they wanted to live in, the group originally planning an interfaith event saw the import for the wider Philadelphia community. Directly responding to the shattered relationships made real by 9/11, the group planned a public event to bring together religious leaders in response to interreligious violence, with the hopes of sharing information toward interreligious peace. The event was a success, but key members of the group felt that a single event was not sufficient for the kind of long-standing relationships that needed to be in place to sustain and create a world that could be otherwise. Interfaith relationships needed to be part of a regular faith practice. They discussed the possibility of meeting more regularly for dialogue. The Philadelphia Area Women's Interfaith Group had begun.

Over the last ten years, the group has grown—inviting new members by word of mouth and gathering monthly to build interfaith relationships. In the beginning, the group functioned in largely the same way as most 'interreligious dialogues' one might think of. A topic was chosen and different members brought the perspective of their tradition into conversation about the similarities and differences between their religious understandings. But the group soon gave its own flavor to these investigations. Recognizing that 'religion' is not just about what one believes but about how one's life is shaped by both belief and practice, members of the group began to invite one another into their homes for religious celebrations: a Jewish seder, the Baha'i spring celebration. As members of the group began to recognize the expanding dimensions of their neighbor's faith and began developing relationships, there was a freedom to extend the dialogue conversations to a more personal investigation. About three years into their monthly meetings, the process of sharing shifted to a format of presenting each individual's 'spiritual autobiography', and a new understanding of 'religion' and 'interfaith' emerged.

The format of the interreligious-dialogue meetings reflects an ever-widening understanding of what 'religion' means. The dialogue of doctrine and expert opinions is but one, limited way of conceiving what religion is or does. In this format, dialogue is primarily about belief. While belief was not taken off the table in the changing format, the women in this group expanded the recognition of 'religion' by insisting on practices as also key to understanding. But their pattern of interreligious dialogue further expanded to include not just proscribed beliefs and discrete practices but the very ebb and flow of their lives. Indeed, in this dialogue, nothing is off the table, as the women bring all of who they are to the monthly meetings—sharing their beliefs, their faith, their stories, and their lives.

Telling Stories

A key turning point in the process of developing the monthly meeting into an interfaith community was the sharing of personal life stories, or, as they group members describe it, 'spiritual autobiographies'. The group's description of the process was this: "In the context of the Multifaith Women's dialogue, we are interested in stories of how our life's experiences, values and beliefs have shaped our religious identification and practice. Sharing our spiritual journeys promises to give life to the distinctiveness and richness of our diverse faith traditions, while deepening relationships and understanding."[10] Each woman was given twenty minutes to share her spiritual autobiography, guided by the question *What have been the formative and transformative experiences in your life that have shaped your core beliefs and led you to practice your faith as you do?* After the presentation of an individual's spiritual autobiography, the remaining twenty minutes of the session were devoted to clarifying questions and deepening understanding of the particular life story that had been shared. This emphasis on *particularity* and *experience* demonstrate a distinctive approach to interreligious dialogue, one that begins from the particular and seeks live engagement with that particularity. It is an approach that requires a great deal of time. With membership at about twenty-five and a core group of eighteen within that, the process of sharing spiritual autobiographies extended over a year and a half. This commitment to the particularity of the other, not merely to her religious tradition, afforded a network for relationality that has come to characterize the group. They meet regularly now, as they have for the past ten years, and continue to nurture those relationships.

The telling of stories was not only an important way into the building of friendships. It also enabled the presentation of 'religion' in a way more akin to the way it is lived. In traditionally formatted dialogue, the 'expert' speaks as if distanced from his actual life to describe 'the religion' as if it stands somewhere apart from the messiness of actual lives. But in sharing stories as the entry point, the women of Philadelphia recognize that 'religion' is found only in its enactment in the world, in the messiness of lives:

> The entry point that has always spoken the most to me is the narrative. Tell me a story. Tell me a story about your belief and how that's affected you. And it has so much more meaning then. . . . So there are certain times when I look at people in religions that I didn't know . . . like the Baha'i religion. I didn't know or even know existed until I came to this group. Or listening to Homara talking about her experiences after 9/11 and how she was treated. I mean these kinds of things bring the whole view of religion to life and it brings it in a different way.
>
> Fran[11]

The process of the 'spiritual autobiography' in this practice of inter-faith dialogue illuminates many things about our religious lives. First and foremost, our religious identities and our relationship to 'religion' are dynamic. As each of the women recounts her spiritual autobiography, it is evident that one's relationship to one's home tradition takes different shapes at different times in one's life. These differences emerge through changing contexts and are interwoven with material conditions and interpersonal relationalities. Each participant described the variety of ways she has been engaged in her home tradition and shifting relation-ship to that faith. As a result, it is not surprising that the group exhibits religious diversity not only among persons of different traditions but within the traditions themselves. In the words of one member:

> No, no we're not the same. I am not the same as even the other Jews in the group. In fact, I'm very different than some of the other Jews in the group. So, it's not anything about sameness. It's about recognizing and accepting the differences. I am never going to know what it's like to be a Catholic, to go to mass to do all those things. But I can accept you without knowing what it's like to do all those things. And I think that's what's happened in the group. It's a lot of acceptance of who you are. Amina . . . she prays five times a day. Now Homara doesn't. Homara says her husband prays five times a day, and she doesn't. . . . Of course, it's just who you are: some-times you do and sometimes you don't.
>
> Amira[12]

'Internal religious diversity' can refer, then, to religious diversity within a given tradition as well as to the diversity of practice and belief that constitutes the individual at different times of her life. Our recognizing this reminds us to hold 'religion' not as a static reality but as a living and dynamic category woven into complex lives.

In the process of recounting their own autobiographies, so many of the women demonstrate the hybridity of our lives not only in the way our identities are dynamic and shifting but also in that our stories can be impacted and shaped by encounter with the 'other'. In a sense, then, even before these women joined the Philadelphia Multifaith Women's Group, their lives had been structured in and through interfaith encounter. One woman was raised Roman Catholic and, experiencing a deep trouble in this community, left to find a home as a Unitarian Universalist. A Muslim participant grew up in Hindu India where she was educated at a Catholic convent and taught in a Protestant school; a Jewish woman describes an early encounter with Christian prejudice that shaped her own religious self-understanding; an Episcopalian found a religious home with Quaker friends and Unitarian Universalists. In relationship with various communities through marriage and history, one participant professes affinities with Catholic, Episcopalian, and Presbyterian communities. Through marriage, one participant identifies with the Episcopal and Jewish communities; the marriage of another Jewish participant's son led her to learn more about Catholicism—the faith of her new daughter-in-law. Raised Presbyterian, yet another studied in Japan and was shaped by the Buddhist family with whom she shared a home. These and many other examples demonstrate that our 'religious' identities are not static entities hemmed in by the boundaries of home traditions. Rather, the tracing of spiritual biographies demonstrates the dynamism and 'interfaith' that shapes persons' lives.

Interfaith Hurt / Interfaith Healing

The interreligious biographies that characterize these women's lives reflects also the way that 'religion' is communicated not primarily as belief through teachings or scripture but fundamentally through relationships and interpersonally. In her spiritual biography, one woman indicated that a shift from one congregation to another was precipitated not by a change in doctrine but by a change in the community. As her father was ill in the hospital, not one member of her religious congregation reached out in support. As she recalls, "In the meantime my dad had a heart attack and the—for whatever reason—the Episcopal priest at our church. . . . Nobody came to see him. So my parents left the church and joined a Presbyterian

Church, so I was in a Presbyterian Church for a number of years."[13] Another member recalls the process of her own Jewish identity shaped by a life with Christians. Having had an interfaith childhood, she recalls that "the reason my parents decided to join a synagogue was because they heard me upstairs building with my blocks and singing, 'Jesus loves me, that I know, because the Bible tells me so.' Which is what my friend right next door had taught me, because she was going to Sunday school every week and my father and mother, they thought they heard this; they came upstairs and said, 'I think it's time to join a synagogue.'"[14]

In recounting what sorts of interfaith encounters preceded her participation in the interfaith dialogue, one Jewish participant recounts a story buried deep in her consciousness from when she and her young daughter were shopping at Christmastime. She overheard her daughter saying to the women shopkeepers,

> "I know why the stockings are hanging on the fireplace." So one of them says . . . and they're all interested in her, there's nobody else in the store. And she is very winning-looking, at that age she was very beautiful. And they said, "Why?" And she said, "Because Santa Claus is going to come down here and put presents in the stockings for all the children." And this woman: "Well, dear, actually this is a store and Santa Claus doesn't really come down and it's just for decoration, but I'm sure . . ."—which is very important for her to tell her—". . . but I'm sure Santa Claus will come to your house and bring you lots of toys and put a lot of things in your stocking." And Sarah—I'm listening to this, I have my back to them, and I'm kind of looking around, and I'm kind of thinking, "Oh my god . . . what . . ." And Sarah looks at them and puts her hands on her hips and says, "Oh, no, he won't!" And these women are like riveted, and they say, "What do you mean he won't?!" And Sarah says, "Santa Claus doesn't come to my house, I'm Jewish!" And they . . . and this is the point of the story, this one woman who is conducting this conversation with this three-year old, she laughs. She really, really laughed. And she says, "Look at this! This child thinks she's Jewish!" She . . . and this all didn't penetrate on me completely. I mean, I'm listening to the whole thing. She could not believe that this was, this little adorable child, who didn't look any different, was Jewish. Now I, I said, "Oh my gosh, it's five o'clock. Bye! Merry Christmas!" And we left. I never really forgave myself for that. Because there was . . . there will never be a more opportune time for me to have said . . . the couches were there, I really didn't

have to go . . . I should have said, "Well, what makes you think she's wrong about that? How do you know she really isn't Jewish, and let's talk about it." But I didn't and I always never forgot that.

Elizabeth[15]

In the narrative of her life, the participant connects to this moment of interfaith hurt and missed opportunity as something that she long carried with her and that constituted a part of her identity and desire to work toward interfaith understanding. In recognizing interfaith auto-biographies, we might begin to see that while interreligious dialogues provide an opportunity for mutual understanding and friendship, inter-religious encounter has more often been the source of discrimination and rejection on the basis of religion. The women of Philadelphia bring to the dialogue all of who they are, but they recognize also, importantly, how their religious identities in particular have served as sites of vulnerability. Indeed, the very narrative that tells the critical moment in this group's history (9/11) serves as global and personal example of how religious difference tends to function. We've witnessed this in the opening experience of fear and distrust, of terror and brokenness articulated by a Jewish member of the group, and the autobiographical account above of more subtle, yet pervasive, forms of religious devaluation of difference. These self-reflective women suggest that religious division, rather than inter-religious solidarity, is the norm that structures our interactions in the world. Asked what prompted her to engage in interfaith dialogue, one participant recalls:

We had brought a piece of property, right down on Montgomery Avenue. . . . It's called the Foundation for Islamic Education. And . . . going through zoning hearings and everything else. And the neighbors put up a very stiff resistance. There were predominantly Jewish neighbors there and they did not want Muslims in their midst. And the one lady, it was very heated and very unpleasant at times and the lawyers on either side had the idea that they should get everyone together and find out that the other doesn't have horns and that they were normal people. And so we were sitting in this room and you know the Muslims were sitting on the one side and everyone else was sitting on the other side of the room. And this one lady looked at me in my face and she said, "I don't want you building bombs in my neighborhood," and I said, "Where do you even come up with that idea?"

Homara[16]

A Baha'i member of the group recalls in her autobiography the deep experience of systemic exclusion and persecution of a minority group in her home country of Iran, but she narrates this reality also as reflected in the contemporary moment of her home country of the United States.

> I was in the elevator [of a hotel] going up and then before us there was another function. I think it was some type of Christian workshop or something. And then this woman who was, I would say, middle age, she came and I was talking to some one else and I think she picked up my accent. And she said, "Where is your accent from?" And I said, "I am Persian and we are celebrating our New Year." And she said, "Are you Christian?"—just like that! [Sarai laughs.] And I said, "No, I'm Baha'i. And we are celebrating our New Year." And she said, "You are going to go to hell." [Sarai laughs.]
>
> Sarai[17]

In retelling this encounter, Sarai laughs as she recounts the absurdity of the exchange. But a deeper underlying realization is that the United States is structured by discrimination and injustice that is racial, cultural, and religious. That someone with a way of speaking marked by difference in 'accent' could be the target for religious interrogation and hate speech would seem to those who have not experienced it unlikely. "I was at a convention. . . . The Islamic Society of North America had a meeting in Philadelphia. And in front of the convention center were these Christian people, with their placards in their hands saying, you know, 'You won't be saved until you follow Jesus.'"[18] Persons marked by features of the nondominant race, culture, and religion are regularly targets in our broken world. Asked to comment on the verbal accosting, Sarai's ironic laugh is followed by the reality: "Being Baha'i in Iran, we are not strangers to persecution and execution."[19]

Witnessing the interfaith hurt that constitutes so many interreligious relations in our world, the women of Philadelphia recognize the need to create a different space in their dialogue setting. Again and again, when reflecting on their experience in sharing their spiritual autobiographies, the women reflected not only on the content of the stories shared but also on the process of getting to know one another, a process that the sharing facilitated. This process was not an easy one, it required deep self-reflection: "That person spent a lot of time . . . getting ready to present it, presenting it, and then we asked them questions."[20] The process of sharing took time as well. But it also required a "willingness to hear" the stories that were being shared.[21] In the reflection of one member, the process of sharing enabled the group to move from superficial encounters to understanding, connectedness, and acceptance. But it was only after meeting already for three years that the group was able to create the space of sharing such intimate stories. Knowledge of the 'other' is intimate, and gaining knowledge of the other requires intimacy. Such intimate knowledge and friendship, however, is crucial in this group's understanding of the role of interreligious encounter as a function that repairs the brokenness of the world:

> It's like we have a job and we can't just say, "Where is God?" because we have to do our part of the job, which is to love other people. And not just *some* other people. And you can't love other people unless you know them. You can love them in the abstract, but that's not going to do it. And it's not going to hold up when . . . they bomb your twin towers or something. You have to know those people—not the ones who bomb the twin towers. But you have to be able to say in the face of all the evidence thrown at you to the contrary, "Yea, but that's not who those people really are, and that's not what their God really says or wants or whatever." So if you don't, um . . . find a way . . . it doesn't have to be in a multifaith group. But it has to be some way to relate to these other people. . . . You are not going to be able to do the job, or help do the job. And I'm sorry to say that 99 percent of people don't know the other. And that's why we're in—one reason—why we're in such a fix.
>
> Elizabeth[22]

The naming of this process by this Jewish participant is framed in a way that is echoed by other members of the group, and while she does not employ this term, she may be drawing on the Jewish tradition of understanding Judaism's aim as 'repair of the world', or 'tikkun'.[23]

From experience, the women of Philadelphia recognize that they live in a world where embracing religious identity is a dangerous thing. On the one hand, there are those who mobilize religious identities for exclusion—whether recognized within their own tradition or experienced as discrimination from persons of other faiths. In his work on religious identities in our globalized world, Arjun Appadurai warns his readers to take stock of how religious identities can be mobilized. From out of the many affiliations and the ways of relating to others and of understanding oneself in relation to the world, leaders often employ religious identities as means of gaining leverage against rivals and of securing social and material resources. Cautioning against the dangers of projecting only one aspect of identity in this way, Appadurai writes, "When these identities are convincingly portrayed as primary (indeed as primordial) loyalties by politicians, religious leaders, and the media, then ordinary people self-fulfillingly seem to act as if only this kind of identity mattered and as if they were surrounded by a world of pretenders."[24] On the other hand, and in response to the mobilization of religion for violence, there are others who reject religion precisely because it does provide a platform for exclusion. But in the space of vulnerability, these women hold out the hope that their religious identities can be mobilized for the transformation of the world. Many of the women in the Philadelphia Area Multifaith Group do not claim their religious identity as 'primary'; they are reluctant to speak for any one tradition and, at times, to claim their primary location as from within one tradition. They do not speak as spokespersons for a tradition that seeks to be homogenous. They do, however, seek to mobilize toward action rooted in their religious identities. Reflecting on their meetings, one participant indicated that

> [the meetings are] really not [focused on] which person is which religion so much as that these are people who are trying to [find] a better way to be in the world or who are trying to make the world a better place even if it's only for their family, or whoever it's for. And when we share, we are always sharing both richnesses of our own culture or our own religion and frustration.
>
> Elizabeth[25]

Desiring a more peaceful world and recognizing their religious traditions as having a part in that process, the women mobilize their religious identities not for division but for solidarity across divisions. Far from the disengaged dialogue of doctrinal comparison, the purpose of their time together is forged in solidarity, responding to a world in need. Having come together originally after the divisions they experienced at 9/11, they continue to see themselves as constituting a practice of interfaith reparation. Homara relates her sense of the group in this way: "I think it helps us understand each other's religions and thought processes and seeing where each other comes from. . . . When we come together we sort of put a salve on each other's wounds. And we try to find out or try to sort through the issues and how they affect us as individuals and us as members of the larger society."[26]

Hybridity That Works

In the process of engaging one another 'religiously', the women of
Philadelphia demonstrate yet another critical component of interreligious relationship in their dialogue: that we meet one another not merely
as 'religious others' but through complex identities that are multiple and
hybrid. While the description thus far has focused on the sharing of
religious traditions and religious identities, the reality of this group is
that their dialogue space is just as often filled with stories that are not
about 'religion' as it is filled with those that are. When the group gathers,
the women weave throughout the discussion the stories of their lives in
all the challenges and triumphs, tragedies and celebrations. The women
of Philadelphia remind us that 'religion' is not just about what happens
in the 'sacred space' of temple and mosque but that the spiritual journey
is one that is traced through the complex and comprehensive stories
of our lives. The story of the pastor and congregation who did not come
to visit the sick father, the story of the encounter of being Jewish in
a 'Christian' store, these examples recognize that 'being religious' is
not identifiable only in the space of our church or synagogue but is interwoven into the very fabric of our lives.

When the tracing of complex lives broadens the sphere of 'religion',
it also enables greater opportunities for dialogue. That is because while
we may not inhabit our dialogue partner's home tradition or attend
her mosque or synagogue, and while we may not understand the
comprehensive pattern of her religious practice, in the living dialogue
that is wide in scope we are offered innumerable opportunities for
connections from out of the complex hybridity of our dynamic identities.
Our religions do not capture all of who we are. The approach of 'sharing
stories' witnesses a richer and more complicated approach to interreligious dialogue, as it reminds us that 'religion' cannot be reduced to
doctrines and scriptures, to 'what I believe' or 'what I do'. 'Religion' is
always 'found' embedded in and intertwined with other aspects of our
lived condition: economics, gender, social relations, material conditions,
politics, and so forth. Our 'religious' identities are entangled in and
impacted by all of these features and more. The very complexity and
multiplicity invites dialogue partners to make any number of connections, not just on the basis of religious belief. The particular location of
the religiously identified speaker in dialogue is always a complex place
which informs the articulation of that 'religion' as the speaker attempts

to speak it forth. To pretend otherwise by focusing only on what 'my tradition' believes or what the tradition 'teaches' ignores the way that the description of 'religion' is always filtered through the biography of the one who articulates it.

In her study of a wide range of women's interreligious engagements— from national and international conferences over the past several decades to more local engagements of women across traditions and including very particular case studies of interreligious dialogue—Helene Egnell summarizes the findings of what might be distinctive of women's interreligious dialogue. She highlights several components that are in line with feminist methodologies and insights. Among the distinctive features, she found that women's interreligious dialogues included the integration of 'traditional experience', including "telling of life stories," concluding also that "the women's interfaith dialogue tends to emphasise faith as lived rather than as expressed in scriptures and doctrine."[27] Simultaneously, "none of the participants claimed to speak as a representative of her tradition, but would rather say, 'I can only speak for myself.'"[28] Among the Philadelphia women, these two central characteristics are reflected in their ongoing dialogue. And, indeed, this reflects what Egnell indicates in her study, namely, that "acknowledgement that not only are there many strands within one religious tradition [recognized by participants in women's interreligious dialogue] but each person has her own interpretations and emphases on what is most important within that strand."[29] Maura O'Neill similarly underscores the internal diversity that might characterize dialogue participants in her study of women's interfaith discussions.[30] One woman in the Philadelphia dialogue reflected on this internal multiplicity of religious perspectives in this way:

> It was the first time I realized there isn't *a* Muslim faith, there isn't *a* Lutheran faith, it's what your personal spin of it is. The women who are Muslim, you know they don't wear the headscarf. And that *is* something that is in the Qur'an. They are very quick to say, "It's between me and God." They do their prayers, they do everything else. But that's where they draw the line. There was a Jewish woman . . . she says that her Orthodox religion says that women cover their hair. She says, "That's where I draw the line. I'm not covering my hair." And I realize that that's where the Catholic women, they had practiced birth control or whatever. The religion becomes personal with each person that you know.
>
> Joanne[31]

The recognition of particularity in our religious articulations illumines how 'hybridity' and 'multiplicity' are features of identity that make dialogue possible. That is to say, the particular emphasis a speaker calls forth will be shaped by the other stories of her life into which her religion is woven. These diverse strands shape her experience of 'the religion' in scripture, tradition, and community. The converse of this is that the 'religious' speaker *has* a multiplicity of strands and stories that shape her. Reflecting on her belief in 'God', one participant says, "whether I look at it as a scientist or as a physician or as a regular human being or as a mother, there is no way that all of this works without there being a higher authority."[32] In this she does not consider herself a 'religious person' alone, and the questions of 'theology' are not addressed by 'religion' alone. But rather, she attends to theological questions from out of the variety of perspectives that are constitutive of her hybrid identity. This recognition is the very foundation for dialogue. If we only had the singular story of our 'religion' as the place to meet, interreligious dialogue would be impossible, as the sacred story of 'the other' may be foreign to us. Furthermore, the complexity of the other's story as it is interwoven with history, ritual, and practice makes it so irreducibly distinctive as to admit understanding principally for those who inhabit it. But with multiple stories that shape us, in narrating our lives and religion within them, our dialogue partners are offered a multiplicity of strands with which to make connections. It is the multiplicity of our lives—and our willingness to share that multiplicity and complexity—that provides the place for weaving our lives together, for becoming an interreligious community, and for building the friendships required to stand in solidarity in a world that divides on the basis of religion. Thus, the hybridity of our religious identities can work to bind us across difference *and* do the work of reparation, as we've seen in the example of the women of Philadelphia.

Where Is 'Religion'?

We can read the dynamics of 'sharing stories' analytically as the means by which we might encounter the other, not in 'pure otherness' but in the multiplicity and hybridity that provides for overlapping narratives and experiences. But we can also read the sharing of stories theologically. The insistence on speaking from out of one's own life experience is the insistence that the divine encounters humanity in and through that lived experience. The women of Philadelphia recognize that this is given through the patterns of their religious traditions, such that they 'touch Spirit' in reading the Qur'an, or in Jewish ritual, or at a Christian eucharist, as their spiritual autobiographies insist; but they equally recognize that Spirit at work beyond the bounds of their own home locations. A Christian participant talks about how hearing others discuss their practices has sparked in her a desire not only to know more about the religious practices but even to try them herself. She states: "I just find it fascinating and enriching to learn so much about other faiths and religion . . . sometimes I think that I'd like to, you know, try out a few of those. Not the religion itself but some of those practices: like the spring celebration in the Baha'i [faith]—it was beautiful! And it was different than a Passover, different than an Easter."[33] Ava, who is grounded in her Jewish practice, makes similar remarks about what she feels when she hears other members describe their practices: "If when she is talking about prayer, or talking about her experience with communion, I can just watch her light up, I want to know what that is about. I want to understand that. If I see it in her, I know it's accessible in me. And I know it's accessible in others. I want to pay attention to that—when she lighted up, talking about her experience on hajj."[34] A Christian participant recounted: "To hear Homara talk about going to Mecca and . . . that is such a moving scene and I'm kind of walking around imagining people walking around this big stone and oh! I've seen pictures of a million people packed into one area and it is just awesome to me. It's just awesome."[35]

In addition to communicating a power at work in and through traditions not their own, the women of Philadelphia indicate that they have 'touched Spirit' in and through the interreligious dialogue itself. In describing interfaith encounter, one participant said, "I had definitely experienced this as sacred space in a different way, like maybe I should say it had expanded my awareness of what sacred space is and that it can be created, and that, that there are many . . . just to be attuned to, you know, the . . . the awareness of that when it happens."[36] For this participant, the creation of sacred space occurred fundamentally in the sharing of stories, in the deep self-reflection and listening that characterized the distinctive process of this group. In her words:

> I think that where I kind of became most aware of that kind of sacred space that you asked about was in the listening part. In the air, in the way people really were present, and not judging, and not going to the place of offering advice and not going to the place of asking questions about the

facts of the situation, or questioning, 'Was this really their experience?' but just hearing, and accepting. . . . So as a group that learned to hold a story . . . I just felt really a profound sense of sacred space there.

Ava[37]

Other group members share the feeling of connectedness and sacredness that characterizes their monthly meetings. One of the women describes being present with the group each month as "important to the fundamental of my personal spiritual core, my spiritual being."[38] Yet another states: "[The group] is my spiritual home in huge, huge ways. So, I find that my spiritual home is where, is with, is in interactions with those who are awed by spirit and awed by divine and whatever form that takes. Which is why this group is so important to me. And the seriousness with which we all hold spirit is what draws me and what nourishes me."[39] One member comments: "I think one of the reasons it works when we are together is because we are in deep trusting conversation-relationship, that there is a sense of the sacred presence."[40] In their ongoing encounter, they have created a space in which they recognize the ineffable among them: "That sense that we can evoke, you know, when we are together, in that place, just something luminous—whatever word we put on it, and if we put a word on it in that moment we would probably lose it, right?"[41] When they are together they sense the presence of a reality greater than themselves, a reality that speaks to them both in their home tradition and in this interreligious space. In the view of a Muslim member, it is a presence of spirit 'inside' each person that forms the 'common bond' they experience when they are together.[42]

In the foregoing description of their experience in interreligious dialogue the women of Philadelphia do not simply describe being enriched by 'the other'; they repeatedly speak of being 'bound to' one another. Participants describe the relationships built over time as "years of bonding."[43] In the telling of their stories they were bound together: "I think it's in the telling of those stories, of those narratives, not just for me, but within this group—it binds us together."[44] This binding together may be formally the very structure of 'religion' itself. According to W. C. Smith, one of the ancient sources of the word 'religion,' from the Latin 'religio', may be 'religare', meaning 'to bind'.[45] In various contexts, this meaning of the word has been identified as 'binding' to precepts, a 'binding' to other members of the community, and a 'binding' to the Divine. All three of these senses are in evidence in the dialogue practice of the Philadelphia women. They describe being 'bound' together, and the divine, 'Spirit', is what forms the common bond between them and what they experience whenever they are in contact. Their interreligious community has become a place to enact a set of binding precepts as well. The precepts of the dialogue space itself—shared ownership, rotating leadership, listening to all voices, respectful disagreement, recognition of similarities, honoring particular life stories, and more—are principles that the Philadelphia women enact in the carved-out space of each month and that they hope carry over into the world. "The world demonstrates to us the consequences of living in a world where we are not connected to one another; we see that and ask what is more important to us—being connected? Or, being in the world as it is?"[46] They report experiencing a wholeness in community with their friends of other faiths, a wholeness that stands in contrast to a world of divisions. Together, they are bringing forth a better world.

The experience of interreligious dialogue—and more particularly, *this* experience of interreligious dialogue—raises questions about just what 'religion' is. If interreligious dialogue doesn't include just the 'religious' markers of belief and ritual but all of one's story, what is the boundary between 'religion' and 'not-religion'? Further, if interreligious dialogue itself constitutes a sacred space, what does this say about the traditionally defined sacred spaces of authoritative traditions? Many who take our interreligious world as their point of departure for theological thinking are beginning to argue that the examination of other faiths is, indeed, an intra-theological project and that studying the faith tradition of one's neighbor is part of one's own spiritual practice. This is articulated most compellingly by proponents of 'comparative theology', which, as Francis Clooney writes, "is not primarily about which religion is the true one, but about learning across religious boundaries in a way that discloses the truth of my faith, in the light of their faith."[47] Indeed, the project of inter-faith work and interreligious theology might begin from the question 'What is the meaning of my neighbor's faith for mine?' The disciplines of comparative theology and theologies of religious pluralism are developing to consider that question as one at the heart of the theological enterprise.

But what if, as we witness in the experience of the Philadelphia Women's Multifaith Group, it is not that a singular, discrete 'religion' alone nourishes human spirits but rather that the meeting with the religious other has the potential to create an interreligious space that also nourishes spirit? If religions are frameworks for shaping the way persons understand the world and their place within it, then what is the function of interreligious conversation as a space that reshapes one's understanding of one's place within the world? What do we 'learn' in the interfaith context that shapes our understanding of the world, our place within it, and the mystery that brings it ongoingly into being? To pursue this question, I return to theological anthropology—this time, through the lens of our human capacity for knowledge.

6 The Dynamic Self as Knower

INSIGHTS FOR THEOLOGICAL
ANTHROPOLOGY

I found it difficult at times. . . . I had to do research: what do Episcopalians
say about something? You know, because . . . I think we experience things
sometimes through our own . . . personal experience as opposed to . . . I mean
there were things I knew, but . . . other things I had to . . . I had to find out some
more about.

The Philadelphia Area Multifaith Women's Group provides a context for
considering the phenomenon of interreligious dialogue. It simultaneously presents a point of departure for asking again the question "What
does interfaith encounter have to say about what it means to be human?"
While this interfaith group demonstrates an essential relationality in
multiplicity (connecting with the discussion of 'love' at the heart of
theological anthropology, as examined in chapters 1 and 2), and provides
examples of 'creativity under constraint', as reflected in the women of
the dialogue making creative choices about their home traditions and
religious belonging (connecting with 'freedom', which was the focus of
chapters 3 and 4), the exchange of ideas also witnesses to a fundamental
characteristic of our human experience, which Karl Rahner focuses on
in his investigation of 'knowing'. As in the preceding chapters, I am
affirming the method of Rahner, assuming that the everyday experiences
of our humanity can be illuminating for theology. Rahner invites us to
suspend the terms of theology and start instead with experience of 'the
matter itself', and only after having examined our lived experience bring
the theological language to bear.[2] In the process, I am also bringing the
lived experience of women in interreligious dialogue and across traditions to bear on the modern constructions of theological anthropology.

The Knowing Self in Modern Theological Anthropology

The turn-to-the-subject of modern theology has embraced the idea that a fundamental characteristic of the human person is found in our capacities for thought. As René Descartes articulated, so much is uncertain and able to be questioned, but at least this we can know with certainty: There is thinking going on, and the 'I' is the one who is doing the thinking. 'I think, therefore I am' was his famous dictum, rooted in his Third Meditation, *On God, That He Exists*:

> Now I will shut my eyes, I will stop up my ears, I will divert all my senses, I will even blot out from my thoughts all images of corporeal things—or at least, since the latter can hardly be done, I will regard these images as nothing, empty and false as indeed they are. And as I converse only with myself and look more deeply into myself, I will attempt to render myself gradually better known and familiar to myself. I am a thing that thinks, that is to say, a thing that doubts, affirms, denies, knows a few things, is ignorant of many things, wills, rejects, and also imagines and senses. As I observed earlier, although these things that I sense or imagine may perhaps be nothing at all outside me, nevertheless I am certain that these modes of thinking—which I call sensations and imaginations— insofar as they are only modes of thinking, are within me.[3]

Descartes' shutting out of the external world envisioned the human person as knower, with two important corollaries. First, thought is independent of what is outside the person; after all, even if I stop my ears and shut my eyes, and cut off all perceptions, I am still able to think. Second, the certainty that I am the one who thinks is a solid foundation, free from external influences, for grounding further assertions. Hence, knowing is assumed to be a universal process available to all through the internal universality of reason, where the 'I' precedes the knowing as a condition of knowing's possibility.

When Karl Rahner continues a Cartesian trajectory in his theological anthropology, he similarly identifies 'knowing' as an essential constitutive of the human person. The process of knowing demonstrates for Rahner that there is an 'I' irreducible to the external world and preceding the experience within it, albeit, for Rahner, inextricably conditioned by this world. He writes:

> In the fact that man raises analytical questions about himself and opens himself to the unlimited horizons of such questioning, he has already

transcended himself and every conceivable element of such an analysis or of an empirical reconstruction of himself. In doing this he is affirming himself as more than the sum of such analyzable components of his reality. Precisely this consciousness of himself, this confrontation with the totality of all his conditions, and this very being-conditioned show him to be more than the sum of his factors.[4]

In unpacking Rahner, we might see that the human ability to comprehend not only the external world but also to comprehend oneself in all one's component parts indicates that there exists an 'I', which is more than the sum of said parts. Importantly for Rahner, as for Descartes, this ability to raise analytical questions about the self opens oneself up to a reality beyond the self, a reality whose foundational existence gives rise to the human person, namely, the reality of God.

While such an intimate relationship between knowing subject and God provides a compelling warrant for celebrating human knowledge, this construction of the human person as knowing subject is not without its problematics. As T. M. Rudavsky explains:

> The feminist critique of reason is part of [a] long tradition within philosophy. Feminists have extended this historical critique by arguing that concepts of reason are reflections of gendered practices passing as universals . . . .Following Kant's espousal of the intellect as an active creator of knowledge, feminists have argued that if the human mind constructs knowledge, then the identity of the knower becomes relevant to the process of knowing.[5]

The feminist lens interrogates knowledge systems for the traces of human subjectivity embedded within them. That is to say, reason is not a disembodied and disinterested project, but knowledge itself is the product of human contemplations and constructions of 'the way things are' informed by and informing the very specific experience of living in the world. In this, feminist epistemology follows more closely the outlook of theorists like Thomas Kuhn, who shed light on the way 'knowledge' is constructed by particular communities, seeing disciplines like science and religion and philosophy not as disentangled from the world, but as part of the "social process."[6]

Economies of Knowledge: Access and Alternatives

To unpack further the particular understanding of 'knowledge' that Kuhn opens up for this theological anthropology, a closer look at his proposal is in order. Beginning from an understanding that 'reality' or 'nature' presents uniform but ambiguous stimuli to all persons and that each person is endowed with similar neural apparatus, Kuhn argues that the stimuli presented are shaped into 'data' based on the framework of ideas and concepts each person brings to them. These categories have been made available to the individual (have become the way s/he 'sees' the world) by the particular methods or paradigms the individual has learned from his/her community. The data presented by the universe is organized through the forms that the paradigms provide.[7] Here, we see how Kuhn's explanation sees knowledge as a social project informed not simply by 'the way things are' or by the individual as knower but by the way s/he has been shaped by a community of thought and practice. The paradigms of a community shape the way an individual sees the world; they shape his/her understanding of 'the way things are'. While this offers an understanding of how different religious traditions, scientific views, or communal understandings render the interpretations of the world diverse, Kuhn presses the function of the framework even further to suggest that each paradigm blocks out certain stimuli (as irrelevant, or beyond its scope) and has categories that access and emphasize other stimuli. Therefore, paradigms limit what can be 'known' or accessed of reality, because they necessarily focus on some details and disregard others as irrelevant to the community's concerns. As Kuhn notes from within scientific practices, procedures and applications inevitably "restrict the phenomenological field accessible for scientific investigations at any given time."[8] While the paradigm functions to organize stimuli, Kuhn argues that the use of a specific paradigm reciprocally programs one's neural apparatus to perceive the world in a particular way. This means that it is not just the interpretation of data that differs among communities employing different paradigms but that the perception of the stimuli or construction of the 'data' itself is different. The 'training' or 'programming' of one's neural apparatus takes place as the individual adopts the methods of a community.[9] He follows the lead of others in the community and applies the paradigmatic examples the community offers. Thus the initiate learns by doing, by applying paradigmatic exemplars in a variety of contexts. These exemplars teach more or less intuitively the rules that govern the community's life form or language game.[10]

If knowledge is not the disembodied access to universal reason but participation in the life world and language game of particular communities, then we might be encouraged to think about the knowing subject embedded in systems of knowledge or 'economies of knowledge', wherein what is 'known' is shaped by and constructed within particular, localized communities. In feminist understanding, these might be described as 'epistemic communities' that produce and reproduce knowledge by shaping members within the community to see, and therefore to experience, the world in similar ways. At the same time, since our experience is impacted also by our social location in the world, what we 'know' is informed by the particularities of our experience. What we 'know' is conditioned by where we are situated, in terms both of conceptual frameworks that shape us and of social location that impacts our experience.[11] Utilizing the term 'economy' might bring to mind the material realities that inform constructed knowledge systems and 'what's at stake' in thinking in particular ways.

The basic suggestion that knowledge is created by communities seeing the world in particular ways is relevant to the distinctiveness of religious communities shaping people's thought and practice. In fact, George Lindbeck argues, 'religions' are very much like 'epistemic communities' of persons who see and experience the world in similar ways based on the shaping of their epistemic-apparatus by living deeply within a particular community. For Lindbeck, it is the sacred scripture of a religion that functions as the communal paradigm providing the categories for organizing and understanding reality.[12] As he describes this intratextual process, "one privileged text [the sacred scripture] functions as the comprehensive interpretive framework."[13] Thus, just as communities of scientists see the world in a particular way based on the paradigms they employ, so too religious communities see the world in a particular way based on the sacred texts that function as paradigms for them. Believers see the world imaginatively through scriptural lenses allowing the structure of the narrative itself to organize the sensory stimuli of the world. Within the pages of the sacred text are found the categories that shape religious persons' experiences of the world.

Following Kuhn, Lindbeck concludes that different paradigms create different and often incompatible modes of community life that do not offer points of contact for comparative conversations. In the conversation between communities, Kuhn notes the difficulty of adjudicating between claims:

To the extent, as significant as it is incomplete, that two scientific schools disagree about what is a problem and what a solution, they will inevitably talk through each other when debating the relative merits of their respective paradigms. In the partially circular arguments that regularly result, each paradigm will be shown to satisfy more or less the criteria it dictates for itself and to fall short of a few of those dictated by its opponent.[14]

Paradigms answer specific questions. In doing so, they limit what can be known and they shape what is known about reality. In adopting different paradigms, distinct communities know and experience 'reality' in different ways. Since perceptions are shaped by particular paradigms, "there is no standard higher than the assent of the relevant community" for assessing the conclusions reached.[15]

Because persons of differing religions are born into communities with specific language systems, and because these language systems provide distinctive categories for organizing sensory data, two persons of different faith cultures not only speak different languages with regard to faith experiences but, indeed, they have different experiences. Lindbeck writes that "there are numberless thoughts we cannot think, sentiments we cannot have, and realities we cannot perceive unless we learn to use the appropriate symbol system."[16] Taking up particular postmodern strands of thought, Lindbeck through his construction challenges the modern form of identity and knowledge that opened this discussion—namely, from a postmodern perspective, the 'I' never precedes language, cannot stand apart from it, and is always constructed through it.[17] Thus, without fluency in the language of a given religion, one cannot perceive the reality identifiable through the categories of that religious tradition.

This way of visualizing religions as frameworks and stories that shape us makes interreligious dialogue both a compelling and a challenging project. The ideal participants might be open to the adventure of encounter with the other. But as they begin their explanations, the words uttered by conversation partners raise as many questions as they do answers. This is because each word is linked not only to a particular idea but to an interconnected life world of sacred stories, ritual remembrances, and religious practices. As Sallie King describes it:

> Living in the Buddhist world, one lives in the world of the serenely smiling Buddha; a world whose vista embraces lifetime after lifetime of countless rebirths held in tension with an invitation to complete selflessness; a world in which one strives to remove all 'thought coverings,' to erase

everything and plunge again and again into vast emptiness; a world in which one feels one's connectedness with all things and has compassion for all beings, the insect as well as the human. Say 'Buddha Nature' and all this is implicit.[18]

Thus, as the Buddhist participant begins by affirming that all who are gathered share in 'Buddha Nature', her hearers are bewildered by the many ideas that are connected and require further explanation. As evidenced in the examination of the Philadelphia Area Women's Multifaith Group, the stretch of interreligious conversation each month over the past ten years suggests that the communication across religious frameworks is an ongoing and enriching process but one that must necessarily be extended because of a lack of easy understanding.

To add another layer to this discussion, however, one must recognize that 'the religions' are composed of a variety of internal economies of knowledge. The production of knowledge may draw from foundational texts and the authoritative interpreters of the tradition, but it also includes the practitioner's own experience. This means that knowledge production within a religious tradition itself is variously understood and variously accessed. A poem by Merle Feld captures some of the sentiment of how gendered expectations and divisions of roles have left the production of so-called authoritative knowledge in the hands of men in many religious traditions of the world, while women's knowledge might expand the story.

My Brother and I were at Sinai
He kept a journal
Of what he saw
Of what he heard
Of what it all meant to him

I wish I had such a record
Of what happened to me there

It seems like every time I want to write
I can't
I'm always holding a baby
One of my own
Or one for a friend
Always holding a baby
So my hands are never free to write things down

And then
As time passes
The particulars
The hard data
The who what when where why
Slip away from me
And all I'm left with is
The feeling

But feelings are just sound
The vowel barking of a mute

My brother is so sure of what he heard
After all he's got a record of it

If we remembered it together
We could recreate holy time
Sparks Flying[19]

For the better part of human history, in so many cultures and religions, it is the case that women have been barred from education and religious education, which means that they have been barred from access to authoritative knowledge and that they have been excluded from being producers of knowledge. The production of that knowledge (so-called, as an authoritative discourse) has been out of bounds for many women:

I have heard "I really don't know enough," or some variant of that phrase, at every conference of Jewish women, almost every time a Jewish woman gets up to speak of Jewish matters. At the 1992 First International Conference on Judaism, Feminism, and Psychology in Seattle, it was an opening remark that punctuated informal conversations in the hallways, as well as formal presentations and workshop discussions. I realized that I too, whether I voiced it or not, had a similar feeling of not really being entitled to my opinions or observations because I was not sufficiently steeped in Jewish texts. I have become aware of my own anxiety about speaking on the topic of Jewish women's issues, and I have realized that my sense of not knowing enough is not unique to me but is shared by other Jewish women. This may, in fact, be central to understanding certain element (sic) in the lives of Jewish women today.

Jewish women's collective sense of not knowing enough has many roots and manifests itself in many forms. It could well be called Jewish women's "learned ignorance." We have learned to remain ignorant for several, sometimes opposite, reasons. Chief among these is a Jewish tradition of keeping women out of the male bastions of Jewish learning and synagogue ritual, a tradition that has only begun to be questioned and open to change within my lifetime, starting timidly in the 1950s, and more vigorously since the 1970s.[20]

Articulated eloquently through the experience of Jewish women, it is not an experience limited to Jewish women. Even while many religious ideologies teach the equality of women and men in one form or another (pointing to sacred scriptures as evidence), practices exclude women from full participation in leadership roles, as is the case in contemporary Roman Catholicism and Sikhism, even when women have gained access to the highest forms of learning available within these traditions.[21] This has been the case in just about every religious tradition, in places where women have been barred from education and religious education.[22]

The lack, or perceived lack, of understanding of even one's own economy of knowledge informs participation in interreligious dialogue. Asked to reflect on what she experienced as the challenges of interfaith dialogue, one respondent replied, "my lack of biblical knowledge and my inability to express myself articulately about my faith."[23] Perceiving 'my faith' as knowledge held by some other authority (the economy of biblical knowledge experienced as authoritative within the community) limits the fullness of participation and the ease with which one might participate in interreligious settings. The construction of interreligious dialogue as a conversation among experts comparing the 'knowledge' of discrete traditions further excludes women and other nonexperts from the table.

The construction of economies of knowledge produced largely by men has the result that women often find themselves both within and outside their tradition. They are 'within' the tradition as active members of the community, having been shaped by sacred scripture or liturgy or ritual, but they are 'outside' the tradition in its instantiation of knowledge. Having been produced by men, the knowledge systems of the tradition continue to privilege certain male experiences and have the ring of 'truth' to masculinist ways of being in the world. Existentially, often inchoately, women then experience themselves 'othered' by their own tradition.[24] This leads to a relationship of tension for women in many religious traditions. At the height of the women's movement in North America, some thirty years ago, one Christian woman reflected, "So many times I've tried to decide whether I should just drop out and forget the church or whether I should hang in there."[25] Now, more than a quarter of a century later, Catholic women still write that "the voices and experiences of women have been marginalized within official Church teachings and practices. Although women constitute the majority of Church membership, they have continuously been denied full participation in the Church by virtue of their sexed/gendered identities. For many women, the consistent devaluing of their gifts and resources has led to a dilemma: 'should we stay or should we go?'"[26]

Recognizing structural exclusion from the economies of knowledge that shape them, feminist thinkers have obviously been frustrated by the persistent exclusions rooted in gender discriminations in evidence across the traditions. But such persistent exclusion from full participation in their tradition's economy of knowledge has propelled many women from across the traditions to seek greater access to the educational forms that would situate them more closely with authoritative strands of knowledge in their tradition.

Access to Education

Across the religious traditions, across the three waves of feminism, women strove to gain access to education, religious education, and the right to interpret sacred texts that would provide them with access to authoritative knowledge. In the late nineteenth century, Elizabeth Cady Stanton's *The Woman's Bible* argued precisely this need for women to be able to have authoritative access to the Christian scripture, which was being used to enforce patriarchal roles. In 1928 and 1929, Lebanese Muslim Nazira Zayn al-Din published two texts that argue for women's religious right to interpret the qur'anic texts that have to do with women. As Zayn al-Din argued, women "are more worthy of interpreting verses that have to do with women's duties and rights than men, for they are the ones that are directly addressed."[27] As a leader in the movement for women's rights in India, Hindu activist Sarojini Naidu championed women's right to education also in the late nineteenth and early twentieth centuries.[28] Recalling Naidu's words: "I think it is inevitable that one should become interested in politics if one is a true Indian. I lived in a Muhammadan city, and you see, I had so many Muhammadan friends . . . I have taken part in all their political and educational meetings. I have presided over their meetings and spoken at mosques."[29] Concern for education crosses lines of religious affiliation; and the concern for religious education is related to access to secular forms of education as well.

In recognizing the relationship between knowledge and power within religious traditions, many women across the traditions, in the first and second wave and beyond, have attempted to become authoritative in the traditions of learning within the religions. In the second-wave movement of Christian feminist theology, women entered institutions of higher learning to gain access to the training once reserved for male priests and clergy. Jewish women gained access to training in becoming rabbis and pursuing traditionally male forms of study and learning. From the perspective of Muslim feminists, they too have become experts in their field. As Miriam Cooke comments:

> What does it mean to intercalate scripture with history as an Islamic feminist? It entails study of the life of the Prophet, of the many strong women around him, and of his founding *umma* in the seventh century, and also direct engagement with the foundational texts, rather than merely reaction to their interpretations. It involves looking at the context in which the Qur'an was revealed and these texts were written. Finally, it means applying this understanding to the present so as to question the ways in which Islamic knowledge has been produced.[30]

Mehrezia Labidi-Maiza, a Tunisian Muslim, reflects on the religious warrants that sustain Muslim women's access to knowledge:

> On many occasions I heard my father defending his choice of education by invoking God's Messenger Muhammad, who was the father of four daughters and who promised eternal happiness to fathers who were benevolent with their daughters . . . inspired as he was by the Prophet and firmly convinced that a girl's greatest protection was and always would be Knowledge. . . . If today I had to choose which measure to adopt in order to promote better conditions for women in a country where rights were being denied them, I should say without hesitation: access to education without caveats![31]

As in the feminist movement in society, the feminist movements in religion have sought access to systems that might produce greater equality. Participation in knowledge accumulation and knowledge production has been key. Because each of us is historically and socially conditioned, what will count as 'knowledge' or the type of knowing that is passed along to each will vary. On some accounts, this is precisely why women have been historically excluded from interreligious dialogue, because they have not acquired the 'correct' knowledge to be equipped to participate. Organized as a discourse among 'experts' in the traditions, the learned and/or ordained members of various religions are gathered to represent their communities. When women are systematically barred from taking a leadership role in their religious community (for example, in the case of the Roman Catholic Church), they are not thought of as properly representative of 'the tradition.' The women of the Philadelphia Area dialogue group are active in their home communities, interreligious networking, and interfaith activism, but only a few of them would be recognized as 'experts' by their tradition's leadership.

Even if not ordained leaders, women are increasingly becoming 'experts' in the various traditions through the avenues of higher education and learning. The story of the women's movement and the emergence of feminist theology tells clearly the tale of women challenging their male-centered traditions by acquiring the academic credentials that have allowed them to do so. Whether through doctorates in theology or religious studies, or through ordination as rabbis or priests, the women's movement has empowered women to move into the ranks of experts through their participation in religious study. But in many parts of the world, women continue to be limited in their access to education. According to the United Nations, the vast majority of women around the globe achieve lower levels of education than do men in their respective region. Of the 130 million children worldwide who were not in school in 1997, two-thirds of them were girls. That this disparity is of real urgency is recognized by the UN Millennium Development Goals, on which elimination of educational disparity appears second on the prioritized list.[32] Even in areas where women have equal access to education, gendered expectations surrounding childcare limit the assigned and acquired leadership of women as spokespersons of the faiths rooted in a traditional understanding of knowledge.

Alternative Economies of Knowledge

If a fundamental dimension of who we are as human beings rests in our capacity to create knowledge and to participate in the production of secular and religious insight, the denial of access for women appears to have been a fundamentally compromising constraint on the very human being of women. At the same time, the feminist perspective in thinking from the experience of women recognizes that the authoritative, male-constructed forms of knowledge are just one form of knowledge. That is to say, when women approach these traditions of knowledge and the sacred texts from their gendered experience, the understanding that will grow out of the encounter may be very different. This is akin to Rudavsky's explanation of how feminist epistemologies found an opening to gender-inflected knowledge in Kant's assessment that the knower is an active participant in the production of knowledge. But what this means for the authoritative economies of knowledge has not been fully considered. We might pursue this consideration with the texture of the lived experience of one Jewish feminist scholar. Rachel Josefowitz Siegel writes:

> I remember sitting next to my mother in the women's gallery in the balcony of our beautiful little synagogue in Lausanne, Switzerland. I could have been eight, or ten, or eleven, or it happened every year. I hardly knew enough Hebrew letters to follow the prayers in the prayer book. I did not know the order of the service and never knew what page we were on or what to say, or do. I assumed that my mother knew, since she was a rabbi's daughter and competent in other areas, yet I was never sure that she really did. Only a few of the women in the women's gallery appeared to be immersed in prayer or to know when to stand up and when to sit down. I followed my mother's cues, embarrassed and ashamed at faking it.
>
> I remember the mixture of feeling deeply connected to the assembled Jewish community, but feeling strangely excluded from what was really going on in the main sanctuary downstairs, where I saw my father and brothers participating in the Torah service. While I could not have named these feelings at the time, I wanted *in* most desperately, and I also wanted *out* and away from the unnamed tension of ignorance and exclusion. . . .
>
> I see no contradiction in wanting access to the male privileges of ritual and wanting to feminize the very same ritual by bringing female wisdom and consciousness into it. . . . Much like women in other spheres of male dominance, having partly achieved some of those goals I then began to question the words that I had been excluded from saying all those years. As I learned more, I became aware of my aversion to the sexist, hierarchical, and vengeful messages that are embedded in Jewish texts. I began to ask myself whether this was what I really wanted

to perpetuate. The question that emerged was whether it is possible to retain the positive elements of Jewish teachings, while reframing or rejecting the objectionable elements. In answer to that question, I have fought for the inclusion of women in Jewish prayer, in Jewish institutions, and in Jewish communal leadership; at the same time I have initiated changes in the text and challenged the status quo.[33]

As Siegel indicates, access to authoritative sites of knowledge often brings with it a desire to change that knowledge system from the resources of an alternative system. We know from a study of women in the various religious traditions of the world that gender has been one factor for systematic exclusion from access to knowledge—whether academic knowledge or religious knowledge—especially in the reception of knowledge but then, therefore, simultaneously in the production of authoritative knowledge. When excluded from patriarchal forms of religiosity, women have often developed their own patterns of religiosity. In addition to this distinctiveness arising from exclusion, the mere fact that we inhabit a world where gender impacts our experience of being human means that women's experiences in the religions have been distinctive. Women have woven their religious traditions into their child-rearing practices and outlooks on the everyday; they have served as storytellers within communities through which embodied knowledge and religious practice has been transmitted. Thus, feminist approaches across the traditions also recognize women's gendered experiences as producing alternative sites of knowledge.

The work of Muslim scholar Leila Ahmed demonstrates the many aspects of introducing women's voices to our understanding of knowledge rooted in the religions. A scholar, Ahmed has undertaken the requisite learning to be considered an expert on women in Islam. She has written numerous books and teaches university courses on the topic. But in her memoir, *A Border Passage*, she indicates that the knowledge passed along to her of Islam was not simply the knowledge that came from books, lectures, and research. It was an embodied Islam that was woven into the many dimensions of her life. It was an Islam communicated in and through the lives of the women in her community: "It is easy to see now that our lives in the Alexandria house, and even at Zatoun, were lived in women's time, women's space. And in women's culture."[34] Not only barred from leadership and learning but also discouraged from communal participation in religious services in the mosque, Ahmed was raised in what she terms 'women's Islam'. It is worth returning to the passage already quoted in chapter 2:

> For although in those days it was only Grandmother who performed all the regular formal prayers, for all the women of the house, religion was an essential part of how they made sense of and understood their own lives. It was through religion that one pondered the things that happened, why they had happened, and what one should make of them, how one should take them.
>
> Islam, as I got it from them, was gentle, generous, pacifist, inclusive, somewhat mystical—just as they themselves were. . . . Being Muslim was about believing in a world in which life was meaningful and in which all events and happenings were permeated (although not always transparently to us) with meaning. Religion was above all about inner things. The outward signs of religiousness, such as prayer and fasting, might be signs of a true religiousness but equally well might not. They were certainly not what was important about being Muslim. What was important was how you conducted yourself and how you were in yourself and in your attitude toward others and in your heart.
>
> . . . What was passed on, beside the very general basic beliefs and moral ethos of Islam, which are also those of its sister monotheisms, was a way of being in the world. A way of holding oneself in the world—in relation to God, to existence, to other human beings. This the women passed on to us most of all through how they were and by their being and presence, by the way *they* were in the world, conveying their beliefs, ways, thoughts, and how we should be in the world by a touch, a glance, a word. . . . And all of these ways of passing on attitudes, morals, beliefs, knowledge—through touch and the body and in words spoken in the living moment—are by their very nature subtle and evanescent. They profoundly shape the next generation, but they do not leave a record in the way that someone writing a text about how to live or what to believe leaves a record. Nevertheless, they leave a far more important and, literally, more vital, living record.[35]

Quoting Ahmed at length, I'd like to draw attention to two important challenges she raises to the questions of what 'religion' is and of how religious knowledge is transmitted. While textbook descriptions of 'Islam' will include the mosque as a primary site of ritual practice, women are often not active participants in the mosque community and often have been barred from such active participation. This means that what textbooks describe as the 'religion' of Islam is the religion of 'men's Islam'. Presenting 'religion' in public forms, academic economies of knowledge identify primarily male forms of religion: texts, public ritual gatherings, legal codes. But in Ahmed's description, 'religion' designates the way an economy of knowledge rooted in the Qur'an allows the world to be permeated with meaning and provides the structure for conducting oneself within that meaningful world. The sacred text creates the world as one might live within it. As a way of living, 'religion' for Ahmed is transmitted in an embodied and relational way, passed on without written record but nonetheless having a powerful and distinctive living presence. As Ahmed recalls: "I spent a great deal of my childhood and adolescence among the women of Zatoun, whether at Zatoun itself or at the family home in Alexandria. My view of that world, and of the nature and meaning of life, I learned from the women, not the men."[36] Her reflections lead us to imagine the many living ways women throughout time and across cultures and religions have livingly created and informed their traditions. It is this sort of living enactment of traditions in its 'non-textbook' manifestation that also comes through in the Philadelphia women's dialogue. Religion, life, and personal story are alive in women's distinctive social locations.

Merle Feld's poem about being written out of the events of Sinai communicates another dimension related to this theme—namely, that in gendered constructions where the child-rearing falls to women almost exclusively, the record of events is not written by woman's hand. But, importantly, as Feld describes the woman's perspective, the symbolism of holding the next generation communicates a particular mode of shaping the community. Jewish feminist theologian Judith Plaskow underscores the importance of this way of passing on knowledge through ritual and communal presence. As Plaskow explains it, the critical moments of Jewish religious history recorded in the Bible are not merely past record or source of information but shape Jewish memory and consciousness. This happens through "the liturgical reenactment and celebration of formative events." She writes, "The weekly renewal of creation with the inauguration of the Sabbath, the entry of the High Priest into the Holy of Holies on the Day of Atonement, the Exodus of Israel from Egypt every Passover—these are remembered not just verbally but through the body and thus doubly imprinted on Jewish consciousness."[37] Plaskow also raises to the surface the traditions of home-based liturgical practice and women's prayers and rituals as an extension of the communal celebrations of liturgy that take place in public spaces of synagogue. Rachel Josefowitz Siegel insists, "Let us celebrate the beauty of women's voices affirming the varied ways of Jewish knowing."[38]

The passing on of tradition in ways not captured in texts enables us to recall also cultures where orality is the primary mode of communicating tradition—for example, in many African societies. The practice of embodying tradition in voice and movement carried over for African women under inhumane conditions of the Middle Passage and was the means by which they maintained traditions even under the duress of enslavement when external power in slave-owning societies aimed to willfully break the continuity of these traditions. The power of the oral and embodied traditions, carried by women and men from African societies, witnesses the power of this practice for shaping religious sensibilities.[39] In the words of Trinh T. Min-ha, "From Africa to India and vice versa. Every woman partakes in the chain of guardianship and of transmission. Every griotte [storyteller] who dies is a whole library that burns down."[40]

The passing on of religious knowledge through ritual practice is central to understanding the important role of women in Hindu traditions. In her *Guests at God's Wedding*, Tracy Pinchman describes the present-day rituals that sustain a community through women's participation.[41] The distinctive knowledge embedded in celebrating the deity enacts the community's understanding of the divine in ways that particularly convey also the specific experiences and social realities of the women themselves. Assessing such alternative sites of knowledge in Hindu cultures, Madhu Khanna writes: "Women have preserved a large number of traditional knowledge systems. Firmly grounded in religious revelations they have drawn inspiration from folklore, epics and age-old models of virtuosity."[42]

A distinctive form of 'women's knowledge' was recognized by the Catholic women of Maryknoll who traveled to China on mission. As Sister Paulita Hoffmann relates:

Every word would have to be said in their colloquial language. . . . So you really had to. . . . that was, explain the characters so that they would understand the meaning of those prayers. The Mass prayers the same way, they were very literary. . . . Then you had the catechism which was in Pai Hua. So that was more understandable. That was understandable to students but not to the women from the kitchen! Because that's not what they spoke!

Then you had tutom. And what was 'tu' is the language and 'tom' was the earth language. Well, the tutom was the way, woman-to-woman, would speak over the back fence. You know, 'how is your kitchen stove?' 'and I burn this and I burn that, and I burn fire.' It's a completely different language!!

So we studied the catechism, we studied the doctrine and all those. Bishop Ford, I guess about the second year the sisters were there or the third year, he said, 'You know, we're never going to get to these people until we get into their kitchens. And the women are in the kitchens. The women really have the feel of the sentiment of the children. They instill knowledge into those children—into the heart. And we won't know them until we get into (he always used the word kitchen) the kitchen.'[43]

The Human Condition: Receptive to the Speech of God in Our Everyday Existence

The alternative knowledge systems that women have cultivated have only rarely been identified as sources of religious knowledge. In approaches that separate the sacred from the mundane, the everyday is discarded as unimportant to understanding what is holy. But this theological anthropology has insisted that what counts as 'religion' and therefore what can be included as 'sacred knowledge' cannot be contained in the so-called 'sacred spaces' but rather flows through the world as we find it. Such an insistence about the nature of our human condition *as holy* is rooted in a broader Catholic Christian outlook that recognizes a nearness as well as a mystery to the reality that is named 'God'. The nearness of God and God's ultimate mystery sustains a wide variety of economies of knowledge, including those produced by women in the everyday habits of their lives.

Remaining mystery always, the transcendent reality that Christians name 'God' exceeds all economies of knowledge but nevertheless is affirmed as a reality toward which our economies of knowledge might bend. 'God' is available to us precisely because 'God' is understood as what brought us into being ultimately and what continues to sustain us moment to moment. The sustaining power of God courses through our everyday existence, cooperating with those realities that bring us into being proximally and continuing to sustain us moment to moment. God, world, and humanity are deeply interconnected, and our awareness of

'God' emerges in and through the everyday. Our economies of knowledge may attempt to speak of this power and presence in human tongues.

Karl Rahner articulates this through his characteristic method of taking our human experience as starting point and connecting traditional theological language to the various profound experiences of our lives. Using 'revelation' to describe the very deep insights humans achieve into their own condition, Rahner writes: "When and where this innermost self-communication of God, which is already revelation, is wholly and correctly reflected in consciousness, and is objectivated in words, there we have what one calls—I might say—in the common (and correctly common) theological sense *revelation*. It has always a double component: the original self-communication of God and at the same time the reflective awareness of this original self-communication as it occurs in the history of humankind—of course not only individually, but also collectively."[44] Rahner continues:

> The reflective awareness of this original revealing self-communication of God is not the product of mere introversion. It occurs in concrete, historical, human experience. People do not experience what love is, what responsibility is, by sitting and asking themselves in some psychological introspection: Who am I really? They make this experience of freedom, of responsibility, of love in concrete life, in their concrete activity, in their concrete historical reality.[45]

Those crucial experiences—of love and relationality, of freedom as creativity under constraint—are fundamental to the human capacity to ask those questions of ultimate meaning: Why am I here? Who am I to become? Our ability to reflect on those experiences as sites that pose the questions to us is central to Rahner's understanding of the human relatedness to the ultimate source of these questions and their answers. In the many and diverse ways that human beings reflect on their experiences, grab flashes of insight into their human condition, or touch authentically a moment for which it was made, they encounter the meaning, purpose, and being of existence. For Rahner, such awareness and experience indicate an encounter with the power and presence that is ultimate—that is, an encounter with God.

In such a conceptualization, our human self-reflection and our human 'speaking-forth' of the experience (which Rahner identifies as 'revelation') is subsidiary to an originary movement that transcends us (the 'God speaking' part of revelation). If 'God speaks', God speaks in and through the world as we know it. If God speaks, it is through the data of our world, but recalling Kuhn, we realize the power of our inherited paradigms to shape this data into meaning. The data of our world and God's speaking forth within it requires paradigms to shape our reception of it. Invoking Kuhn again, he describes how all persons need a conceptual paradigm through which to organize the data of an otherwise chaotic world. He writes that "something like a paradigm is prerequisite to perception itself. What a man sees depends both upon what he looks at and also upon what his previous visual-conceptual experience has taught him to see. In the absence of such training there can only be, in William James's phrase, 'a bloomin' buzzin' confusion.'"[46]

If God 'communicates', if Ultimate Reality 'speaks', it is through diverse economies of knowledge that humans are able to 'hear' and organize this speech into understanding. God may speak through our religious economies of knowledge, but the economy of knowledge itself does not exhaust the 'communication' of God. As forms of knowledge, our religious traditions in their multiplicity arise out of the meaning-making of human experience embedded in distinctive economies of knowledge that order the chaos of a world that can be interpreted in a multiplicity of ways, always opening outward to the expanse of a horizon that is Ultimate.

Theologians such as Lindbeck may describe Christian scripture as "God's word to his people"[47] and insist that persons are "addressed directly by God speaking in and through Scripture,"[48] whereby "God speaks in particular words in particular settings to his people by means of the Bible."[49] Taken literally, such a position on religious knowledge would dangerously guarantee the economy of knowledge particular to the Christian scripture and its guardians. Understood poetically, however, such conceptualization might have meaning beyond a fundamentalist interpretation. If 'God speaks', and our human organization of that communication comes through our economies of knowledge, then the concretized form of that speech captured from out of experience and into scripture can subsequently be a way that God speaks. But, it is also the case that this simultaneously can be held together with the insistence that God continues to speak and that the speech of God is not captured once, for all, in a singular economy of knowledge or a single scripture. There is a distinction here that is theologically essential: 'God' is not the words and worlds spoken forth by our economies of knowledge, but these words may be affirmation of those places and ways that the human person is in touch with that reality, that mystery, rightly and really, but not exhaustively.

Continuing the trajectory of theological anthropology begun by my modern philosophical predecessors in their thinking through knowledge, I was set on a path that elevates certain rational forms of thinking as the means by which knowledge is produced. The expansion of our investigation to the ways in which women have formed alternative economies of knowledge in the everyday might encourage us to consider the nonrational, embodied, emotive production of knowledge such that economies of knowledge are transmitted not simply in language but in bodies and through practice. This might allow us to recognize diverse types of knowledge not limited to neuro-typical practices of rational thought—to recognize, that is, diverse knowledge systems that pass along insight, awareness, and the nearness of God in many and diverse ways. Such multiplicity relativizes any one economy of knowledge.

The Human Condition: I Think Toward 'I Am'

If we can recognize the multiplicity of knowledge systems—ways of knowing and economies of knowledge—we must inquire as to the *why* of inhabiting certain patterns of thought. Seeing how systems of knowledge have been sources of exclusion, it is incumbent on us to interrogate our own systems of knowledge for the part they play in guaranteeing material well-being or withholding it. A knowledge system is not power-neutral. Speaking of the academic study of Eastern peoples in Western scholarship under the heading 'Orientalism', Edward Said illumines the way that the construction of knowledge is implicated and entangled with other areas of human life. Said writes:

My principal operating assumptions were—and continue to be—that fields of learning, as much as the works of even the most eccentric artist, are constrained and acted upon by society, by cultural traditions, by worldly circumstance, and by stabilizing influences like schools, libraries, and governments; moreover, that both learned and imaginative writing are never free, but are limited in their imagery, assumptions, and intentions; and finally, that the advances made by a 'science' like Orientalism in its academic form are less objectively true than we often like to think. . . .

A field like Orientalism has a cumulative and corporate identity, one that is particularly strong given its associations with traditional learning (the classics, the Bible, philology), public institutions (governments, trading companies, geographical societies, universities), and generically determined writing (travel books, books of exploration, fantasy, exotic description).[50]

Said lays bare the economies of knowledge and the collective nature of any learned enterprise, illuminating further the idea from chapter 4 that the human person is characterized by 'creativity under constraint': We are acted on by our frameworks and communities even as we produce new knowledge within them. But Said widens Kuhn's scope of what will impact the production of this knowledge. It is not only one's localized community that shapes the framework and economy of knowledge; knowledge production emerges in an interconnected system rooted in particular historical, social, and material locations, bearing an interest in those locations and their relationship to others. Said points toward the material repercussions of how knowledge will be employed. He sees the links between production of knowledge about the 'other' and knowledge produced in classic texts, biblical texts, government and trade interests, universities, travel books, and more. He raises for us the questions: How is the production of our internal religious knowledge connected with biblical texts, material outcomes, social relationships, popular writings, cultural production, and political, governmental, and economic interests? How is the production of knowledge about our religious others similarly intertwined with material outcomes, social relationships, popular writings, media and cultural production, political, governmental, international, economic interests, and more?

Knowledge does not simply exist for human beings to access it; rather, it is produced in communities that are now globally interconnected and materially interested. What counts as 'knowledge' and 'truth' is constructed within fields of discourse and culture and passed along through educational and embodied means. This way of thinking about knowledge enables us not only to see 'knowledge' as constructed but also to witness in that construction the possibility for privilege and exclusion. Given the many different ways that 'knowledge' can be construed, we can interrogate systems of knowledge to ask what material conditions are supported by particular ways of knowing. What structures of power and exclusion inform particular 'economies of knowledge' in ways that create and invisibly defend privilege and dispossession? Those who serve as 'guardians' of knowledge within a community have power while those with no access to the systems that will pass on this 'knowledge' do not. Economies of knowledge can enrich the guardians with evident material gains and livelihoods as well as social capital. The exclusion from access can be built on cultural, religious, or gendered differences; it can be patrolled with discriminations of economics, class, and race. There is a crucial intersection, then, between the guardians of Christian knowledge (which have been patriarchally conferred) barring the access of women *and* their resistance to the presence of religious others. Why is it so often the case that the same authoritative guardians reject the insights of women *and* refuse the wisdom of other faiths?

As corrective to this patrolling of religious knowledge and containing it in privileged certainties, Rahner's conceptualization of knowledge and the quest for the living God are essential. His vision of the encounter with God evidenced in practices of knowing was that God stood as the horizon of mystery, beckoning humanity to ever deeper engagement with the complexity of existence. Drawing on the concept of divine mystery in Thomas Aquinas, we are pressed toward an invitation to wonder. Thomas writes: "Nothing can be wearisome that is wonderful to him that looks on it, because as long as we wonder at it, it still moves our desire. Now the created intellect always looks with wonder on the divine substance, since no created intellect can comprehend it. Therefore, the intellectual substance cannot possibly become weary of that vision."[51] In face of God as mystery, Rahner pressed into the very being of the human person as characterized by knowledge, writing: "Hence the existentiell question for the knower is this: Which does he love more, the small island of his so-called knowledge or the sea of infinite mystery?"[52] Embracing the human production of knowledge invites us to see our knowledge as tentative and revisable, always pressing new horizons toward the ever-receding horizon of mystery.

Knowledge serves a function that is proximate: It is interested and invested in the everyday. So, too, religious knowledge is invested not just in some ideal Truth or Hereafter but in the social, material, and political contexts in which the knowledge is constructed. As we recognize the way economies of knowledge are interested and implicated in material social conditions in the world, we are guided by what philosophers call a 'retroductive warrant' in participating in the creation of economies of knowledge.[53] That is to say, in thinking about what will count as author-itative thought and practice, we must consciously recognize the practical outcomes of each distinct way of thinking. How does a particular way of construing reality have specific social, material, and political effects? Given the mystery that serves as backdrop for all knowledge, reasoning, and theologizing, and recognizing the manifestly multiple ways of struc-turing that experience and knowledge in the face of mystery, we are freed to be guided by pragmatic aims in our participation in a given system of knowledge. Does this way of thinking bring life and well-being? To whom? Does it restrict the well-being of others? In feminist theology, the retroductive warrant has often been framed as 'the well-being of women', and it has been employed to assess and critique religious economies of knowledge. The use of such a retroductive warrant seems to be in play implicitly when many women actively respond to their received tradi-tions and innovate changes in their lives. As one participant in the Philadelphia Area Multifaith Women's Group reflects:

> It impressed me that each of us, no matter what our professed faith, somehow added a personal interpretation to the precepts of her faith, e.g. the Jew who also had a Christmas tree, the Moslem who chose not to cover her hair, the Catholic who did not always go to Sunday mass. This exercise, which was often very moving, strengthened my belief that faith is very personal and that no one should generalize about a particular faith being violent, for example, based only on the media's presentation.[54]

There is a personal dimension attendant in our own production of knowledge. For women, this often comes out of the experience of a 'cognitive dissonance' between their received tradition and their experi-ence in response to which they make their own choices. But in their sharing this experience with others, in speech or practice, these alternatives are not simply relegated to the 'personal', but rather they become communal through the production of an alternative economy of knowledge.

Recognizing diverse economies of knowledge and our willed partici-pation in them, we are now in a position to recast Descartes' famous idiom in a new key. Descartes envisioned thought as something inde-pendent of the social and material world. He posited a fundamental 'I' who precedes all thinking, asserting: "I think, therefore I am." Thinking itself demonstrated one's own 'reality' that one could access foundation-ally by turning inward in introspection. But if knowledge is not some-thing sui generis to be grasped but rather something constructed by a community as a life world and framework within which one will live, the dictum must now be, "I think *toward* I am." The framework of knowledge within which I live shapes how I understand the world and how I will be within that world. Recognizing the diverse economies of knowledge I might inhabit, my willingness to be shaped by a particular economy of knowledge comes into relief. I must own my assent to the knowledge system that shapes me, embracing its revisability and recognizing that there are other stories to be told.

If religions are a form of knowledge system and if they shape who we are in the world, we might also recognize that these knowledge systems are of a particular kind—that is, that they not only speak of this world but also project into 'the next'. Here we enter the realm of 'ultimacy' with which religions deal and which is often at the heart of projects that theologize about religious difference. The central question might be framed thus: If we inhabit different religious 'worlds' with our different religious economies of knowledge, which one of these 'worlds' is ultimately true? Which one best represents things 'as they are'? Many theologians will respond to this with the idea that we will not know until 'the eschaton', beyond this world. And the area of Christian theology that is 'eschatology' functions as anticipation of what the Christian hopes will be the case. But in thinking about the production of life worlds that economies of knowledge create, we might see eschatology as shaping our 'next world'—that is, as imaginatively creating a new world into which we might live. Drawing on the insight and practice of the Philadelphia Area Multifaith Women, we might vision this future interreligiously.

The Story of Salvation: An Interreligious Eschatology

The poetry that is theology draws not only on the particularly religious economy of knowledge of 'scripture' and 'tradition'; it also reshapes that knowledge by incorporating 'experience'. So theology is not simply a reflection on the past; it articulates also our current understandings of ourselves. As we have seen in previous chapters, Christian theological anthropology as it emerges in this process draws on scripture, tradition, and experience to consider the human person in discussions of God as creator of the human person (where the Genesis account is key). It draws as well as on christology, where Jesus Christ offers a vision of the fully human person. Indeed, theological anthropology is woven through all areas of systematic theology. For example, when Christians talk about God or Jesus, they simultaneously disclose something of how they understand themselves. The same is true for 'eschatology', whereby we consider our final destiny in salvation. In the words of Peter Phan, in Christian tradition, "eschatology is anthropology conjugated in the future tense on the basis of christology."[55] The term 'eschatology' encompasses the theological poetics of those places where thinking is applied in the direction of the 'last things.' That is, who are we finally as human beings? What is our ultimate destiny? When transposed into the medium of doctrine, Christian teaching on eschatology is centered primarily on what happens after death.[56] Yet in every Christian eschatology, present and future stand in creative tension, as the tradition has insisted on a continuity between them. So while we do not, indeed, cannot know with certainty what lies beyond our life in this world ('no eye has seen' [1 Corinthians 2:9]), nevertheless Christians hope for a certain future based on present experience.[57] In writing the faith forward into the future, we see the project of eschatology as hope-filled expression of the whole of the faith and as a deep witness to Christian theological anthropology. Adopting the dictum "I think toward I am," eschatology creates the 'next world' into which we might live.

While 'eschatology' functions as Christian theological language embedded in its own economy of knowledge, I'd like to suggest that it serves also as a node for recognizing a fundamental aspect of who we are as *elastic* human beings. That is to say, we see that there are diverse ways within the religious traditions to shape our perception of the world and our lives within the world. The human person is malleable in and through diverse frameworks for our being and becoming. Eschatology is that aspect of the framework that envisions who we are 'ultimately', or 'in the end', and seeks to shape us toward that particular end. Those strands of the tradition that emphasize the way such an envisioned future breaks into the present are described as "realized eschatology." Here a foretaste of the future emerges within the living texture of the present; thus, the fulfillment that is the future is painted from the palette of the present and is imbued with elements drawn from lived experience in particular contexts.

We see this sort of "realized eschatology" in the life and teaching of Jesus as remembered in the gospel witnesses. Jesus' teaching was not just about some future 'kingdom' beyond the everydayness of our being human in the world. His teachings on the 'kingdom' and the economy of knowledge it produced encompassed the here and now of human living and human being. In the gospels, Jesus' own eschatological vision might be captured in his preaching of a coming kingdom where the poor and the poor in spirit are found and where mercy, peace, and righteousness reign (Matthew 5:3–12; Luke 6:20–23). This vision is mirrored in Jesus' practical ministry, where work among the outcast foretells a future in God's kingdom, where 'the last will be first' (Mark 10:28). In the words of Elisabeth Schüssler Fiorenza, "The *basileia* [kingdom] of God is experientially available in the healing activity of Jesus."[58] Following Jesus' vision, Christians ought to be living in the world in ways that allow mercy, peace, righteousness, and healing to reign.

While Jesus is remembered to have preached a vision of the kingdom wherein "whoever does the will of God is my brother and sister and mother" (Mark 3:31–35; see also Luke 8:19–20), the Christian tradition developed to a more exclusivist stance of identifying the kingdom with the Christian church alone. Two early arguments of this are found in Cyprian of Carthage (~~second~~ *third* century) and Augustine of Hippo (fifth century), both bishops of an emerging Christian church. Cyprian's lasting contribution to the eschatological imaginings of the Christian tradition is neatly summed up in the axiom 'outside the Church, no salvation'. There is no more succinct statement of a Christian economy of knowledge that proximally and ultimately distances Christians from their neighbors of other faiths. Augustine, too, had his part in shaping Christian imaginations, as his division of humanity into the 'earthly city' and the 'city of God' further cemented a Christian economy of knowledge that denigrated alternative faiths and elevated Christian faith and practice. While the fullness of the city of God remains eschatological and beyond this world, a present division anticipates an everlasting one, in Augustine's view. Those who reside in the city of God have eternal happiness to look forward to, and "they who do not belong to this city of God shall inherit eternal misery."[59] According to Brian Daley, it is Augustine who laid down the pattern for identifying "the Kingdom of God, at least in its first stage of existence, with the institutional Catholic Church."[60] For Augustine, and so many who follow him, the present Church and the future kingdom are linked in eschatological and ecclesial continuity.

While early thinkers of the Christian tradition fundamentally set the economy of knowledge on an exclusivist trajectory, both Cyprian and Augustine (and every other theologian we might name) was informed in his vision of the future by the context of his particular 'present'. Although Cyprian's dictum found its way into the tradition as a stance against people of non-Christian faiths, Cyprian actually was speaking to an intra-Christian debate over particular social and embodied practices. Cyprian and fellow bishops wrote to Pomponius to "say what we thought of those virgins who, after having once determined to continue in their condition, and firmly to maintain their continency, have afterwards been found to have remained in the same bed side by side with men . . . [yet] declare that they are chaste."[61] Cyprian determines the proximity of male and female bodies in sleep (and otherwise) to be contrary to Christian discipline and offers guidelines to be used for these dedicated women and the men with whom they have been sleeping. He provides ways for repentance and return to the community; however, if they continue in their practice, they will not be let back into the Church. Cyprian heightens the threat of this social exclusion, writing, "Nor let them think that the way of life or of salvation is still open to them if they have refused to obey the bishops and priests. . . . For they cannot live out of it, since the house of God is one, and there can be no salvation to any except in the Church."[62] The axiom arose not to discriminate against non-Christians but to discipline Christian bodies.

Augustine similarly did not envision his eschatological division in a vacuum but was promoting a Christian community under threat in a troubled social and political landscape. As he announces in the opening of *City of God*, his concern is for those who "impute to Christ the ills that have befallen their city"—that is, Rome, which had recently fallen to the Goths.[63] The political fall of Rome and the loss of power were being blamed on Christians by Romans who worshiped other gods. Rising to Christian defense, Augustine turned the tables to argue for an elevated Christian community, not the debased one his interlocutors would see. The eschatological visions of who we are as human beings ultimately take shape from out of our experience of being human proximally. They are informed by social, material, and political contexts in which we do our visioning. And our visioning creates the economy of knowledge within which we live. When Augustine in the fifth century and Thomas Aquinas in the thirteenth century portray humanity's "future glory" exclusively through the Catholic-Christian Church and its sacraments,[64] we can imagine how this would have shaped Christians' perception of religious others. Becoming embedded in the economy of Christian knowledge, it shaped actions toward religious others not only in their own time but down through the centuries, even to our own day.

As Christians increasingly encountered the embodied life practices of persons of other faiths, the twentieth century gives witness to eschatologies that aim to reconsider the reality of religious differences in resistance to the exclusivism that has been Christian heritage. While certainly there are still strands of thought that focus the future of eschatology narrowly through the doors of the Church, there are also strands of the tradition that reclaim a universal restoration in the end times, or 'apokatastasis'. Traceable back to the third-century thought of both Origen and Clement of Alexandria, this way of conceiving the end times rests on the affirmation that God, as creator of all, brings about a final consummation *for* all.[65] Just what this might entail, given the reality of religious difference, is worked out in a variety of ways in contemporary Christian theology.

In the middle of the twentieth century, theologians began to take note of what we today call 'globalization', where the world is recognizable as 'a single place'. Karl Rahner, for example, recognized the intertwining of histories and the multi-religious landscape that is the Christian's home, writing that

> where formerly the individual nations were independent of one another in their lines of historical development, nowadays these lines are tending to become fused into a single great world history. And the result of this is that the non-Christian religions and philosophies of life such as Islam, Hinduism and Buddhism, no longer constitute an area of foreign folklore which has no bearing upon the course of life modern man maps out for himself and raises no radical problems for him. Instead of this, these non-Christian religions have come to be regarded as the philosophies of life of men who have become neighbors to modern man, men in whom he cannot fail to recognize just as high a degree of intelligence as that with which he credits himself.[66]

Given this new social and political context, and recognizing that discriminations against people of other faiths were rooted in Christian theological thinking, Rahner insisted on a fundamental sameness among human beings in this life *and* the next. Desiring that well-being and restoration of wholeness be made possible for everyone, regardless of religious tradition, he forecasted that *all* humanity would be brought to salvation through Jesus Christ. In Rahner's words, "the relationship of God to man is basically the same for all men, because it rests on the Incarnation, death and resurrection of the one Word of God made flesh."[67] Therefore, "the achievement by any man of his proper and definitive salvation is dependent upon Jesus Christ."[68] In Rahner's eschatological imagining, our future fulfillment is rooted in a theological conviction of the universal efficacy of Christ, rendering persons of other faiths 'anonymous Christians' as they reach their final destiny of human being and becoming.

When theological thinking impacts the social, material, and political well-being of persons of another faith through Christian privileging, it is understandable that a theologian might want to repair that breach by expanding the boundaries of the Christian community to include all people, Christian or not. But in doing so, Rahner very clearly erases the distinctiveness of the persons about whom he is speaking while maintaining the privileged position of Christians. In response, other theologians tried to work out a vision of our future humanity where such elevation of Christian thought and practice was resisted in appreciation and embrace of all faith traditions. John Hick, for example, challenges Rahner's eschatology as a form of Christian imperialism and sees instead a similarity of practice across traditions such that none is guarantor of 'the Truth'. In fact, no religion holds the Truth in its perspective of the present or future because each is merely framing an encounter with an inaccessible Reality beyond the reach of any framework. In visioning our common human future, Hick pictures a universal source that lies "outside the scope of our human conceptual systems" and calls all people to a shared salvation.[69] He posits that "the great world religions are all inspired and made salvific by the same transcendent influence [which propels us beyond] the historical figure of Jesus to a universal source of all salvific transformation."[70] While shared salvation is the goal, no single tradition can claim to have insight into its form, as the Real remains beyond human reach. Further, the distinctiveness of the religions themselves are erased in the process of attempting to vision a future where all are equally capable of attaining the very same salvation, regardless of which religious tradition one is part of.

While Hick's eschatology attempts to resist the privileging of the Christian story, his visioning invites us to erase the particularity of *every* religious tradition. The practical outcome of Hick's philosophically grounded theology is that the distinctive strains of our sacred stories, the life-shaping practices they call forth, and the way they invite us to inhabit the world are all almost meaningless except insofar as they all foster a turn away from self-centeredness and produce moral fruits. Still other theologians in the late twentieth century, having had increasingly greater interaction with persons of other faiths, resist the erasure of particularity that Hick's pluralism seems to encourage. Responding to both Rahner's erasure of all but Christian particularity and Hick's erasure of all particularity, Mark Heim visioned our human future rooted in the specificity, complexity, and beauty of each religious tradition, embedded as it is in distinctive stories, beliefs, communities, and practices. Consider instead, he suggested, that our religious traditions really are comprehensive frameworks of thought and practice that really do shape us to see and experience the world in particular ways. The stories put forth in our differing eschatologies, intertwined as they are with the person of the Buddha or the poetry of the Qur'an, provide the "material for a thorough pattern of life."[71] As eschatological visions themselves provide worlds into which persons are shaped, the distinctiveness of these embodied practices conceivably brings people to very different religious ends, or, in Heim's terms, we arrive at diverse 'salvations'.[72]

Inviting as it is to take seriously the particularity of our religious frameworks, stories, and practices, the conceptualization of these practices leading, ultimately, to diverse ends in salvations doesn't seem to match the deep intertwining of persons of religious difference evidenced in the women we met in chapter 5. Continuity between embodied religious practices here and now and those 'beyond' *may* result in eschatological divisions that reflect our present particularity (as Heim's eschatology forecasts); *or* could it be that the embodied practice of interreligious friendship may provide the palette for envisioning a different future restoration?

The women of the Philadelphia Multifaith Group, who have been meeting regularly for more than ten years, suggest an alternative. Their home traditions range from the variety of Christian denominations (Episcopal, Catholic, Methodist, and more) to Judaism, Islam, and Baha'i. While their commitment to interfaith work began as a way of getting to know neighbors of other faiths and picked up steam in response to the divisions experienced after 9/11, their primary aim when they gather is fellowship. They meet every month, sharing their faith journeys, their stories, and, by now, their lives. They are in a dynamic conversation and relationship; they are the best of friends. And they give witness to the possibility of interreligious restoration in the future.

One member explains that "I think one of the reasons it works when we are together is because we are in deep trusting conversation-relationship, that there is a sense of the sacred presence."[73] In the words of a Muslim member, it is a presence of spirit "inside" each person that forms the "common bond" they experience when they are together.[74] One of the

Christian women describes being present with the group each month as "important to the fundamental of my personal spiritual core, my spiritual being."[75] Yet another, a Jewish participant stated: "[The group] is my spiritual home in huge, huge ways. So, I find that my spiritual home is where, is with, is in interactions with those who are awed by spirit and awed by divine and whatever form that takes. Which is why this group is so important to me. And the seriousness with which we all hold spirit is what draws me and what nourishes me."[76] In binding themselves to one another, they have created a space in which they recognize the ineffable among them. Another participant commented: "That sense that we can evoke, you know, when we are together, in that place, just something luminous—whatever word we put on it, and if we put a word on it in that moment we would probably lose it, right?"[77] In this meeting of women across religious lines, the binding of their lives together has created a sacred space that illumines for them who they are as human beings in their relation to one another and to Spirit, or the presence of the divine, which transcends them. This binding power and fullness of relationality is an interreligious community that stands in contrast to a world that divides them. The interreligious community anticipates a restoration of creation. "The world demonstrates to us the consequences of living in a world where we are not connected to one another; we see that and ask what is more important to us—being connected? Or, being in the world as it is?"[78] Together, the members of the community are bringing forth a better world.

In reaching out across religious boundaries and embracing their neighbors of other faiths, aren't these women—Christian, Jewish, Muslim, Baha'i—experiencing a fullness of life as Luke's gospel remembers Jesus to have envisioned?

> Just then a lawyer stood up to test Jesus. "Teacher," he said, "what must I do to inherit eternal life?" Jesus said to him, "What is written in the law? What do you read there?" The lawyer answered, "*You shall love the* LORD *your God with all your heart, and with all your soul, and with all your strength, and with all your mind; and your neighbor as yourself.*" And Jesus said to him, "You have given the right answer; do this, and you will live."
>
> Luke 10:25–28

In this first-century witness to the life and ministry of Jesus of Nazareth, the teacher describes a path to life that is marvelously simple yet profound. He suggests that a life of abundance, the inheritance of eternal life (or 'salvation') is rooted, quite simply, in love. All dimensions of the human person—the emotional (heart), the rational (mind), the spiritual (soul), the physical (strength)—are bound up in a 'centered act' of relationship between the individual and the divine.[79] Loving God with this intensity and focus, the dynamic love between self and God overflows to envelop also the neighbor. This brings life. While the lawyer asks after 'eternal life', Jesus' answer reminds us of the inbreaking of a realized eschatology: Love God, and your neighbor as yourself. Do this, and you will live.

The women of Philadelphia have found in their time together a realized eschatology in which the healing of interreligious relations is found in love: She-who-is-neighbor is part and parcel of a life of fullness as she enables one to deepen one's relationship with God. This is the case even when, sometimes especially when, she is rooted in a different faith tradition. As they report an experience akin to sacramental restoration of wholeness, might their experience of interreligious dialogue foretaste the eschatological apokatastasis, when the Creator of all in particularity brings creation to its completion? Present and future stand in tension, but the present gives a foretaste of what may be to come. The women of Philadelphia are not awaiting the eschaton. They are part of the process. And they themselves do not name it as such, do not give it form and vision and projection into the future. Nevertheless, in the paradox of the mystic, they do speak forth in invitation that being together, sharing lives across difference, weaving ourselves in interreligious friendships might both be a site of sacred presence and a space for sharing stories—and for telling those stories that might shape us anew to bring forth a world as we live in it 'as if' it were the case.

The ability to craft a new vision and to inhabit it connects fundamentally to the theological anthropology emerging in this work. In chapter 2 we followed feminist theories of identity to argue that the self is not best conceptualized in individual isolation but that the self is an event constituted by relationality in interaction with others. Chapter 4 built on this, recognizing that human relationality creates constitutive contexts in which we experience our humanity in distinctive ways because of the community into which we are born and because of those with whom we are fundamentally in contact and therefore shaped. Rather than constituted by 'freedom' (as modern theological anthropologies would have it), we are most helpfully conceptualized as human beings who demonstrate creativity under constraint. Among the constraints that shape us are, certainly, our religious stories that provide the framework through which we understand ourselves and our world. This relationality and creativity under constraint have brought us to the investigation of this chapter in which we have pressed further into the knowledge systems (religious knowledge systems being within them) that constitute those frameworks of our creativity. The eschatology that closes this chapter invites us to see the women of Philadelphia engaging in the creative production of a new knowledge system of interreligious knowledge that might serve as a new framework of relationality for more humane human becoming.

In this theological anthropology, the basic structure of the human person, constituted by relationality, exhibiting creativity under constraint and participating in the knowledge systems that shape us, has been read also through the metaphor of motherhood. Just as developmental theory identifies the m/other as the first figure to relationally form the self, we are invited to see ourselves as human beings who are characterized by our m/othering—that is, by our relationality and responsibility to others. The invitation to such m/othering in this Christian theological anthropology raised up Christ and the women who followed Jesus to vision Christianity as a movement of m/others, where Christian creativity is played out within the narrative constraints of the one who cares for the least among us. The expansion of our investigation into interreligious encounters invites us to consider the diverse patterns of m/othering that might be available in the symbol systems of the religious traditions of the world. And dwelling at length on the women of the Philadelphia Multifaith Dialogue Group offers another extension of the motherhood metaphor.

The m/other serves a fundamental role in language acquisition as s/he forges the first relationship with the child, and so the m/other's inter-action is crucial in the most basic shaping in language and the categories embedded within it. In modern child development theory,

> there have been those (for example, Piaget 1955; 1971; Slobin 1977; Bates, Bretherton and Snyder 1988) who view language as one of the many cognitive capacities or skills the child has to acquire, like memory or attention. The linguistic system is build up [*sic*] by the child in interaction with his/her caretakers and this language development goes hand in hand with the development of general forms of knowledge.[80]

Language acquisition forms the groundwork for the knowledge systems that will be embedded within it. So fundamental is the role of the mother that language-acquisition theories attentive to child development employ the term 'mother talk' as a way of capturing the fundamental role of the primary caregiver in shaping the linguistic patterns of the child as well as his or her emotional states.[81] The role that the mother has traditionally played in laying the foundation for language acquisition impacts future understanding in a profound way. Contemporary theorists describe the way infants are shaped neurologically in their acquisition of language, suggesting that the very early 'neural commitment' to a certain pattern of linguistic formation forms the neural apparatus that will function throughout a lifetime (offering a theory of why the learning of a second language and language acquisition late in life have proven more difficult than the acquisition of a first language in childhood).[82] The amazing ability of the primary caregiver to shape the future of a child through language makes 'mother' a powerful metaphor for how we might shape anew our language, thoughts, and knowledge for the future.

The language I hear week after week in the mother tongue of a Christian liturgical setting that turns in on 'ourselves' as a Christian community profoundly shapes imaginings and becomings. What language do we need to learn, what stories do we need to tell, to shape our generation and generations to come into a new interreligious family? In their commitment to the well-being of each other and in their learning together a new language of interreligious dialogue, the women of Philadelphia might be mothering us all in the practice of a new linguistic system that does not shut the other out but forges a new linguistic community, a new economy of knowledge. They are mothers to us all, teaching us a new language for interreligious becoming.

Conclusion: Seeking Salvation

When we come together we sort of put a salve on each other's wounds.

—HOMARA, *interview by Mara Brecht*[1]

Among the Igbo of Nigeria, to be creative is to turn the power of evil, sin, and suffering into the power of love. When things are not going well in a community, in order to restore harmony and mutuality of existence, this African community requires artists to camp together, to work together to heal the society by their sacrifice. . . . The artist symbolically recreates the clan in its pristine state through artifacts and the result is salutary for the real clan. It becomes once again a wholesome people in a wholesome community.

—MERCY AMBA ODUYOYE, *"Creation, Exodus, and Redemption"*[2]

The Christian narrative is a story of seeking salvation, of enacting the means by which to right the wrongs we encounter in our lives and in the world. Like the artist of the Igbo people or the women in the Philadelphia dialogue group, the Christian theologian fashions a people anew, seeking wholeness where brokenness has reigned. For the Christian this emerges through a retelling of the story of Jesus so as to bring forth a patterning of human lives on the life and practice of Jesus of Nazareth toward wholeness and well-being. Rooting our weaving in the story of Jesus, theology as storytelling occurs in the space between mystery and memory.

Our human existence is characterized by mystery. There is simply too much that we do not know about our world, our cosmos, and our selves to ignore that the fundamental context of our existence is mystery. It is in the face of mystery that our lives unfold in dynamic exchange between divine mystery and the stories that frame our existence. As Catherine Keller suggests:

> For any divinity I can unfold is unfurling, unfinished, unfolding in our own unpredictable becomings, which fold or crumple back as her multiplicative body. Under the sheets, perhaps, of the old luminous darkness. Or of some new dark energy. . . .
>
> Amidst the bottomless waters of becoming—*genesis*—we need our edges, our shorelines. . . .
>
> . . . All the love in the universe cannot evaporate for us the uncertainty of what is coming.[3]

In light of the mystery that we are to ourselves and that our world is to us, we tell stories to orient ourselves to this mystery. These are our shorelines that structure our encounter with the face of the deep. They are stories of history, of science, of art, of literature, and of theology. But these stories do not drop from the sky; they emerge from our making sense of our experience of the mystery in and through memory. For the Christian theologian this includes the memory of Jesus of Nazareth and those who followed him, but it must be always framed along the lines of what Emilie Townes describes as a living, breathing, shifting, dynamic memory. "Memory . . . is life, always carried on by living societies, and therefore it remains in permanent evolution, open to the dialectic of remembering and forgetting, unconscious of successive deformations, vulnerable to all appropriations and manipulations, susceptible to long periods of latency and sudden revitalizations."[4] Between mystery and memory are the stories that save us. These are stories of our lives, which are sometimes the tragic stories of human existence, the trauma of our pain and human brokenness. They also might be stories of how that pain and brokenness could be refashioned and held in the story of Jesus and the Christian community. But stories of Jesus and the Christian community can also be stories that traumatize. The task before us is to find those ways of telling the story that bring life and to keep in awareness the ways our story might damage another.

With the backdrop of mystery, the story of theological anthropology has been woven through the experience of Jesus and the experience of women in these pages. The story it tells of who we are as human beings is one that presses modern thought in new directions; it is a story that pulls out new strands of the ancient story of Christianity while interweaving also the wisdom of other faiths. In this Christian theological perspective, then, we see that we are fundamentally called to be a movement of mothers, relationally bringing into being a new world through nurturing care for the least. As human beings, we recognize the great variety of ways that are available to us for being human in the world; as Christians, we agree to be shaped in our particular instantiation of human diversity by the pattern of Jesus. Engaging our creativity within certain constraints, we recognize also the patterns of other faiths and so align ourselves in trans-religious solidarities with our sisters and neighbors of other faiths. Together we create new knowledge of who we are as human persons, and together we create anew the world.

Mother-Love and the Fullness of Life

If theology is storytelling with the symbols of a tradition, then we need to seek ways to tell stories that are no longer dehumanizing, degrading, or death-dealing but to tell them in ways that are salve-ific, that they might be healing stories. In the words of the Philadelphia woman whose reflections on her interreligious-dialogue practice opened this conclusion, the stories we tell must put a salve on one another's wounds. But to be salve-ific, they must take seriously the world that we actually live in and they must attend to our brokenness. They cannot claim a deadly neutrality in the face of evil but must advocate for justice even while admitting to being implicated in injustice. To the question *What must I do to inherit eternal life?* Jesus is remembered to have replied (quoting Deuteronomy 6:5): Love the LORD your God with all your heart, mind, soul, and strength; and your neighbor as yourself (Luke 10:27). Marvelously simple, yet profound: Love God and neighbor. But, the interlocutor in this story, wanting to justify himself, pushes Jesus further: *To whom must my love extend? Who is my neighbor?* And Jesus tells him this story: "A man was going down from Jerusalem to Jericho and fell into the hands of robbers, who stripped him, beat him, and went away, leaving him half dead" (Luke 10:30). It has become the classic story of the Good Samaritan, and Christians have become complacent in their hearing of it, identifying themselves not with the pious leaders who walk past the man to leave him in his suffering but seeing themselves in the 'good' Samaritan. When the Christian hearer of this first-century tale too easily identifies with the 'good Samaritan', it sometimes comes at the expense of Judaism, as the pious leaders are seen as Jews and the good Samaritan something other. (Too often, I suspect, the Christian hearer scoffs at those who walk by precisely because they are Jews and sees the Samaritan as a proto-Christian.) But if we hear this story and too easily identify *ourselves* with the Samaritan, we are missing something that Jesus' hearers would have heard. That is, in answer to the question 'Who is my neighbor?', Jesus does not go to the leaders of the community, and he does not even go to the margins of his community. In answering the fundamental question of what pattern brings life, Jesus reaches *outside* of his own community and raises the 'other', the despised, as the model to follow toward salvation.

The Samaritan would have been seen as someone culturally and religiously other to Jesus' hearers. Yet while Samaritan and Jew were separated by cultural and religious differences and divisions, while they were considered 'foreign' to one another, the Samaritan nevertheless somehow saw his life wrapped up in the life of the broken other. It was the Samaritan, the outsider, who bound his life up with the man broken by the side of the road; it was the Samaritan who brought him life and, in doing so, bound himself up with the life of the 'other'. The Samaritan does not simply bind the man's wounds but binds his life to the one who was broken: He brought him to an inn, asked the innkeeper to look after him, and told the innkeeper, "I'll be back, and I'll repay you when I return" (Luke 10:35). This is not a random act of kindness but a commitment to the well-being of the other through the binding of his wounds and the binding of two lives together. When we name this unnamed character the 'Good Samaritan', we elevate him from out of the everydayness of life, as if his goodness were something exceptional. But in the telling of this story in common language, with familiar characters, and in the everyday setting of his hearers, Jesus is responding to the lawyer's query with an everydayness that must be enacted. This is not the exceptional moment of all goodness but the neighborly gesture of what must be done. In binding the wounds of the other, in making her whole, and, in so doing, binding oneself *to* the other in compassion and care, one finds 'life'. The mothering care of Christian witness must be an everyday practice that pervades the rhythm of our lives in the social and the political and extends beyond the bounds of biology, family, nation, and religion. At the same time, the mothering care of Christian witness must not only be extended *to* these many neighbors but must be seen *within* them as well.

How difficult has it been to extend this mother-love to bring about a better world? Given the transnational movements of people, ideas, world-views, and religions that constitute 'globalization', and given that material resources are unequally distributed around the globe, our constituting ourselves as a global family and practicing the pattern of mother-love for all has been more than challenging. Indeed, while neighbors of difference encounter us daily, the response to difference has not always been one of hospitality. As Linell Elizabeth Cady describes it, "A major response to the increased pluralism and globalization of life in the late twentieth century has been a reassertion of tightly bounded personal and communal identities, what some have called tribalization."[5]

Mothering in a tribalistic mode is the mothering of nationalism, biology, and family. It is a mothering that turns in on one's own—culturally and religiously—and against the 'other'.

But theorist of globalization Ulrich Beck also sees enacted in the world alternative postures of relating to difference. Conceptually, socially, and politically, another response to our globalized world of increasing difference is what Beck names as 'sameness universalism', which looks out on the world and paints it all with one brush. We can mother our others because they are basically the same; we will grant them the same rights so long as their way of being doesn't challenge too much our own. This sameness universalism, however, runs the risk of ignoring real differences when "the voice of others is granted a hearing only as the voice of sameness, as self-confirmation, self-reflection and monologue."[6] The mother-love of Jesus patterned in the Everyday Samaritan sees in the other genuine difference but crosses boundaries of care nonetheless.

Beck offers yet another option in framing a response to our globalized world, one in which persons simultaneously view themselves as part of a narrow, localized collective *and* as part of a wider, global world. While differences exist, including the distinctiveness of my own localized community, our pasts and our futures are bound up together. This Beck describes as a 'cosmopolitan outlook'. In Beck's words, a cosmopolitan outlook is one "in which people view themselves simultaneously as part of a threatened world and as part of their local situations and histories."[7] In cosmopolitan vision, one sees oneself not as in an enclave of distinctiveness, cut off from those who are different, but rather interwoven with the lives and futures of those whose culture, religion, and outlook are different. For Beck, this interweaving of lives with a view toward the future is particularly pressing in light of the risks we face as a global interreligious, intercultural, and international community. A cosmopolitan vision requires a concern for nothing less than the future of humanity. As a way of being Christian, 'cosmopolitan Christianity' would invite us to see ourselves as part of a local/narrow 'Christian' community but simultaneously woven into a wider world in solidarity with our sisters and brothers of the many faith traditions of the world.

The 'cosmopolitan Samaritan' points us in the direction of allowing our cultural and religious others to show us the way of a mother-love that binds our lives and our futures together.

What would it look like to practice this pattern in our everyday lives, in the spaces where religious identities place persons on the margins of society, denying even social and political rights?

Structured as our world is, by divisions that run deep and religious patterns that keep us from our neighbors of other faiths, how do we pursue the life-giving path that Jesus sets forth?

Jesus is remembered to have directed those who followed him thus: "Whenever you enter a town and its people welcome you, eat what is set before you; cure the sick who are there, and say to them, 'The kingdom of God has come near to you'" (Luke 10:9). The direction is to eat and to heal and, in so doing, to recognize that the kingdom of God draws near. The kingdom practice of fellowship that feeds and heals is not only the directive that Jesus gives to his disciples in this gospel; it is also the means by which those who seek him find Jesus after his death. Glossing the story of the disciples, on the road to Emmaus, transformed by the trauma of Jesus' trial, torture, and death, Serene Jones writes, "Jesus is finally made known to them in an event of life-giving communion. In this moment, we find the reality of grace breaking into their midst not through an act of exclusionary compassion, but rather through a bodily gesture that is deeply embracing. This is no escapist meal of commodified junk food, a gathering of surface pleasures; it is a meal that nourishes and strengthens, and most important, it is a meal that opens their eyes."[8] In Christian tradition, Jesus is found in the healing meal, and those who follow him seek out his healing in meals of celebration and remembrance.

It is a fundamental understanding of historical-biblical scholarship and the re-creation of the earliest Christian communities that the meal of remembrance was one that characterized how the faithful followed Jesus in his lifetime and after his death. But in the story of Luke's gospel and Jesus' sending of the seventy disciples out to spread his healing mission, the meal is not one of faithful Christian remembrance, it is the meal set out by the stranger. "Whenever you enter a town and its people welcome you, eat what is set before you; cure the sick who are there, and say to them, 'The kingdom of God has come near to you'" (Luke 10:9). The first act of the Christian, in this case, is to be welcomed *by* the stranger. To go out into the world, and to be welcomed by those who do not know you, by those who do not know Jesus and his message. And to eat what is set before you, accepting the hospitality of the stranger. The second act of the Christian is to cure the sick, heal wounds, and bind the brokenness. And in this, the Christian announces the coming near of the kingdom of God. The very act of Christian mission, in this particular story, is interreligious: the acceptance and demonstration of hospitality. Is this not the witness we saw when the Maryknoll women were welcomed into the homes of the Chinese women, eating what was set before them? Did their mission and their friendship not rely first on the hospitality of the non-Christian toward them? Similarly, the women of Philadelphia constitute their healing practice in the process of sharing sustenance through tea and scones and salad and bread. Eat what is set before you, by the non-Christian who welcomes you, and only then might you cure the sickness of our world and announce the coming near of the kingdom.

Mothered by Our Others

The Jesus of Luke's gospel sends those who would follow him out into the world for the encounter with the neighbor. They were sent out into the world, to be welcomed into the others' home, and to be taken care of by them before the possibility of healing could occur. The gesture of Christian mission was a reciprocal mothering. The task of the Christian today is to continue to recognize that we are mothered by our others.

In 2004, at the Parliament of the World's Religions, representatives from all faith traditions of the globe gathered in Barcelona, Spain, for workshops, panel presentations, and the sharing of practices. Over nine thousand participants lived and talked together for a week. And amid the great range of memories of new ideas and different ways of seeing the world, one particular stands out as a shining possibility of being religious in the world today. The Sikh community, it was announced, would be happy to have you come to dinner tonight, tomorrow night, and every night this week. Not 'you', as in 'me', but 'you' as in all nine thousand of you, welcomed into our makeshift 'home' to celebrate a meal prepared in the style of our tradition. You are welcomed to sit with us, to eat together, and perhaps to learn something about our faith.

And so, at the end of each day, we made the quarter-mile trek along the waterfront in the descending sun, and we talked with new friends and strangers as we went to be welcomed in the 'home' of the Sikhs.

We took off our shoes at the door (as we were entering holy ground) and were given a cloth to cover our heads. We sat on the floor, and they served us. Young Sikh men brought us drinks, and old Sikh women made sure we had utensils, and young women came out from the kitchen, and old Sikh men served us heaping plates of vegetarian fare. They smiled.

If we wanted, we could stay and walk around the larger 'house' area and read something of the words of the founder Guru Nanak—and we could listen in, if we'd like, on a talk being given about the outlook of the tradition. But many of us did not, and there was no suggestion that we ought to. They welcomed us in and took care of us, they fed us, they made sure we were well. Mothering anyone who would come, every day that week.

I later learned that the langar offered at the gudwara is the Sikh practice of hospitality and that this is the way all Sikhs worship regularly—taking care of one another and anyone who comes to eat and sharing the faith vision of the founder of the community. And for the past seven years I have carried around this witness. Whenever I think of the Parliament of the World's Religions, or the Sikh community, I think to myself, "I love the Sikhs. They are so welcoming. And they feed me."[9]

If we are looking for salve-ific stories to shape our mothering in the world and mothering across religious lines, for me, this certainly is among them, as my neighbors of the Sikh faith welcomed me into their home so that I might eat what was set before me and together we might heal the brokenness that has reigned, experiencing in everyday life the world as it was meant to be—the kingdom of God.

Serendipitous Creativity and the Future of the Planet

In Christian perspective, the healing power that courses through Jesus' life and ministry and vivifies the lives and practices of those who follow him is none other than God's own power at work in the world. Participating in the healing practice, we touch the very power of God; we do God's work in the world. But recognizing what we have in the preceding chapters—how the story of the Christian tradition is but one story among many—we might at every turn reaffirm that the mysterious power that courses through creation and made possible Jesus' life-affirming ways is also coursing through the whole world in many and diverse religious and nonreligious ways. Theologian Gordon Kaufman highlights this ancient affirmation by identifying precisely God's presence in the world through the language of 'serendipitous creativity.'[10] By definition, the serendipitous is something that surprises us, something that we don't anticipate but that nevertheless is agreeable and beneficial to us. God's creative power, then, arrives in the world in unexpected times and places, and in this theological anthropology, through unanticipated actors. God's creative power courses through us in the miraculous and in the mundane; it is God's creative power we witness in the horizon of possibility before us.

The healing story of Jesus gives texture to this power in striking and challenging ways, ways at odds with the pull and pressures of the world as we know it.

> An argument arose among them as to which one of them was the greatest. But Jesus, aware of their inner thoughts, took a little child and put it by his side, and said to them, "Whoever welcomes this child in my name welcomes me, and whoever welcomes me welcomes the one who sent me; for the least among all of you is the greatest."
>
> Luke 9:46

In Jesus' day as in our own, human nature evidences a self-referential drive for security, for *my* self, for my well-being, for my position, recognition, and honor. And yet it was the mothers among them who were the first to welcome the child. So there she is and there they are, finding themselves in the following of Jesus not by leaving family and relationships behind (for hermetically sealed institutional spaces) but by caring for the least right there in the following of Jesus. They were doing what the Chinese women were doing when they met with Maryknoll Sisters with their babies on their backs; they were doing what the suffragettes did when they marched with children in their carriages; they were doing what I do when Thea looks out from her baby bjorn on the steps of city hall or in the pews of church. They were multitasking for their future, for, as they were seeking the life-giving stories Jesus might, tell they could *not* also be wrapped up in life itself; they could not forgo their commitment to the least. Christian feminist theology has its roots in these unnamed, unmentioned, literally invisible biblical women who follow Jesus with their everyday lives; theology in interreligious perspective sees their companions in the women of Buddhism, Islam, Judaism, Hinduism, and countless indigenous practices. In following them we are following him, seeking salvation.

Generations of Christians would agree that the principal aim of telling the Christian story is for the purposes of 'salvation'. 'To save souls' is what both Ignatius of Loyola in the sixteenth century and Sister Rosalia Kettl of Maryknoll in the twentieth century propose as their mission and goal. But, as may come as no surprise, the concern for salvation has been primarily focused quantitatively on 'who' is saved.[11] Following the liberationist trajectory of Gustavo Gutierrez, we might ask instead after the *quality* of salvation—that is, what is its texture and how does it come about?[12] As witnessed in chapter 6, this qualitative question of salvation inheres in a realized eschatology that sees salvation in terms of 'wholeness'.[13] In the living dialogue among the women of Philadelphia, this wholeness was found in friendships that crossed boundaries of religious difference, but even more so it was found in the relationships that heal, those that put a 'salve' on our wounds of injured interreligious relationships. That salvation might be found in the salve of interreligious healing is, indeed, a new way of conceptualizing Christian salvation, and this interreligious pattern of seeking salvation has not been the practice heretofore. We have been seeking salvation as an inherently Christian reality, and so we have been seeking our own wholeness with dimness of vision.

Seeking Salvation with Dim Vision

In Christian theology, the aim of salvation is part and parcel of our human story precisely because we find ourselves broken. If who we are as human beings is fundamentally constituted by relationality, sin consists in ignorance of that relationality, in promoting primarily the self. This ignorance of relationality can be willful ignorance (that self-referentially constructs the self as priority over and against others) or it can be structural ignorance (a socially constructed prioritizing of some members of the human family over others because of race, economic standing, gender, sexual orientation, religion, and more). The story of Jesus of Nazareth invites a retelling that challenges both of these forms of self-referential prioritization. "The least among all of you is the greatest." In this Lucan passage, like so many others in which Jesus' pattern of being in the world is remembered, Jesus invites the fundamental reversal of our social striving. The one who has nothing, the least among us in status, and power, and acceptability, is the greatest. Really? What would this mean if we took it seriously? How would this shape our interfaith relations, our social interactions, our political visions?

Jesus' challenging reversal here has tremendously fruitful reverbera-
tions as it is placed in conversation with Buddhist ways of being in the
world. A fundamental wisdom of the Buddhist tradition lies precisely in
that our human nature has seen that we strive for our own self-referential
well-being and ignore the fundamentally relational nature of our existence.
In Buddhist perspective, nothing *is* apart from anything else; we are
all—humanity and the rest of the created world—bound together in our
interbeing. More radical even than Jesus' invitation to reversal, the
wisdom of the Buddha insists that there is no *self* on which to rest one's
self-referential concerns. Instead, there is only the illusion of self created
and perpetuated by these self-referential longings. We grasp at the self
as if it were static, as if it were something we could build up, as if we
could finally achieve security by means of power, economic standing,
status, education. But, Buddhist wisdom insists, we are instead always in
the process of dying, always in the permanent flux of impermanence,
always in the process of rebirth. We are not ourselves, then, but are
constantly being called into existence by what is not ourselves, in the
hybridity of enmeshed relationships between 'self' and the surrounding,
infinite world.

The suggestion of 'no-self' in Buddhist perspective meets resistance in
the Christian feminist theological tradition precisely because of the way
Western Christianities of self-abnegation have fallen too often squarely
on the shoulders of women.[14] And yet, as women seek their own well-
being, too often they are blind to the relationality that constitutes them
as well. If we have come this far in our exploration of this theological
anthropology, we might see three fundamental characterizations of who
we are as human beings in the preceding chapters. We are fundamentally
relational, we exercise creativity under constraint as embedded and
embodied beings within this relational nexus, and we have the capacity to
think ourselves forward or to know ourselves into interbeing in community with others. If we're willing to grant these ways of being in the world
as characteristic of our own humanity, 'sin' points to our refusal to act as
if this were the case. Sin is the grasping at selfness to the exclusion of
otherness, the fundamental denial that who we are is constituted in our
relationality. Michele Saracino writes that, in the midst of a hybrid existence that is constituted by relationality with otherness, "sin occurs when
we fail to attend to the needs, feelings, memories, and stories of another.
We sin not necessarily because we are mean-spirited or even because we
are consumed by hubris, but perhaps, as Bernard Longeran explains,

because the sin is a result of scotoma, of being blinded to our hybrid existence."[15] Steeped in our own sinful self-absorption, we've been seeking salvation with dim vision.

If we are constituted by our relationality, coming into being across time in dynamic interrelationship, then a classic understanding of 'sin' as 'de-creation' seems apt as a description of the reality to which the category points. Explaining this understanding of sin, Richard Clifford and Khaled Anatolios write that, as 'de-creation', sin "brings about a state of death and corruption 'phthora'—both physical and moral—which is really a decline from being toward nothingness."[16] In our futile attempts to save ourselves, we bring about our own de-creation from out of the reality of relationality and into the dark illusion of independent selfhood. Returning to Elizabeth Cady Stanton as champion of women's rights in the first wave of feminism: Cady Stanton visions a theophany of equal rights and the flourishing of women. But that she was enabled by racist ideologies drawn from social-scientific spheres demonstrates scotoma. Returning to the women of Maryknoll in their work with native Chinese women, we see that their desire to save souls often lead them to devalue the native religious practices of their new friends. This, too, is scotoma. How do we also, today, and in our place and time, come to terms with our own dimness of vision? How do we recreate ourselves by enacting new relationships of mother-care for our others so that together we might birth forth a better world?

Birthing Forth a Better World

"It's like we have a job and we can't just say, 'Where is God?' because we have to do our part of the job, which is to love other people. And not just *some* other people."[17] The power of serendipitous creativity courses through creation and abides within the world. In the vision of Karl Rahner, "through the Word of God, we learn that deep in our own nature God dwells, and that this is no mere metaphor for the reflection of the infinite things within us, but the expression of a literal truth."[18] The embodied and embedded experience of growing into our roles as mothers invites us to bring forth divinity anew.

It is both miracle and metaphor that something new lives inside me. Miracle that I hold within my self that new life, yet unformed, yet unborn, and yet filled with the potential of all that it is to be human. Anonymous cells inside of me are organizing to become a fully human being.

Miracle that such transformation and such potential are possible. The actual growth of a new life within my own living being is miracle indeed in its concrete actuality, but it is metaphor as well. It is metaphor for the potential and newness that lies within each one of us. Within every human being dwells the possibility for what is new. We birth into existence all sorts of realities—in ideas, in love, in experiences, in words, in physical constructions, in artistic creations, and in intellectual reflections. Possibilities await their birth in each of us. When we realize this potential for our own human becoming and for the introduction of newness into the world, we glimpse the infinite mystery that is the source of all existence, all newness, and that Christians name God. And we might recognize that in bringing forth what is new, we co-create our world and participate in the very being of God. We bring forth what is new, as Eve and Mary proclaimed, "with the help of the Lord."

If we can begin from our very embodied human experience to recognize that newness and new life spring forth from our very selves, how might we think our way forward to envision interfaith relationships anew? A new existence is something we have in our power to create . . .

I never could have imagined what the realization of this miracle might feel like. It made me feel queasy. It was as if the future was far more uncertain and filled with the unknown and with possibilities than I had ever fully realized. There is, in fact, nothing I can do to control the growth of those anonymous cells within me. I cannot slow or speed up their development. As I continue on in my work and play, in my everydayness, something that I cannot change continues anonymously within me. It is my life and my self we are talking about here, but I am not in control. It is disorienting. But the loss of control is the condition of possibility for a new and deeper insight into the nature of existence. Our lives are not altogether our own. We are dependent on God for our coming into being, and this contingency remains, as we are not fully in control of the forces of our existence. The realization of my own lack of control gave way, for me, to trust.

When resistance surfaces to interfaith being and learning and appreciation, Christians must be reminded that whatever we mean by the word 'God', we mean that power that brought forth humanity, all of humanity, all of creation. We *all* are dependent on this mystery of creativity. If there is possibility for new life of interfaith relations in the world, we must trust that it is God's will that is being done.

The author of the Gospel according to Luke placed these words on the lips of Mary at the discovery of her own pregnancy: "Here I am, the servant of the Lord; let it be with me according to your word" (Luke 1: 38). Like Mary, I am not entirely in charge of what happens to me next. As the story of Luke unfolds, there is much evidence that the newness of life within is a miracle. Mary's *magnificat* gives praise to God in a way that echoes the song of her spiritual ancestor Hannah (1 Sam. 2:1–10), and we can see Mary in a long line of voices that give praise to God both for the gift they receive in this newness of life and for the life that this new life will be. The pregnancy of her cousin Elizabeth is no less a miracle and is recognized as such when the angel Gabriel announces it to her husband Zechariah. So remarkable are the events surrounding Elizabeth's naming of her child 'John' that their neighbors ponder aloud, "What then will this child become?" The anticipation of a future life that stretches out from the womb is a miracle of awe and wonder at the possibilities and potential of each new life, of each life.

As interfaith relations bring about new ways of being in the world, we recognize that the future *is* unforeseen and will take on a life of its own. We will be transformed. Our faiths will be as well. The newness of the mother-subject-position and the expanding possibilities for care embedded within it have applications for our relationship with people of other faiths. It is precisely the power of the unknown—of God—that brings forth the new child in the womb. And it is the power of the unknown that calls forth new fruitfulness across religious lines. This fruitfulness requires nurturing, commitment, attention, and more. The theology that emerges from the second child helps us to remember that the power that brings newness into the world carries with it the expanding possibilities of love. In Rahner's vision, there is no limit to the limitless source of love that is God. In the mother's experience, the love for the second *and* the third is not the splitting of love from the first but rather an exponential increase in new ways of loving.

The theological anthropology with which I began was modeled on Karl Rahner's orientation toward being human as characterized by knowledge, will, and love. To this, the investigation of women's interreligious encounters has expanded the contemplation of love to witness radical relationality (which also has a shadow side). The history of the women's movement and women's studies in religion has shown quite clearly the reality that our freedom, our creativity is always under constraint. And explicit interreligious dialogues proffer the foundational challenge that all knowledge is shaped by particular contexts and forms an 'economy of knowledge' with material, political, social, and economic outcomes. These fundamental features of our human condition meet the theological tradition of Christian thought and suggest new ways of thinking about ourselves as fully human, fundamentally Christian, and formatively interreligious.

If we believe that our very selves are shaped in distinctive economies of knowledge, we see that the story of our interreligious context and the stories of our Christian heritage shape us as hybrid selves with a multiplicity of stories. We are invited to see the story of our Christian heritage as one that must be mobilized toward a creativity that resists the damaging constraints of inequality and injustice, of racial and religious discrimination and the dehumanizations that have been grounded in sexual difference. We might mobilize these stories anew toward an interreligious solidarity that feeds not only our selves but all our others.

We feed them milk
We feed them love
We feed them hatred.
Whatever we feed them they will eat
And they *will become.*

NOTES

Introduction. We Feed Them Milk: Theological Anthropology as a Labor of Love

1. Elana Rozenman, Ibtisam Mahameed, Zriek Randa Sabag, and Siham Halabi, "Peace-Building for Women—Taught by Middle East Interfaith Women," panel presentation at the Parliament of the World's Religions, Barcelona, Spain, 10 July 2004.
2. Karl Rahner, *Foundations of Christian Faith: An Introduction to the Idea of Christianity*, trans. William V. Dych (New York: Crossroad, 1994), 112.
3. Ava (pseud.), interview by Mara Brecht, transcription from digital recording, West Philadelphia, Pa., 20 July 2007.
4. Rahner, *Foundations*, 29.
5. Ibid., 30.
6. Ibid., 35. In recognition of the androcentric language embedded in Rahner's writing, Antoinette Gutzler writes, "Personal conversations with one of Rahner's translators, William V. Dych, indicated that, if Rahner were writing at this time in history, he would use inclusive language in his writings." Antoinette Gutzler, "Reimagining the Body of Christ: Women's Body as Gospel Proclamation" in *The Body and Sexuality: Theological-Pastoral Perspectives of Women in Asia*, ed. Agnes M. Brazal and Andrea Lizares Si (Manila: Ateneo de Manila University Press, 2007), 185.
7. Elizabeth Cady Stanton, "Comments on Genesis II," in *The Woman's Bible*, part 1, *Comments on Genesis, Exodus, Leviticus, Numbers, and Deuteronomy*, by Elizabeth Cady Stanton et al. (1895; reprint, North Stratford, N.J.: Ayer, 2002), 21.
8. Elisabeth Schüssler Fiorenza, *In Memory of Her: A Feminist Reconstruction of Early Christian Origins* (New York: Crossroad, 1992), xv.
9. In chapter 4, I will interrogate the very categories of 'women' and 'men' with the aid of Judith Butler and Virginia Ramey Mollenkot.
10. Rita Nakashima Brock, "Feminist Theories," in *Dictionary of Feminist Theologies*, ed. Letty M. Russell and J. Shannon Clarkson (Louisville: Westminster John Knox Press, 1996), 117.
11. Elisabeth Schüssler Fiorenza, "Feminist Hermeneutics," in *Dictionary of Feminist Theologies*, 99. Schüssler Fiorenza coined the term 'patri-kyriarchal' to expand the understanding of patriarchy not only to connote 'rule of the father' but also the interlocking systems of rule (kyriarchy) by which some (men) have control of other persons (men and women).

12. Enid M. I. Sefcovic and Diane Theresa Bifano, "Creating a Rhetorical Home for Feminists in the 'Masters House' of the Academy: Toward a Gendered Taxonomy of Form and Content," *Women and Language* 27, no. 1 (Spring 2004): 55.

13. J. E. Walsh, *Mission Manual of the Vicariate of Kongmoon (South China)* (Hong Kong: Nazareth Press, 1937), 207.

14. The encounter with religious 'others' has been an important part of much of Christian history, although this deep intertwining with the histories and futures of persons of other faiths has often willfully been ignored or erased. A retelling of Christian history to include the encounters with the faith traditions of ancient Greece and Rome, those of India as Christianity spread across trade routes, the recognition (as, for example, by Clement of Alexandria) of Buddhist wisdom seekers, the particular syncretism of Christian monks in Xi'an China in the seventh century, Thomas Aquinas's drawing on Jewish and Muslim interlocutors, mission encounters that changed Christian theology, and much more—all give witness to the long-standing way Christian theology, and perhaps even theological anthropology, has been intertwined with the thought and lives of persons of other faiths.

15. Julia Hannigan, *Living History*, interview by Sister Joanna Chan, 8 July 1980, Maryknoll Archives, Ossining, New York.

16. Hannigan, *Living History*, 4–5.

17. Sarai (pseud.), interview by Mara Brecht, transcription from digital recording, Philadelphia, 1 August 2008.

18. Joanne (pseud.), interview by Mara Brecht, transcription from digital recording, Villanova, Pa., 15 December 2007.

19. Homara (pseud.), interview by Mara Brecht, transcription from digital recording, Philadelphia, 16 December 2007.

20. Elizabeth (pseud.), interview by Mara Brecht, transcription from digital recording, Philadelphia, 1 August 2008.

21. Elizabeth Cady Stanton, diary entry, 25 November 1880, in *Elizabeth Cady Stanton as Revealed in Her Letters, Diary, and Reminiscences*, ed. Theodore Stanton and Harriot Stanton Blatch (New York: Harper and Brothers, 1922; New York: Arno and New York Times, 1969), 2:180. Cady Stanton is quoting Reform Rabbi Felix Adler of the Ethical Culture movement. See Kathi Kern, *Mrs. Stanton's Bible* (Ithica, NY: Cornell University Press, 2001), 66.

22. Ava, interview.

23. Elizabeth Cady Stanton, diary entry, 28 October 1881, in *Elizabeth Cady Stanton as Revealed*, 2:187. While Susan B. Anthony was among Stanton's closest collaborators, Stanton's diary shows her engaged in many different conversations, not reserved to intra-Christian debate. As quoted above, she was influenced by the thought of Reform rabbi Felix Adler; on November 25, 1882, she met with Annie Besant, leader in the nineteenth-century theosophical movement, which drew on both Buddhist and Hindu thought. In her diary she also writes of meeting Jewish women at her New York residence, April 19, 1895: "A delegation of orthodox Jewish women called on me yesterday to talk over with me the Bible matter" (Stanton and Stanton Blatch, 312). A global traveler, she met also with Siberian and Russian émigrés. Concerned not only with the plight of women in the suffrage movement, Cady Stanton writes powerfully of her concern for political oppressions around the globe and the "working masses" in her own country.

24. Julia Ward Howe, "What is Religion?" in *The World's Parliament of Religions: An Illustrated and Popular Story of the World's First Parliament of Religions, Held in Chicago in Connection with the Columbian Exposition of 1893*, ed. John Henry Barrows (Chicago: Parliament Publishing Company, 1893), 2:1251.
25. Elizabeth Cady Stanton, "The Worship of God in Man," in Barrows, 2:1236.

1. Encounter in the Mission Fields: Engendering Dialogue with Women of China

1. Caption on original 1929 poster at Maryknoll Archives, hallway of main building, Maryknoll, Ossining, N.Y.
2. Caption on original 1928 poster at Maryknoll Archives, hallway of main building, Maryknoll, Ossining, N.Y.
3. Penny Lernoux, *Hearts on Fire: The Story of the Maryknoll Sisters* (Maryknoll, N.Y.: Orbis, 1993), 26 and 30.
4. *The Field Afar*, January 1935, 14.
5. *The Field Afar*, January 1935, publication page.
6. Father Thomas V. Kiernan, "Chinese Sisters," *The Field Afar*, July–August 1936, 209.
7. Sister Mary Rose Liefels, "Roots in China," 8; in *Creative Works*, 9-5, Maryknoll Archives, Ossining, N.Y.
8. Sister Rosalia Kettl, interview by Sister Virginia Unsworth, 8 June 1981, Maryknoll China History Project, Maryknoll Archives, Ossining, N.Y.
9. For an overview of the many ways this axiom has shaped the Catholic understanding of people of other faiths, see my *Monopoly on Salvation? A Feminist Approach to Religious Pluralism* (New York: Continuum, 2005), chapter 2; and Francis Sullivan, *Salvation Outside the Church? Tracing the History of the Catholic Response* (New York: Paulist Press, 1992).
10. Lernoux, 30.
11. Quoted in Lernoux, 30.
12. Kwok Pui-lan describes the traditional social segregation of the sexes in Chinese society and the emergence of a women's movement in China in the early twentieth century. See her *Chinese Women and Christianity, 1860–1927* (Atlanta: Scholars Press, 1992). Ono Kazuko chronicles women's revolutionary activity in her *Chinese Women in a Century of Revolution, 1850–1950*, ed. Joshua A. Fogel (Stanford, Calif.: Stanford University Press, 1989). See also Sharon K. Hom, "China: First the Problem of Rights and Law," in *Women's Rights: A Global View*, ed. Lynn Walter (Westport, Conn.: Greenwood Press, 2001), 29–42.
13. Sister Mary Imelda Sheridan, unpublished talk on "direct apostolate" (Kaying, China), Creative Works Box 14, Maryknoll Archives, Ossining, N.Y. In 1934 the July–August edition of *The Field Afar* included an announcement that the following women were going to Kaying: Sister M. Imelda Sheridan, of Scranton, Pa.; Sister M. Madeleine Sophie Karlon, of Brooklyn, N.Y.; Sister Anna Mary Moss, of Los Angeles, Calif.; Sister Rita Marie Regan, of Fairhaven, Mass.; and Sister M. Jean Theophane Steinbauer, of Owatonna, Minn.
14. Bishop Francis X. Ford, "Retreat to MK Srs in Philippines," 1935, 85, Ford Collection, file 2/15, Maryknoll Archives, Ossining, N.Y.
15. Anna Mary Moss, letter from Mission of the Holy Child, Tung Shek, 29 December 1934, Maryknoll Archives, Ossining, N.Y.

16. In February 1936 (58), *The Field Afar* included this announcement: "In groups of two these young American women will journey from village to village, living in the peoples' houses and, as concerns material comforts, 'going native' for Christ and souls."

17. Jean-Paul Wiest, *Maryknoll in China: A History, 1918–1955* (Armonk, N.Y. / London: M. E. Sharpe, 1988), 101.

18. Lernoux, 62.

19. House-to-house visitation was also an approach undertaken by Protestant women in mission as early as 1867, but it was a new approach for Catholic women in mission who had primarily worked in institutional or social-service settings in mission contexts. See Kwok Pui-lan, *Chinese Women and Christianity, 1860–1927* (Atlanta: Scholars Press, 1992), 74. What was unusual about the Maryknoll approach as compared with the approach of women in mission outlined in Kwok's text is the degree to which the Maryknoll Sisters engaged in interfaith encounter in the rhythm of the Chinese women's daily lives.

20. Sister Paulita Hoffmann, interview by Sister Joanna Chan, 12 March 1981, Maryknoll China History Project, Maryknoll Archives, Ossining, N.Y.

21. Hoffmann, Maryknoll China History Project, 73.

22. Sister M. Marcelline, "Catechetical Work," 1938, in file "Kaying Vicariate, Letters, Mission Trips, Mission Work" (used for promotion), box 37, file 11, Maryknoll Archives, Ossining, N.Y.

23. Anna Mary Moss, letter, 20 January 1935, Maryknoll Archives, Ossining, N.Y.

24. Kaying Vicariate, letters, mission trips, Mission Work, box 37, file 11.

25. *The Field Afar*, November 1941, includes an advertisement for the publication of Kettl's *One Inch of Splendor*.

26. Sister Mary Rosalia of Maryknoll (Mary Martha Kettl), *One Inch of Splendor* (New York: Field Afar Press, 1941), 46.

27. Anna Mary Moss, letter, 28 April 1935, Maryknoll Archives, Ossining, N.Y.

28. Kettl, Maryknoll China History Project, 40.

29. Ibid., 11.

30. Lernoux, 65.

31. Liefels, "Roots in China," 89.

32. Kettl, *One Inch of Splendor*, 50–51.

33. Kwok, *Chinese Women and Christianity*, 79.

34. Lernoux, 66–67.

35. Sister Mary Paulita Hoffmann, quoted in Jean-Paul Wiest, *Maryknoll in China*, 112.

36. Anna Mary Moss, "Maryknoll Sisters, Catholic Mission, Tungshek, Pingyun Via Swatow, China," 28 March 1940, Maryknoll Archives, Ossining, N.Y.

37. Hoffmann, Maryknoll China History Project, 23.

38. Ibid.

39. Kettl, *One Inch of Splendor*, 52.

40. Anna Mary Moss, "Explanatory Information and Translation of Hakka Catechism, Book 25—Women's Question," Creative Works box 35A, file 1, Maryknoll Archives, Ossining, N.Y.

41. See, e.g. Sue Bradshaw, O.S.F., "Catholic Sisters in China: An Effort to Raise the Status of Women," in *Women in China: Current Directions in Historical Scholarship*, ed. Richard W. Guisso and Stanley Johannesen (Youngstown, N.Y.: Philo Press, 1981), 201–13.

42. Hoffmann, Maryknoll China History Project, 60.

43. Kwok, *Chinese Women and Christianity*, 13.

44. Anna Mary Moss, "Hakka Catechism Explanatory Information."

45. Hoffmann, Maryknoll China History Project, 61.

46. Kwok Pui-lan reports: "The discussion on concubinage demonstrated similar ambivalent attitudes, since some condemned the practice as contrary to Jesus' teaching on marriage, while others pleaded tolerance, citing cases of polygamy in the Old Testament as their support. Some of the missionaries probably realized that only those from families of some means could afford having several wives, and they did not wish to offend them. Others were careful to point out that concubinage was not merely a question of sexual appetite but was rooted in the culturally informed need to have a male heir in order to continue the patrilineal line." *Chinese Women and Christianity*, 104–5.

47. Julia Hannigan, interview with Sister Joanna Chan, 8 July 1980, Maryknoll China History Project, Maryknoll Archives, Ossining, N.Y.

48. Leifels, "Roots in China," 8–9.

49. Hoffmann, Maryknoll China History Project, 24.

50. Sister Julia Hannigan, interview by Sister Joanna Chan (transcript of third of three tapes), 4 August 1981, Monrovia, Calif., Maryknoll China History Project, Maryknoll Archives, Ossining, N.Y., 11.

51. Hannigan, Maryknoll China History Project, 12.

52. Kettl, *One Inch of Splendor*, 27–28.

53. Sister M. Imelda (Mary Imelda Sheridan), "Rosary Convent, Kaying, March 20, 1938," in Kaying Diaries, box 37, Maryknoll Archives, Ossining, N.Y.

54. Kettl, *One Inch of Splendor*, 82–83.

55. Sister Miriam Louise, "Outline of a Mission Story (8-25-39)," in Kaying Diaries, box 37, file 11. Maryknoll Archives, Ossining, N.Y.

56. Hannigan, Maryknoll China History Project, 4–5.

57. Ibid.

58. Kettl, Maryknoll China History Project, 40–41.

59. Paulita Hoffmann, interview by author, Maryknoll residence, Ossining, N.Y., 7 December 2007.

60. See my "As Long as We Wonder: Possibilities in the Impossibility of Interreligious Dialogue," *Theological Studies* 68, no. 3 (September 2007): 532–54.

61. Kwame Anthony Appiah, *Cosmopolitanism: Ethics in a World of Strangers* (New York: Norton, 2006), 77.

62. Hannigan, Maryknoll China History Project, 4–5.

63. Hoffmann, Maryknoll China History Project, 6–7.

64. Kettl, Maryknoll China History Project, 40–41.

65. Hoffmann, Maryknoll China History Project, 33.

66. Chung Hyun Kyung, "Seeing the Religious Roots of Pluralism," *Journal of Ecumenical Studies* 34, no. 3 (Summer 1997): 401.

67. Pamela Dickey Young, *Christ in a Post-Christian World: How Can We Believe in Jesus Christ When Those around Us Believe Differently—or Not at All?* (Minneapolis: Fortress, 1995), 30.

68. Chung, 401.

2. *We Meet in Multiplicity: Insights for Theological Anthropology*

1. Karl Rahner, *Foundations of Christian Faith: An Introduction to the Idea of Christianity* (New York: Crossroad, 1994), 112. In describing the theological reflection on 'original sin', Rahner writes: "We should rather acquire enough theology so that, starting with experience and with a description of the existentiell human situation, we can talk about the *matter itself* without using this word. Only at the end would we have to indicate that this very actual reality of one's own life and one's own situation is called 'original sin' in ecclesiastical language."

2. Rosemary Radford Ruether, "Feminism and Jewish–Christian Dialogue," in *The Myth of Christian Uniqueness: Toward a Pluralistic Theology of Religions*, ed. John Hick and Paul F. Knitter (Maryknoll, N.Y.: Orbis, 1987), 147.

3. Mercy Amba Oduyoye, "Women and Ritual in Africa," in *Beads and Strands: Reflections of an African Woman on Christianity in Africa* (Maryknoll, N.Y.: Orbis, 2004), 88.

4. Linell Elizabeth Cady, "Identity, Feminist Theory and Theology," in *Horizons in Feminist Theology: Identity, Tradition and Norms*, ed. Rebecca S. Chopp and Sheila Greeve Davaney (Minneapolis: Fortress, 1997), 19.

5. Cady, 19, quoting Iris Marion Young, *Justice and the Politics of Difference* (Princeton, N.J.: Princeton University Press, 1990), 45.

6. Rahner, *Foundations*, 26.

7. Rahner, "The Dignity and Freedom of Man," in *Theological Investigations*, trans. Karl H.-Kruger (London: Darton, Longman and Todd, 1963), 2:237.

8. Rahner, "The Dignity and Freedom of Man," 239.

9. Rahner, *Foundations*, 31.

10. For an attempt to relate Rahner's theological anthropology to postmodern constructions of the self, see Kevin Hogan, "Entering Into Otherness: The Postmodern Critique of the Subject and Karl Rahner's Theological Anthropology," *Horizons* 25, no. 2 (1998): 181–202. For an assessment of Rahner's theological anthropology from a feminist perspective, see Nancy Dallavalle, "Feminist Theologies," in *The Cambridge Companion to Karl Rahner*, ed. Declan Marmion and Mary E. Hines (Cambridge: Cambridge University Press, 2005), 264–78.

11. Luce Irigaray, "The 'Mechanics' of Fluids," in *This Sex Which Is Not One*, trans. Catherine Porther with Carolyn Burke (Ithica, N.Y.: Cornell University Press, 1985), 106–18.

12. Luce Irigaray, "When Our Lips Speak Together," in *This Sex Which Is Not One*, 214–15.

13. Luce Irigaray, "This Sex Which is Not One" in *This Sex Which Is Not One*, 31.

14. Catherine Keller, *From a Broken Web: Separation, Sexism and Self* (Boston: Beacon Press, 1986), 184–86.

15. Miriam Louise, "Outline of a Mission Story (8-25-39)."

16. Kettl, *One Inch of Splendor*, 80.

17. Sister Henrietta Marie (Margaret) Cunningham, letter to her family, 9 May 1943, Maryknoll Archives, Ossining, N.Y.

18. Anna Mary Moss, letter from Holy Child Mission, Tung Shek, 27 January 1935, Maryknoll Archives, Ossining, N.Y.

19. For a theological anthropology that also enters the multiplicity and hybridity of our human condition through the lens of motherhood, see Michele Saracino, "Moving Beyond the 'One True Story,'" in *Frontiers in Catholic Feminist Theology: Shoulder to*

Shoulder, ed. Susan Abraham and Elena Procario-Foley (Minneapolis: Fortress Press, 2009), 9–24.

20. The argument is not that 'motherhood' captures the experience of all women but that 'motherhood' is an experience of some women in their concrete embodiment and that this concrete experience can provide a living site from which to consider the human condition *and* that it can provide a metaphor to express the human condition of relationality.

21. Sylvia Barack Fishman captures well the tension many American Jewish women feel in the conflicting desires of self-development encouraged by feminist thinking and traditional family–community connections valued in Jewish thought and culture. See her, "Choosing Jewish Parenthood," in *A Breath of Life: Feminism in the American Jewish Community* (New York: Free Press, 1993), 45–64.

22. Keller, *From a Broken Web*, 186.

23. Sylvia Barack Fishman, *A Breath of Life: Feminism in the American Jewish Community* (New York: Free Press, 1993), 47.

24. Leila Ahmed, *A Border Passage: From Cairo to America—A Woman's Journey* (New York: Penguin, 2000), 104.

25. Muriel Orevillo-Montenegro, *The Jesus of Asian Women* (Maryknoll: N.Y.: Orbis, 2006), 75.

26. Orevillo-Montenegro, *Jesus of Asian Women*, 158.

27. Mercy Amba Oduyoye, "Poverty and Motherhood," in *Beads and Strands*, 60.

28. See, for example, Elizabeth Cady Stanton, *Eighty Years and More: Reminiscences, 1815–1897* (Boston: Northeastern University Press, 1993).

29. Delores S. Williams, "Black Women's Surrogacy Experience and the Christian Notion of Redemption," in *After Patriarchy: Feminist Transformations of the World's Religions*, ed. Paula M. Cooey, William R. Eakin, and Jay B. McDaniel (Maryknoll, N.Y.: Orbis, 1991), 1–14.

30. Ahmed, *A Border Passage*, 120.

31. Radha Kumar, *The History of Doing: An Illustrated Account of Movements for Women's Rights and Feminism in India, 1800–1990* (London and New York: Verso, 1993).

32. See, for example, Jessika Auerbach, *And Nanny Makes Three: Mothers and Nannies Tell the Truth about Work, Love, Money, and Each Other* (New York: St. Martin's Press, 2007); Lucy Kaylin, *The Perfect Stranger: The Truth about Mothers and Nannies* (New York: Bloomsbury, 2007).

33. Michele Saracino, "Moving Beyond the 'One True Story,'" 18. Saracino points the reader to the four avenues by which bias occurs, in a footnote referencing *Collected Works of Bernard Lonergan*, eds. Frederick E. Crowe and Robert Doran, vol. 3, *Insight: A Study of Human Understanding* (Toronto: University of Toronto Press, 1997), 214–20.

34. Orevillo-Montenegro, *Jesus of Asian Women*, 75.

35. See, for example, Maria José F. Rosado Nunes, "Women's Voices in Latin-American Theology," in *Feminist Theology in Different Contexts*, ed. Elisabeth Schüssler Fiorenza and M. Shawn Copeland (London: SCM Press / Maryknoll, N.Y.: Orbis, 1999), 3–17; or Maria Pilar Aquino, "Feminist Intercultural Theology: Toward a Shared Future of Justice," in *Feminist Intercultural Theology: Latina Explorations for a Just World*, ed. Maria Pilar Aquino and Maria José Rosado-Nunes (Maryknoll, N.Y.: Orbis, 2007), 9–29.

36. Valerie Saiving Goldstein, "The Human Condition: A Feminine View," *Journal of Religion* 40, no. 2 (April 1960): 100–12.

37. See Jeannine Hill Fletcher "Rahner and Religious Diversity" in *The Cambridge Companion to Karl Rahner*, 236–37.

38. Karl Rahner, "Anonymous Christians," in *Theological Investigations*, trans. Karl-H. Kruger and Boniface Kruger (New York: Seabury Press, 1974), 6:393.

39. This is an extension of Elizabeth Johnson's understanding of God as power of creation in *She Who Is: The Mystery of God in Feminist Discourse* (New York: Crossroad, 1992), 179.

40. Johnson, *She Who Is*, 138.

41. Ahmed, *A Border Passage*, 121–22.

42. See Helene Stork, "Mothering Rituals in Tamilnadu: Some Magico-Religious Beliefs," in *Roles and Rituals for Hindu Women*, ed. Julia Leslie (Delhi: Motilal Banarsidass, 1992), 89–106.

43. Judith Plaskow, *Standing Again at Sinai: Judaism from a Feminist Perspective* (San Francisco: HarperSanFrancisco, 1991), 49.

44. Gustavo Gutierrez, *A Theology of Liberation: History, Politics and Salvation*, rev. ed., trans. and ed. Sister Caridad Inda and John Eagleson (Maryknoll, N.Y.: Orbis, 1988), 110.

45. Pedro Arrupe, "Rooted and Grounded in Love" (1981). Cited in Kevin F. Burke, "Love Will Decide Everything: Pedro Arrupe Recovered the Ignatian 'Mysticism of Open Eyes,'" *America*, 12 November 2007, http://www.americamagazine.org/content/article.cfm?article_id=10386 (accessed 13 February 2012).

46. Tina Beattie, *God's Mother, Eve's Advocate: A Marian Narrative of Women's Salvation* (New York: Continuum, 2002), 39.

47. Michele Saracino, "Moving Beyond the 'One True Story,'" 16.

48. Nancy Julia Chodorow, "Gender, Relation, and Difference in Psychoanalytic Perspective," in *Feminist Social Thought*, ed. Diana Tietjens Meyers (New York and London: Routledge, 1997), 11.

49. Judith Butler, *Gender Trouble: Feminism and the Subversion of Identity*, 2nd ed. (New York: Routledge, 1990), 78. Butler is revisiting Sigmund Freud's theory of separation and mourning.

50. Recent writings on the role of Mary in Christian theology have tended to see her importance as 'mother of God' substantively in the form of her accepting impregnation, providing the site for gestation and birthing a savior into the world. See, for example, *Mary, Mother of God Mary, Mother of God*, edited by Carl E. Braaten and Robert W. Jenson (Grand Rapids, Mich.; Cambridge, U.K.: Eerdmans, 2004). Feminist reclaimings of an alternative portrait include the historical-critical work of Elizabeth Johnson, *Truly Our Sister* (New York, Continuum: 2006), and, earlier,the work of Rosemary Radford Ruether, *Sexism and God-Talk* (Boston, Beacon: 1983).

51. Judith Butler, "Beside Oneself: On the Limits of Sexual Autonomy," in *Undoing Gender* (New York: Routledge, 2004), 18.

52. Catherine Keller, "Seeking and Sucking: On Relation and Essence in Feminist Theology," in *Horizons in Feminist Theology*, 58.

53. Morwenna Griffiths, *Feminisms and the Self: The Web of Identity* (New York: Routledge, 1995), 92.

54. Cady, "Identity, Feminist Theory and Theology," 24.

55. R.J. Coggins, *Samaritans and Jews: The Origins of Samaritanism Reconsidered* (Oxford: Basil Blackwell, 1975).

56. Elisabeth Schüssler Fiorenza, *In Memory of Her: A Feminist Theological Reconstruction of Christian Origins* (New York: Crossroad, 1992), 135. For a Christology built on Schüssler Fiorenza's work, see Terrence W. Tilley, *The Disciples' Jesus: Christology of Reconciling Practice* (Maryknoll, N.Y.: Orbis, 2008).

57. Clement of Alexandria, *The Instructor*, book 1, chap. 6, On Paul's 1 Corinthians 3:2, in *AnteNicene Fathers: Translations of the Writings of the Fathers down to AD 325*, ed. Alexander Roberts and James Donaldson (Grand Rapids, Mich.: Eerdmans, 1951), 2:218.

58. Caroline Walker Bynum, *Jesus as Mother: Studies in the Spirituality of the High Middle Ages* (Berkeley: University of California Press, 1982), 114.

59. Bernard of Clairvaux, letter 322, in *Patrologiae cursus completus: Series Latina*, ed. J.-P. Migne (Paris, 1841–64): 182, col. 527, quoted in Bynum, 117.

60. Aelred, *De institutione*, chap. 26, *Opera omnia* 1:658, trans. M. P. Mcpherson, in *The Works of Aelred of Rievaulx*, vol. 1, *Treatises and Pastoral Prayer*, Cistercian Fathers Series 2 (Spencer, Mass., 1971), 73, quoted in Bynum 123.

61. Margaret R. Miles, *A Complex Delight: The Secularization of the Breast, 1350–1750* (Berkeley: University of California Press, 2008), 33–53.

62. According to Gail Paterson Corrington, the earliest Christian use of the image of lactating mother echoes pre-Christian religious traditions in the figure of Isis lactans. Corrington's argument is that the image itself becomes dissociated from real women's experiences as it gets transferred to a God-imaged male. See Gail Paterson Corrington, "The Milk of Salvation: Redemption by the Mother in Late Antiquity and Early Christianity," *Harvard Theological Review* 82, no. 4 (October 1989): 393–420.

63. I am especially aware of the diversity of reasons why women do and do not breastfeed, ranging from cultural practices to the economic need *not* to breastfeed, and then there are women for whom breastfeeding is a source of death for the child—for example, in the lives of women with AIDS. My aim is not to identify breastfeeding as the desired practice but rather, recognizing that it is a practice for some women, to draw from this experience theological insights.

64. Butler, *Undoing Gender*, 24.

65. Philip L. Quinn and Kevin Meeker, *The Philosophical Challenge of Religious Diversity* (New York and Oxford: Oxford University Press, 2000), 2. This phrasing represents how interreligious dialogue is often conceived as a conflictual comparison rather than as the source of theological insight and cooperative solidarities.

66. Elana Rozenman, Ibtisam Mahameed, Zriek Randa Sabag, and Siham Halabi, "Peace-Building for Women—Taught by Middle East Interfaith Women," panel presentation at the Parliament of the World's Religions, Barcelona, Spain, 10 July 2004.

67. Aelred of Rievaulx, *De Jesu puero duodenni*, sec. 3, par. 30, *Opera omnia* 1:276, quoted in Bynum, 124.

68. Homi Bhabha, keynote address to "Sex and Religion in Migration" (conference), Yale University, New Haven, Conn., 15 September 2005.

69. Lina Gupta, "Affirmation of Self: A Hindu Woman's Journey," in *Women's Voices in World Religions*, ed. Hille Haker et al. (London: SCM Press, 2006), 90.

70. Chung Ok Lee, *Vision for a New Civilization: Spiritual and Ethical Values in the New Millennium* (New York / Iksan, Republic of Korea: Won Buddhism Publishing, 2000), 185.

71. Aimee Carrillo Rowe, *Power Lines: On the Subject of Feminist Alliances* (Durham, N.C.: Duke University Press, 2008), 27–28.

3. *Encounter in Global Feminist Movements: Enacting Trans-religious Alliances*

1. See "Suffrage Parade, New York City, May 6, 1912," Library of Congress, Prints and Photograph Division, http://memory.loc.gov/cgi-bin/query/D?suffrg:1:./temp/~ammem_ Pp6I.

2. Aimee Carrillo Rowe, *Power Lines: On the Subject of Feminist Alliances* (Durham, N.C.: Duke University Press, 2008), 5.

3. Lieve Troch, "Swimming like Salmons against the Stream: Some Reflections on Interreligious Communication from a Feminist Perspective," in *ESWTR Yearbook: Feminist Perspectives in Pastoral* Theology (Leuven: Peeters, 1998), 107; quoted in Helene Egnell, *Other Voices: A Study of Christian Feminist Approaches to Religious Plurality East and West* (Uppsala, Sweden: Studia Missionalia Svecana C, 2007), 26.

4. Elizabeth Cady Stanton, *Eighty Years and More: Reminiscences, 1815–1897* (Boston: Northeastern University Press, 1993), 122.

5. Elizabeth Cady Stanton, diary entry, 22 February 1881 *Elizabeth Cady Stanton as Revealed in Her Letters, Diary and Reminiscences*, ed. Theodore Stanton and Harriot Stanton Blatch (New York: Harper and Brothers, 1922; New York: Arno and New York Times, 1969), 2:183.

6. Kathi Kern, *Mrs. Stanton's Bible* (Ithaca, N.Y. and London: Cornell University Press, 2000), 3.

7. Cady Stanton, *Elizabeth Cady Stanton as Revealed*, 190–91.

8. Elizabeth Cady Stanton, "The Worship of God in Man," in *The World's Parliament of Religions: An Illustrated and Popular Story of the World's First Parliament of Religions, Held in Chicago in Connection with The Columbian Exposition of 1893*, ed. John Henry Barrows (Chicago: Parliament, 1893), 2:1236.

9. Richard Hughes Seager, *The Dawn of Religious Pluralism: Voices from the World's Parliament of Religions, 1893* (LaSalle, Ill.: Open Court, 1993), 8.

10. *Daily Inter Ocean* (Chicago), 12 September 1893; quoted in Seager, *Dawn of Religious Pluralism*, 31.

11. For a discussion of androcentric historiography and the erasure of women, see Elisabeth Schüssler Fiorenza, *In Memory of Her: A Feminist Theological Reconstruction of Early Christian Origins* (New York: Crossroad, 1992), 26–29.

12. Augusta J. Chapin, closing address to the Parliament, in Barrows, 1:179.

13. Some of the identifying names are ambiguous with only initials included. See also Richard Hughes Seager, *The World's Parliament of Religions* (Bloomington: Indiana University Press, 1995), 91. At approximately 13 percent, women were clearly the minority at this event; yet a scan of women's participation in high profile dialogues and writings on the subject even today indicates that women remain a minority often at a similar percentage to their 1893 foremothers.

14. The World's Congress Auxiliary was the organizing body for the many congresses that were to be held in conjunction with the Columbian Exposition. Many of the women who spoke at the World's Parliament of Religions also participated in the Congress of Representative Women and other congresses in which they introduced a woman's perspective.

15. Ellen Martin Henrotin, closing address to the Parliament, in Barrows, 1:178.

16. The speech of noted suffragist Julia Ward Howe is included in Seager's volume, but the addresses of Elizabeth Cady Stanton and Mary Baker Eddy are not included. Since Mary Baker Eddy, founder of the Christian Science Movement, had her address read by Judge S. J. Hanna, editor of the *Christian Science Journal,* this may have influenced Seager's decision not to include it in his volume. Similarly, Elizabeth Cady Stanton did not present her speech in person; as she writes in her memoir, "[Susan B. Anthony] came to stir me up to write papers for every Congress at the Exposition, which I did, and she read them in the different congresses" (Elizabeth Cady Stanton, *Eighty Years and More,* 449). Yet, given the renown of Elizabeth Cady Stanton both in her own day and in history, it is not clear why Seager did not include in his 1993 volume on the event her address from the 1893 Parliament. According to Seager's words in the introduction to the volume *The Dawn of Religious Pluralism: Voices from the World's Parliament of Religions, 1893,* selection of texts was based, in part, on whether they "were delivered by noteworthy people." Seager writes, "We have worked to make this collection inclusive of the many different voices that gained expression in the first, global, ecumenical assembly in world history" (Seager, *Dawn of Religious Pluralism,* 2).

17. Julia Ward Howe, "What is Religion?" in Barrows, 2:1250–51.

18. Ward Howe, "What is Religion?" 1251.

19. Cady Stanton, "The Worship of God in Man," 1234–45.

20. Schüssler Fiorenza, *In Memory of Her,* 7. Evidence of Cady Stanton's effectiveness can be seen in the invitations she received to preach. See her diary entry, 21 May 1883, in *Elizabeth Cady Stanton as Revealed,* 2:207.

21. Cady Stanton, "The Worship of God in Man," 2:1236.

22. Annis F. F. Eastman, "The Influence of Religion on Women," in Barrows, 1: 752–58.

23. Henrietta Szold, "What Has Judaism Done for Woman?" in Barrows, 2:1052–56.

24. Fannie Barrier Williams, "What Can Religion Further Do to Advance the Condition of the American Negro?" in Barrows, 2:1114–15.

25. Josephine Lazarus, "The Outlook of Judaism," in Barrows, 1:705–15.

26. Rev. Augusta J. Chapin, opening address to the 1893 World's Parliament of Religions, in Barrows, 1:82.

27. Jeanne Sorabji, "Women of India," in Barrows, 2:1037.

28. Sorabji, "Women of India," 1038.

29. May Wright Sewall, introduction to *The World's Congress of Representative Women: A Historical Resume for Popular Circulation of the World's Congress of Representative Women, Convened in Chicago on May 15, and Adjourned on May 22, 1893,* ed. May Wright Sewall (Chicago: Rand McNally, 1894), 242; Harvard University, Open Collections Program, www.ocp.hul.harvard.edu, http://pds.lib.harvard.edu/pds/view/2574452 (accessed August 2, 2010).

30. Sarah B. Cooper, "Discussion [of Woman as Religious Teacher] Continued," in Sewall, 282.

31. See for example, Lady Linchee Suriya (Representative of Siam), "Women in Agriculture in Siam," in Sewall, 765–69; and Hanna K. Korany, "The Position of Women in Syria," in Sewall, 773–77.

32. Manisha Desai, "India: Women's Movements from Nationalism to Sustainable Development," in *Women's Rights: A Global View,* ed. Lynn Walter (Westport, Conn.: Greenwood Press, 2001), 99–112 at page 102.

33. Radha Kumar, *The History of Doing: An Illustrated Account of Movements for Women's Rights and Feminism in India, 1800–1990*. (London and New York: Verso, 1993), 56.

34. Geraldine Heng, "'A Great Way to Fly': Nationalism, the State and the Varieties of Third-World Feminism," in *Feminist Genealogies, Colonial Legacies, Democratic Futures*, ed. M. Jacqui Alexander and Chandra Talpade Mohanty (New York and London: Routledge, 1997), 30–45 at 31. Heng is citing Benedict Anderson, *Imagined Communities: Reflections on the Origin and Spread of Nationalism* (London: Verso, 1983).

35. Sharon K. Hom, "China: First the Problem of Rights and Law," in *Women's Rights: A Global View*, ed. Lynn Walter (Westport, Conn: Greenwood Press, 2001), 29–42 at page 32. See also Kwok Pui-lan, *Chinese Women and Christianity, 1860–1927* (Atlanta: Scholars Press, 1992) and Ono Kazuko, *Chinese Women in a Century of Revolution, 1850–1950*, ed. Joshua A. Fogel (Stanford, Calif.: Stanford University Press, 1989).

36. Leila Ahmed, "Early Feminist Movements in Turkey and Egypt," in *Muslim Women*, ed. Freda Hussain (London and Sydney: Croom Helm, 1984), 119.

37. In the late twentieth and early twenty-first centuries, the veil has a very wide range of meanings in particular contexts, including its symbolic use among politically progressive Muslim women. See Leila Ahmed, *A Quiet Revolution: The Veil's Resurgence from the Middle East to America* (New Haven, Conn.: Yale University Press, 2011).

38. Leila Ahmed, *Women and Gender in Islam: Historical Roots of a Modern Debate* (New Haven, Conn.: Yale University Press, 1992), 172.

39. Ahmed, *Women and Gender in Islam*, 184.

40. See Kumar, *The History of Doing*.

41. Cady Stanton, *Elizabeth Cady Stanton As Revealed*, 2:212–23.

42. Adler's influence can be seen running through her diary from 25 November 1880 to 25 February 1896, *Elizabeth Cady Stanton as Revealed*.

43. Cady Stanton, *Elizabeth Cady Stanton Revealed*, 2:264.

44. Chava Frankfort-Nachmias, "Israel: The Myth of Gender Equality," in *Women's Rights: A Global View*, 127–39 at 129.

45. Ahmed, *Women and Gender in Islam*, 178.

46. Peggy Antrobus, *The Global Women's Movement: Origins, Issues, and Strategies* (London and New York: Zed Books, 2004) 33.

47. Kathleen C. Berkeley, *The Women's Liberation Movement in America* (Westport, Conn.: Greenwood Press, 1999), 19–39. See also, Janann Sherman, ed., *Interviews with Betty Friedan* (Jackson: University Press of Mississippi, 2002).

48. Ann Braude, "A Religious Feminist—Who Can Find Her? Historiographical Challenges from the National Organization for Women," *Journal of Religion* 84, no. 4 (2004): 559.

49. National Organization for Women, www.now.org/history/founders.html.

50. Although Farians's biography initially tells us of the 'secular' women's movement as a hidden location for trans-religious alliances and collaborations, her life's work moves also to more explicitly interreligious work; the website Earthsave describes recent work with a Cincinnati Jain community in advocating for animal rights and vegetarian practice. See cincinnati.earthsave.org/elizabeth.htm (accessed March 15, 2010).

51. Pauli Murray, *Pauli Murray: Selected Sermons and Writings*, ed. Anthony Pinn (Maryknoll, N.Y.: Orbis, 2006), 15.

52. Deborah E. Lipstadt, "Feminism and American Judaism: Looking Back at the Turn of the Century," in *Women and American Judaism: Historical Perspectives*, ed. Pamela S. Nadell

and Jonathan D. Sarna (Hanover, N.H.: University Press of New England / Brandeis University Press, 2001), 292–93.

53. Ann Braude, ed., *Transforming the Faiths of Our Fathers: Women Who Changed American Religion* (New York: Palgrave Macmillan, 2004).

54. The Equal Rights Amendment (written in 1921) states simply: "Men and women shall have equal rights throughout the United States and every place subject to its jurisdiction. Congress shall have power to enforce this article by appropriate legislation." www.now .org/issues/economic/eratext.html (accessed September 19, 2011).

55. Ruth Rosen, *The World Split Open: How the Modern Women's Movement Changed America* (New York: Penguin, 2001), 264–65.

56. Carol Christ, "Roundtable Discussion: Feminist Theology and Religious Diversity," *Journal of Feminist Studies in Religion* 16, no. 2 (2000): 79. Christ's comment is retrospective on a time when this interreligious synergy seemed to be flourishing, and her reflections were in response to an assessment by Rita Gross that feminist theology had lost its interreligious flavor.

57. James C. Livingston and Francis Schüssler Fiorenza with Sarah Coakley and James H. Evans "Feminist Theology," *Modern Christian Thought*, vol. 2, *The Twentieth Century* (Upper Saddle River, N.J.: Prentice Hall, 2000), 420.

58. Livingston and Schüssler Fiorenza, "Feminist Theology," 421.

59. Judith Plaskow, *Standing Again at Sinai: Judaism from a Feminist Perspective* (San Francisco: HarperSanFrancisco, 1991).

60. Riffat Hassan, "Muslim Women and Post-Patriarchal Islam," in *After Patriarchy: Feminist Transformations of the World Religions*, ed. Paula M. Cooey, William R. Eakin, and Jay B. McDaniel (Maryknoll, N.Y.: Orbis, 1991), 39–64.

61. Carol Christ and Judith Plaskow, eds., *Weaving the Visions: New Patterns in Feminist Spirituality* (San Francisco: HarperSanFrancisco, 1989), 8.

62. Robin Morgan, introduction to *Sisterhood is Global: The International Women's Movement Anthology* (Garden City, N.Y.: Anchor / Doubleday, 1984), 3.

63. Countries represented include Afghanistan, Algeria, Argentina, Australia, Austria, Brazil, Britain, Canada, The Caribbean, Chile, China, Colombia, Cuba, Denmark, Ecuador, Egypt, El Salvador, Finland, France, Germany (East & West), Ghana, Greece, Guatemala, Hungary, India, Indonesia, Iran, Ireland(s), Israel, Italy, Japan, Kenya, Korea (South), Kuwait, Lebanon, Libya, Mexico, Morocco, Nepal, The Netherlands, New Zealand, Nicaragua, Nigeria, Norway, The Pacific Islands, Pakistan, Palestine, Peru, Poland, Portugal, Rumania, Saudi Arabia, Senegal, South Africa, Spain, Senegal, South Africa, Spain, Sri Lanka, Sudan, Sweden, Thailand, U.S.S.R., United Nations, United States, Venezuela, Vietnam, Yugoslavia, Zambia, Zimbabwe.

64. Morgan, *Sisterhood*, 3.

65. Morgan, *Sisterhood*, 28.

66. This is the same strategy evidenced by Cady Stanton's speech at the 1893 Parliament where patriarchal religion / Christianity is challenged, while creatively employing a vision of Jesus to do so.

67. Morgan, *Sisterhood*, 29.

68. Although she began her public career alongside noted abolitionists like Frederick Douglass to raise the concern for African American enfranchisement and women's rights, after the passage of the Fifteenth Amendment in 1870, which gave voting rights to

black men, Cady Stanton saw black men and white women no longer as allies. According to Sue Davis, "Cady Stanton also utilized inegalitarian, undemocratic arguments to argue that educated, white, native-born women were far better suited to participate in the political life of the nation than were males who were uneducated, nonwhite, and foreign born." Sue Davis, *The Political Thought of Elizabeth Cady Stanton* (New York: New York University Press, 2008), 2.

69. For a range of ways black women's bodies and subjectivities have been constructed through white supremacist culture, see Emilie Townes, *Womanist Ethics and the Cultural Production of Evil* (New York: Palgrave Macmillian, 2006).

70. Mahasweta Devi, "Breast-giver," in *Breast Stories*, translated and with introductory essays by Gayatri Chakravorty Spivak (Calcutta: Seagull Books, 2010), 38.

71. Gayatri Chakravorty Spivak, "'Breast-giver': For Author, Teacher, Sublatern, Historian . . .," in *Breast Stories*, 125.

72. Devi, "Breast-giver," 54.

73. Devi, "Breast-giver," 73.

74. Spivak, "'Breast-giver': For Author, Teacher, Subaltern, Historian . . .," 106.

75. Spivak, "'Breast-giver': For Author, Teacher, Subaltern, Historian . . .," 109.

76. Arjun Appadurai, *Modernity at Large: Cultural Dimensions of Globalization* (Minneapolis: University of Minnesota Press, 1996), 23.

77. This description of history and genealogy is taken from Appadurai, 74.

78. Appadurai, *Modernity at Large*, 36.

79. Judith Plaksow, "Authority, Resistance, and Transformation: Jewish Feminist Reflections on Good Sex," in *The Coming of Lilith: Essays on Feminism, Judaism, and Sexual Ethics, 1972–2003* (Boston: Beacon Press, 2005), 201. Plaskow cites the work of Sharon D. Welch, *Communities of Resistance and Solidarity* (Maryknoll, NY: Orbis, 1985) and Daniel Boyarin, "Justify My Love," in *Judaism Since Gender*, ed. Miriam Peskowitz and Laura Levitt (New York: Routledge, 1997).

80. Madhu Khanna, "A Conversation on Two Faces of Hinduism and their Implication for Gender Discourse," in *Women's Voices in World Religions*, ed. Hille Haker et al. (London: SCM Press, 2006), 86.

81. Tracy Pinchman, *Guests at God's Wedding: Celebrating Kartik among the Women of Benares* (Albany: SUNY Press, 2006).

82. Lynn Teskey Denton, "Varieties of Hindu Female Asceticism," in *Roles and Rituals for Hindu Women*, ed. Julia Leslie (Delhi: Motilal Banarsidass Publishers, 1992), 213.

83. Vashudha Narayanan, "Women of Power in the Hindu Tradition," in *Feminism and World Religions*, ed. Arvind Sharma and Katherine K. Young (Albany: SUNY Press, 1999), 25–77.

84. Judith Plaskow, *Standing Again at Sinai*, 49.

85. Adele Reinhartz, "Women in Judaism," in *Women's Voices in World Religions*, ed. Hille Haker, Susan Ross, and Marie-Theres Wacker (London: SCM Press, 2006), 18–19.

86. Leila Gal Berner, "Hearing Hannah's Voice: The Jewish Feminist Challenge of Ritual Innovation," in *Daughters of Abraham: Feminist Thought in Judaism, Christianity and Islam*, ed. Yvonne Yazbeck Haddad and John L. Esposito (Gainesville: University Press of Florida, 2001), 35.

87. Miriam Cooke, *Women Claim Islam: Creating Islamic Feminism through Literature* (New York and London: Routledge, 2001), 59.

88. See Rowe, *Power Lines*.

89. Mary Daly, *Beyond God the Father: Toward a Philosophy of Women's Liberation*, 2nd ed. (Boston: Beacon Press, 1985), 35.

90. Leila Ahmed, *A Border Passage: From Cairo to America—A Woman's Journey* (New York: Penguin, 2000), 128.

4. Creativity Under Constraint: Freedom in Theological Anthropology

1. Charles Taylor, *Sources of the Self: The Making of Modern Identity* (Cambridge, Mass.: Harvard University Press, 1989), 285.

2. Ibid., 305.

3. Ibid., 383.

4. Mary Wollstonecraft, *A Vindication of the Rights of Woman (1792)*, chapter 2. Electronic Text Center, University of Virginia Library, http://etext.virginia.edu/toc/modeng/public/WolVind.html (accessed 19 December 2011).

5. Taylor, *Sources of the Self*, 290.

6. Karl Rahner, interview with Karl-Heinz Weger and Hildegard Lüning, South German Radio (SDR), Stuttgart, 19 March 1979, in *Karl Rahner in Dialogue*, ed. Paul Imhof and Hubert Biallowons (New York: Crossroad, 1986), 217.

7. Karl Rahner, *Foundations of Christian Faith: An Introduction to the Idea of Christianity*, trans. William V. Dych (New York: Crossroad, 1982), 38.

8. Cady Stanton, diary entry, 20 May 1896 in *Elizabeth Cady Stanton As Revealed*, 2:318.

9. Rahner, *Foundations*, 36.

10. Ibid., 97.

11. Kathryn Reklis, "A Sense of the Tragic in a Christian Theology of Freedom," *Theological Studies* 70 (2009): 37–60 at 49.

12. Ibid., 47.

13. Judith Plaskow, "Sexual Orientation and Human Rights: A Progressive Jewish Perspective," in *The Coming of Lilith: Essays on Feminism, Judaism, and Sexual Ethics, 1972–2003* (Boston: Beacon Press, 2005), 186-187.

14. Judith Butler, *Gender Trouble: Feminism and the Subversion of Identity* (New York and London: Routledge, 1990).

15. See Virginia Ramey Mollenkott *Omnigender: A Trans-religious Approach*, rev. and exp. (Cleveland: Pilgrim Press, 2007), 2. Mollenkott cites Cherly Chase, "Hermaphrodites with Attitude: Mapping the Emergence of Intersex Activism," in *Transgender Studies Reader*, ed. Susan Stryker and Stephen Whittle (New York: Routledge, 2006) 300–14; Martine Aliana Rothblatt, *The Apartheid of Sex: A Manifesto on the Freedom of Gender* (New York: Crown, 1995).

16. See, for example, Monique Wittig, "One Is Not Born a Woman," in *The Straight Mind and Other Essays* (Boston: Beacon Press, 1992), 14.

17. Adrienne Rich, "Compulsory Heterosexuality and Lesbian Existence," *Signs* 5, no. 4 (Summer 1980): 640.

18. Rich, "Compulsory Heterosexuality," 637.

19. Camara Phyllis Jones, "Levels of Racism: A Theoretic Framework and a Gardener's Tale," *American Journal of Public Health* 90, no. 8 (August 2000): 1212.

20. See, for example, J. Cameron Carter, *Race: A Theological Account.* (Oxford: Oxford University Press, 2008).

21. See Mollenkott, *Omnigender.*

22. Chava Frankfort-Nachmias, "Israel: The Myth of Gender Equality," 129.

23. Riffat Hassan, "Feminism in Islam," in *Feminism and World Religions,* 251.

24. Mary Daly, *Beyond God the Father: Toward a Philosophy of Women's Liberation* (Boston: Beacon Press, 1985), 69.

25. Ibid., 71.

26. Ibid., 74.

27. Linda Clark, "We Are Also Sarah's Children," *Drew Gateway* 48, no. 3 (1978): 11–37 at 28.

28. Elisabeth Schüssler Fiorenza, *In Memory of Her,* xx.

29. Butler, *Gender Trouble,* 198–99.

30. Mark Brett uses this phrase in his review of Andre LaCocque, *The Trial of Innocence: Adam, Eve, and the Yahwist* (Eugene: Cascade, 2006) in *Biblical Interpretation* 18 (2010): 479.

31. For a tremendous sourcebook tracing the trope of Eve-Woman-Evil through Christian history, see *Eve and Adam: Jewish, Christian and Muslim Readings on Genesis and Gender,* ed. Kristen E. Kvam, Linda S. Schearing, and Valarie H. Ziegler (Bloomington: Indiana University Press, 1999). See also Rosemary Radford Ruether, "Anthropology: Humanity as Male and Female," in *Sexism and God-Talk: Toward a Feminist Theology* (Boston: Beacon Press, 1983), 93–115.

32. See, for example, Pope John Paul II, "Gratissimam Sane" (Letter to Families), 2 February 1994, http://www.vatican.va/holy_father/john_paul_ii/letters/documents/hf_jp-ii_let_02021994_families_en.html (accessed 13 December 2012).

33. Deborah W. Rooke, "Feminist Criticism of the Old Testament: Why Bother?" *Feminist Theology* 15. no 2 (2007): 160–74 at 161.

34. Ibid., 166–67.

35. Elizabeth Cady Stanton, "Comments on Genesis III," in *The Woman's Bible,* part 1, *Comments on Genesis, Exodus, Leviticus, Numbers, and Deuteronomy,* by Elizabeth Cady Stanton et al. (1895; reprint, North Stratford, N.J.: Ayer, 2002), 24.

36. Kathi Kern, *Mrs. Stanton's Bible,* 159.

37. Sun Ai Lee, poem (untitled), in *Eve and Adam,* 420; originally published in Masao Takenaka and Ron O'Grady, *The Bible Through Asian Eyes* (Aukland, New Zealand: Pace, 1991), 24.

38. Kenneth Waters contends that 'childbearing' in this context is an allegorical use of the term to indicate the bringing forth of the virtues that follow in the passage. His reading is grounded in parallels in a variety of ancient texts where the virtues are metaphorized as children in a similar way. This reading challenges the history of biblical interpretation that has weighed on contemporary biblical scholarship in reading 'childbearing' as a literal function for the women in the community to whom the letter is addressed. See Kenneth L. Waters Sr., "Saved through Childbearing: Virtues as Children in 1 Timothy: 15–22," *Journal of Biblical Literature* 123, no. 4 (2004): 703–35. Waters suggests the reading of salvation through virtues-bearing and concludes: "For the author of 1 Timothy, the

means of salvation for women remains the same as the means of salvation for men—and vice versa. *All women and men must give birth to and continue in faith, love, holiness, and temperance in order to be saved"* (emphasis in the original).

39. The strategy of reading biblical texts against the grain to reconstruct social and ecclesial practices is outlined by Antoinnette Clark Wire in *The Corinthian Woman Prophets: A Reconstruction Through Paul's Rhetoric* (Minneapolis: Fortress Press, 1990).

40. Benjamin H. Dunning, *Specters of Paul: Sexual Difference in Early Christian Thought* (Philadelphia: University of Pennsylvania Press, 2011), 6.

41. Dunning, *Specters of Paul,* 154.

42. Riffat Hassan, "The Issue of Woman–Man Equality in the Islamic Tradition" in *Eve and Adam,* 465.

43. Ibid., 467.

44. Ibid., 470

45. Hassan, "Muslim Women in Post-Patriarchal Islam," in *After Patriarchy: Feminist Transformations of the World Religions,* ed. Paula M. Cooey, William R. Eakin, and Jay B. McDaniel (Maryknoll, N.Y.: Orbis, 1991), 49.

46. Ibid., 47.

47. Ibid., 59.

48. Judith Plaskow, "The Coming of Lilith: Toward a Feminist Theology," in *Womanspirit Rising: A Feminist Reader in Religion,* ed. Carol P. Christ and Judith Plaskow (New York: Harper and Row, 1979), 206.

49. See, for example, the overview of contemporary feminist rereadings of Eve chronicled in M. Doretta Cornell, "Mother of All the Living: Reinterpretations of Eve in Contemporary Literature," *Crosscurrents* (Winter 2005): 91–107.

50. For a contemporary scholarly discussion of God's dishonesty/truthfulness see James Barr, "Is God a Liar (Genesis 2-3)—and Related Matters," *Journal of Theological Studies* 57, no.1 (2006): 1–22.

51. The history of competing egalitarian and inegalitarian interpretations is chronicled in Kvam, et al., *Eve and Adam.*

52. Sojourner Truth, "Ain't I a Woman?" speech, Ohio Women's Rights Convention, 1851, http://www.fordham.edu/halsall/mod/sojtruth-woman.html (accessed 7 February 2011).

53. Monique Wittig, "One Is Not Born a Woman," 20.

54. On the possibilities and problems in reconstructing historical women in the Jesus movement, see Mary Rose D'Angelo, "Reconstructing 'Real' Women from Gospel Literature: The Case of Mary Magdalene"; and Amy-Jill Levine, "Women in the Q Communit(ies) and Traditions," in *Women and Christian Origins,* ed. Ross Shepard Kraemer and Mary Rose D'Angelo (New York: Oxford University Press, 1999), 105–28 and 150–70. Leading Christian feminist biblical scholar Elisabeth Schüssler Fiorenza writes, "The scant references to women as well as the inconsistencies in our New Testament sources still indicate that women were members and leaders in the early Christian movement and that the formation of early Christian traditions and their redactional processes followed certain androcentric interests and theological perspectives." Elisabeth Schüssler Fiorenza, "Remembering the Past in Creating the Future," in *Bread Not Stone: The Challenge of Feminist Biblical Interpretation,* tenth-anniversary edition (Boston: Beacon Press, 1995), 111.

55. Schüssler Fiorenza, *In Memory of Her*, 105–59.

56. See David Kelsey's *Eccentric Existence: A Theological Anthropology* 2 vols. (Louisville: Westminster John Knox Press, 2009).

57. Marcus Borg, "From Galilean Jew to Face of God: The Pre-Easter and Post-Easter Jesus," in *Jesus at 2000*, ed. Marcus Borg (Boulder, Colo.: Westview Press, 1997), 7–20.

58. Amy-Jill Levine, "Women in the Q Communit(ies) and Traditions," 157.

59. Mary Rose D'Angelo, "(Re)Presentations of Women in the Gospel of Matthew and Luke-Acts," in *Women and Christian Origins*, 185.

60. Mary Rose D'Angelo, "(Re)Presentations of Women in the Gospels: John and Mark," in *Women and Christian Origins*, 138.

61. Elizabeth Johnson, *Truly Our Sister: A Theology of Mary in the Communion of Saints* (New York: Continuum, 2006), 202.

62. Aram Tropper, "Jewish Life in Late Antiquity," *Journal for the Study of Judaism in the Persian, Hellenistic, and Roman Period* 37, no. 3 (2006): 332.

63. Amy-Jill Levine, "Women in the Q Communit(ies) and Traditions," 159.

64. Mayer I. Gruber, "The Status of Women in Ancient Judaism," in *Judaism in Late Antiquity: Where We Stand: Issues and Debates in Ancient Judaism*, ed. Jacob Nuesner and Alan J. Avery-Peck, part 3 (Leiden: Brill, 1999), 2:151.

65. M. Shawn Copeland, *Enfleshing Freedom: Body, Race, and Being* (Minneapolis: Fortress Press, 2010), 101.

66. Tzvi Novick, "Pain and Production in Eden: Some Philological Reflections on Genesis iii 16," *Vetus Testamentum* 58 (2008): 241.

67. Lisa Lassell Hallstrom, "Anandamayi Ma, the Bliss-Filled Divine Mother," in *The Graceful Guru: Hindu Female Gurus in India and the United States*, ed. Karen Pechilis (New York: Oxford University Press, 2004), 88–89.

68. Hallstrom, "Anandamayi Ma," 111.

69. Anne Carolyn Klein, *Meeting the Great Bliss Queen: Buddhists, Feminists, and the Art of the Self* (Boston: Beacon Press, 1995), 171.

70. Chung Ok Lee, *Vision for a New Civilization: Spiritual and Ethical Values in the New Millennium* (New York/Iksan, Republic of Korea: Won Buddhism Publishing, 2000), 184.

71. Klein, *Meeting the Great Bliss Queen*, 97.

72. Ibid., 81.

73. In his work, Thomas Bohache takes Mary as point of departure for a christology in which we are all called to birth new Christs. See his "Embodiment as Incarnation: An Incipient Queer Christology," *Theology and Sexuality* 10, no. 1 (2003): 9–29. See also his, *Christology from the Margins* (London: SCM Press, 2008), 197.

5. Encounter in Philadelphia: Engendered Dialogue Today

1. Anne (pseud.), group interview by author, transcription of digital recording, Radnor, Pa., 12 February 2009. The women's voices in this chapter are drawn primarily from interviews with the Philadelphia Area Women's Multifaith group and were undertaken by Mara Brecht (Fordham University) and Jeannine Hill Fletcher. Interviews were done over a three-year period with initial thirty-minute phone interviews, one-to-two-hour

in-person interviews, observation of their practice in the dialogue setting, informal conversation, and a formal group interview. Interviews were digitally recorded and transcribed. Pseudonyms are used to identify the women. In a collaborative feminist methodology, Mara and I worked together, at times coauthoring reflections on the experience. I am grateful for her companionship in this work. Any similarities in our published work may be traced to these collaborations.

2. Ava (pseud.), interview by Mara Brecht, transcription of digital recording, West Philadelphia, Pa., 20 July 2007.

3. For an awareness of how mission functions as a site of recognizing historical inter-religious encounter, see David Clairmont, "On Hegemonies Within: Franciscan Missions and Buddhist Kings in Comparative Theological Contexts," in *The New Comparative Theology: Thinking Interreligiously in the 21st Century*, ed. Francis X. Clooney (New York: T & T Clark, 2010), 63–88; and Marion Grau *Rethinking Mission in the Postcolony: Salvation, Society and Subversion* (New York: T & T Clark, 2011).

4. For discussions of interreligious dialogue as a component of the interfaith movement, see Catherine Cornille, *The Im-Possibility of Interreligious Dialogue* (New York: Crossroad, 2008); and Aasluv Lande, "Recent Developments in Interreligious Dialogue," in *The Concept of God in Global Dialogue*, ed. Werner Jeanrond and Aasluv Lande (Maryknoll, NY: Orbis, 2005), 32–47.

5. See my "Women's Voices in Interreligious Dialogue: A Look at the Parliament of the World's Religions" *Studies in Interreligious Dialogue* 16, no. 1 (2006): 1–22; and "Sisterhood is Superfluous: Women in Interreligious Dialogue," in *The Blackwell Companion to Interreligious Dialogue*, ed. Catherine Cornille (forthcoming 2013).

6. Ava, interview.

7. Ibid.

8. Ibid.

9. Ibid.

10. "Format for Spiritual Autobiographies," Philadelphia Area Multifaith Women's Group.

11. Fran (pseud.), interview by Mara Brecht, transcription from digital recording, Narbeth, Pa., 1 August 2008.

12. Amira (pseud.), interview by Mara Brecht, transcription from digital recording, Swathmore, Pa., 21 July 2007.

13. Fran (pseud.), group interview by Jeannine Hill Fletcher and Mara Brecht, transcription from digital recording, Radnor, Pa., 12 February 2009.

14. Elizabeth (pseud.), interview by Mara Brecht, transcription from digital recording, Philadelphia, Pa., 1 August 2008.

15. Ibid.

16. Homara (pseud.), interview by Mara Brecht, transcription from digital recording, Philadelphia, Pa., 16 December 2007.

17. Sarai (pseud.), interview by Mara Brecht, transcription from digital recording, Philadelphia, Pa., 1 August 2008.

18. Homara, interview.

19. Sarai, interview.

20. Amira, interview.

21. Ibid.

22. Elizabeth, interview.

23. As Melissa Raphael explains: "The Hebrew term *tikkun olam* is variously translated as the completion, restoration, healing or mending of the world. . . . The conception of *tikkun* can be traced back to the biblical, prophetic vision of a God who is fiercely critical of the ways of the powerful and who wills a just socio-religious order." Raphael looks to Emil Fackenheim to envision *tikkun* across religious lines as a "practical mending of the world." Melissa Raphael, *The Female Face of God in Auschwitz: A Jewish Feminist Theology of the Holocaust* (New York: Routledge, 2003), 135.

24. Arjun Appadurai, *Modernity at Large: Cultural Dimensions of Globalization* (Minneapolis: University of Minnesota Press, 1996) 155.

25. Elizabeth, interview.

26. Homara, interview.

27. Helene Egnell, *Other Voices: A Study of Christian Feminist Approaches to Religious Plurality East and West* (Uppsala, Sweden: Studia Missionalia Svecana C, 2007), 161 and 163.

28. Egnell, 165.

29. Ibid.

30. Maura O'Neill, *To Mend the World: Women in Interreligious Dialogue* (Maryknoll, N.Y.: Orbis, 2007).

31. Joanne (pseud.), interview by Mara Brecht, transcription of digital recording, Philadelphia, 15 December 2007.

32. Homara, interview.

33. Fran, interview.

34. Ava, interview.

35. Joanne, interview.

36. Ava, interview.

37. Ibid.

38. Mary (pseud.), group interview by Jeannine Hill Fletcher and Mara Brecht, transcription from digital recording, Radnor, Pa., 12 February 2009.

39. Anne, interview.

40. Ava (pseud.), group interview by Jeannine Hill Fletcher and Mara Brecht, transcription from digital recording, Radnor, Pa., 12 February 2009.

41. Ava, group interview

42. Amina (pseud.), group interview by Jeannine Hill Fletcher and Mara Brecht, transcription from digital recording, Radnor, Pa., 12 February 2009.

43. Elizabeth, interview.

44. Fran, interview.

45. Wilfred Cantwell Smith, *The Meaning and End of Religion* (New York: Macmillan, 1962), 213n43. Smith explores the diverse meanings and uses of the term 'religion' in chapter 2 of this work.

46. Elena (pseud.), interview by Mara Brecht, transcription from digital recording, Philadelphia, July 21, 2007.

47. Francis X. Clooney, *Comparative Theology: Deep Learning Across Religious Borders* (West Sussesx, UK: Wiley-Blackwell, 2010), 16.

6. The Dynamic Self as Knower: Insights for Theological Anthropology

1. Fran, interview.
2. Karl Rahner, *Foundations of Christian Faith: An Introduction to the Idea of Christianity*, trans. William V. Dych (New York: Crossroad, 1982), 112.
3. René Descartes, "Meditation Three: Concerning God, That He Exists," *Meditations on First Philosophy* (1641) in *Discourse on Method and Meditations on First Philosophy*, trans. Donald A. Cress (Indianapolis: Hackett, 1980), 67.
4. Rahner, *Foundations*, 29.
5. T. M. (Tamar) Rudavsky, "To Know What Is: Feminism, Metaphysics, and Epistemology," in *Women and Gender in Jewish Philosophy* (Bloomington: Indiana University Press, 2004), 184.
6. Rudavsky, 186.
7. Thomas Kuhn, *The Structure of Scientific Revolutions*, 2 nd ed. (Chicago: University of Chicago Press, 1970), 113.
8. Ibid., 60.
9. Kuhn describes the process in this way in *The Essential Tension: Selected Studies in Scientific Tradition and Change* (Chicago: University of Chicago Press, 1977), 309–12.
10. In explaining this intuitive process, Kuhn points to Ludwig Wittgenstein's theory of language games, suggesting that we know by application what a word means even if we cannot describe the rules that govern its use. Kuhn, *Structure*, 44–45.
11. See, for example, Nancy Hartsock, "The Feminist Standpoint: Developing the Ground for a Specifically Feminist Historical Materialism," in *Discovering Reality: Feminist Perspectives on Epistemology, Metaphysics, Methodology and Philosophy of Science*, ed. Sandra Harding and Merrill B. Hintikka, 2nd ed. (Norwall, Mass.: Kluwer Academic, 2003), 283–310.
12. George Lindbeck, *The Nature of Doctrine: Religion and Theology in a Postliberal Age* (Louisville: Westminster John Knox Press, 1984), 117.
13. George Lindbeck, "Barth and Textuality," *Theology Today* 43 (1986): 371.
14. Kuhn, *Structure*, 109–10.
15. Ibid., 94.
16. Lindbeck, *Nature of Doctrine*, 36.
17. Miriam Cooke cites Jacques Derrida: The 'I' never precedes language and "is thus never independent of language in general" (Derrida 1996 *Le Monolinguisme de l'Autre*). Miriam Cooke, *Women Claim Islam: Creating Islamic Feminism through Literature* (New York/London: Routledge, 2001), 43.
18. Sallie King, "A Pluralistic View of Religious Pluralism," in *The Myth of Religious Superiority: Multifaith Explorationa of Religious Pluralism*, ed. Paul F. Knitter (Maryknoll, N.Y.: Orbis, 2005), 100.
19. Merle Feld, "We all Stood Together," www.jwa.org (accessed 20 February 2007).
20. Rachel Josefowitz Siegel, "'I Don't Know Enough:' Jewish Women's Learned Ignorance," *Women in Judaism* 1, no. 1 (January 1997) 1–6, http://www.proquest.com (accessed 20 December 2011).
21. Doris Jakobish, "Sikhism, Interfaith Dialogue, and Women: Transformation and Identity," *Journal of Contemporary Religion* 21, no. 2 (May 2006): 183–99; Laura Taylor, "Redeeming Christ: Imitation or (Re)citation?" in *Frontiers in Catholic Feminist*

Theology: Shoulder to Shoulder, ed. Susan Abraham and Elena Procario-Foley (Minneapolis: Fortress Press, 2009), 119–40.

22. The exclusion from access to education and religious education is chronicled in diverse perspectives in *Women's Voices in World Religions*, ed. Hille Haker, Susan Ross, and Marie-Theres Wacker (London: SCM Press, 2006).

23. Member of the Philadelphia Area Multifaith Women's Dialogue (anonymous), written correspondence, 2007.

24. Michelle Voss Roberts, "Gendering Comparative Theology," in *The New Comparative Theology*, 115.

25. Linda Clark, "We Are Also Sarah's Children," *Drew Gateway* 48, no. 3 (1978): 28.

26. Jeannine Hill Fletcher, Laura M. Taylor, and Elena Procario-Foley, "Ecclesiology Roundtable," in *Frontiers in Catholic Feminist Theology*, 215.

27. Nazira Zayn al-Din, *The Girl and the Shaykhs* (Damascus: Dar al-Mada, 1998), 82. Quoted in Miriam Cooke, *Women Claim Islam: Creating Islamic Feminism through Literature* (New York/London: Routledge, 2001), xiv–xv.

28. See Radha Kumar, *The History of Doing: An Illustrated Account of Movements for Women's Rights and Feminism in India, 1800–1990* (London and New York: Verso, 1993).

29. Kumar, *The History of Doing*, 56.

30. Cooke, *Women Claim Islam*, 62.

31. Mehrézia Labidi-Maïza, "My Father's Heir: The Journey of a Muslim Feminist," in *Women's Voices in World Religions*, 73.

32. For further information on United Nations statistics on women and education, see www.un.org/womenwatch.

33. Siegel, "'I Don't Know Enough.'"

34. Leila Ahmed, *A Border Passage: From Cairo to America—A Woman's Journey* (New York: Penguin, 1999), 120.

35. Ahmed, *A Border Passage*, 121.

36. Ibid., 101.

37. Judith Plaskow, *Standing Again at Sinai: Judaism from a Feminist Perspective* (San Francisco: HarperSanFrancisco, 1991), 57.

38. Siegel, "'I Don't Know Enough.'"

39. See, for example, Albert J. Raboteau, *Slave Religion: The "Invisible Institution" in Antebellum South* (Oxford and New York: Oxford University Press, 2004); and Anthony Pinn, *Terror and Triumph: The Nature of Black Religion* (Minneapolis: Ausburg Fortress, 2003).

40. Trinh T. Minh-ha, *Woman-Native-Other: Writing Postcoloniality and Feminism* (Bloomington: Indiana University Press, 1989), 130. A griotte is a female storyteller in traditional orally constituted societies that hold the community's history in memory and communicate it in song and story. See Joanna Lott, "Keepers of History," *Research Penn State* 23, no 2 (May 2002), http://www.rps.psu.edu/0205/keepers.html (accessed 15 November 2011). In the work of Christian feminist theologians, the role of story is also in evidence in, for example, the writings of Mercy Amba Oduyoye and Chung Hyun Kyung.

41. Tracy Pinchman, *Guests at God's Wedding: Celebrating Kartik among the Women of Benares* (Albany: SUNY Press, 2005).

42. Madhu Khanna, "A Conversation on Two Faces of Hinduism and their Implication for Gender Discourse," in *Women's Voices in World Religions*, 88.

43. Sister Paulita Hoffmann, *Living History*, interview by Sister Joanna Chan, 12 March 1981, Maryknoll Archives, Ossining, N.Y.

44. Karl Rahner, "What Do I Mean When I Say, 'God Speaks'?" in *Karl Rahner in Dialogue*, ed. Paul Imhof and Hubert Biallowons (New York: Crossroad, 1986), 76 (emphasis mine).

45. Ibid., 77.

46. Kuhn, *Structure*, 113.

47. George Lindbeck, "Atonement and The Hermeneutics of Intratextual Social Embodiment," in *The Nature of Confession: Evangelicals and Postliberals in Conversation*, ed. Timothy R. Phillips and Dennis L. Okholm (Downers Grove, Ill.: InterVarsity Press, 1996), 223.

48. Lindbeck, "Atonement," 229.

49. Ibid., "Atonement," 234.

50. Edward Said, *Orientalism* (New York: Vintage, 1979), 201–2.

51. Thomas Aquinas, *Summa Contra Gentiles*, trans. Anton C. Pegis 4 vols. (Notre Dame, Ind.: University of Notre Dame), 2:110.

52. Rahner, *Foundations*, 22.

53. For an explanation of 'retroductive warrant', see Francis Schüssler Fiorenza, "Systematic Theology: Task and Methods," in *Systematic Theology: Roman Catholic Perspectives*, ed. Francis Schüssler Fiorenza and John P. Galvin, 2nd ed. (Minneapolis: Fortress Press, 2011), 58–61.

54. Joanne (pesud.), letter to the author, 22 February 2007.

55. Peter C. Phan, "Eschatology: Contemporary Context and Disputed Questions," in *Church and Theology: Essays in Memory of Carl J. Peter*, ed. Peter Phan (Washington, D.C.: Catholic University of America Press, 1995), 252.

56. Eschatology is traditionally formulated in doctrines of 'the immortality of the soul', 'resurrection of the body', 'personal judgment', 'purgatory', 'the second coming of Christ', 'general judgment', 'heaven and hell', and 'the final consummation of the world'.

57. It is the position of the Catholic magisterium that while neither scripture nor theology provides sufficient data for a proper understand of life after death and that what is to come remains a mystery, nevertheless there is asserted a continuity between this world and the next. See Sacred Congregation for the Doctrine of the Faith, "Letter on Certain Questions Concerning Eschatology," *Acta Apostolicae Sedis* 71 (1979), codice 35910-2, 17 May 1979.

58. Elisabeth Schüssler Fiorenza, *In Memory of Her: A Feminist Theological Reconstruction of Early Christian Origins* (New York: Crossroad, 1992), 123.

59. Augustine, *City of God*, book 19.

60. Brian E. Daley, *The Hope of the Early Church: A Handbook of Patristic Eschatology* (Cambridge: Cambridge University Press, 1991), 134.

61. Cyprian, bishop of Carthage, Epistle 61, in *The Ante-Nicene Fathers*, ed. Alexander Roberts and James Donaldson (Grand Rapids, Mich: Eerdmans, 1951), 5:357.

62. Cyprian, 5:358.

63. Augustine, *City of God*, book 1, chap. 1.

64. Thomas Aquinas, *Summa Theologica*, II q. 60 a. 3.

65. The idea of consummation for all, rooted in Christian scripture, is predicated of a God "who desires everyone to be saved" (1 Timothy 2:4) and related to the Christian hope in an eschatological time when "God will be all in all" (1 Corinthians 15:28).

66. Karl Rahner, "Church, Churches, and Religions," in *Theological Investigations*, trans. David Bourke (London: Darton, Longman and Todd, 1973), 10:30.

67. Karl Rahner, "Christianity and the Non-Christian Religions," in *Theological Investigations*, trans. Karl-H. Kruger, (London: Darton, Longman & Todd; Baltimore: Helicon Press, 1966), 5:118.

68. Karl Rahner, "The One Christ and the Universality of Salvation" in *Theological Investigations*, trans. David Morland (New York: Seabury Press, 1979), 16:200.

69. John Hick, *A Christian Theology of Religions: The Rainbow of Faiths* (Kentucky: Westminster John Knox, 1995), 29.

70. Ibid., 23.

71. S. Mark Heim, "Saving the Particulars: Religious Experience and Religious Ends," *Religious Studies* 36 (2000): 445.

72. S. Mark Heim, *Salvations: Truth and Difference in Religion* (Maryknoll, N.Y.: Orbis, 1995).

73. Ava, group interview.

74. Amina, group interview.

75. Mary, group interview.

76. Anne, group interview

77. Ava, group interview.

78. Elena, interview.

79. Paul Tillich, *Dynamics of Faith* (New York: Harper and Brothers, 1958), 2–3.

80. Beppie van den Bogaerde, "The Role of Language Input in Acquisitions Theory," in "Input and Interaction in Deaf Families" (LOT Dissertation Series 35).,Netherlands Graduate School of Linguistics, http://www.lotpublications.nl/publish/articles/000464/bookpart.pdf (accessed 4 November 2011).

81. See, for example, Mele Taumoepeau and Ted Ruffman, "Mother and Infant Talk about Mental States Relates to Desire Language and Emotion Understanding," *Child Development* 77 (March/April 2006): 465–81.

82. See Patricia Kuhl, "A New View of Language Acquisition," paper presented at the National Academy of Sciences colloquium, "Auditory Neuroscience: Development, Transduction, and Integration," Arnold and Mabel Beckman Center, Irvine, Calif., 19–21 May 2000, http://www.ncbi.nlm.nih.gov/pmc/articles/PMC34178/#__sec9 (accessed 14 December 2012).

Conclusion: Seeking Salvation

1. Homara (pseud.), interview by Mara Brecht, transcription from digital recording, Philadelphia, 16 December 2007.

2. Mercy Amba Oduyoye, "Creation, Exodus, and Redemption—an African Woman's Perspective on the Biblical Narrative," *Journal of African Christian Thought* 6, no. 1 (2003): 7.

3. Catherine Keller, "Returning God: The Gift of Feminist Theology," in *Feminism, Sexuality and the Return of Religion* ed. Linda Martin Alcoff and John Caputo (Indianapolis: Indiana University Press, 2011), 73.

4. Emilie Townes, *Womanist Ethics and the Cultural Production of Evil* (New York: Palgrave Macmillan, 2006), 14.

5. Linell Elizabeth Cady, "Identity, Feminist Theory, and Theology," in *Horizons in Feminist Theology: Identity, Tradition, and Norms*, ed. Rebecca S. Chopp and Sheila Greeve Davaney (Minneapolis: Fortress Press, 1997), 26.

6. Ulrich Beck, *Cosmopolitan Vision*, trans. Ciaran Cronin (Cambridge, UK: Polity Press, 2006), 51.

7. Beck, *Cosmopolitan Vision*, 48.

8. Serene Jones, *Trauma and Grace: Theology in a Ruptured World* (Louisville: Westminster John Knox Press, 2009), 40.

9. When I told this story at an interreligious event, one of the participants came up to me afterward and said that she too was at the 2004 Parliament and carried with her the memory of Sikh hospitality. But, she said, you forgot the old man who stood by the door and shined our shoes while we were eating. Evidence that Sikh hospitality overflowed from the Parliament is indicated by the photos and stories that appear about this event on the Internet. See, for example, go.worldbank.org, whose author writes: "Guru Nanak Nishkam Sewak Jatha is a Sikh organization located in Birmingham, UK. Over 300 Sikhs from the community came to Barcelona to demonstrate to the world how the Sikh faith exemplifies universal interfaith principles. These core universal principles of Sikhism— dya, sath, santokh, nimrta and pyar: compassion, truth, contentment, humility and love—certainly shone through in the generous act of serving 'langar' to over 10,000 people over the course of the week."

10. Gordon Kaufman, *In Face of Mystery: A Constructive Theology* (Cambridge, Mass.: Harvard University Press, 1993).

11. See, for example, my *Monopoly on Salvation? A Feminist Approach to Religious Pluralism* (New York: Continuum, 2005), chap. 2; and Francis Sullivan, *Salvation Outside the Church? Tracing the History of the Catholic Response* (New York: Paulist Press, 1992).

12. Gustavo Gutierrez, *A Theology of Liberation: History, Politics, and Salvation*, fifteenth-anniversary ed., trans. Caridad Inda and John Eagleson (Maryknoll, N.Y.: Orbis, 1988), 84.

13. Elisabeth Schüssler Fiorenza, *In Memory of Her: A Feminist Theological Reconstruction of Christian Origins* (New York: Crossroad, 1992), 113.

14. Valerie Saiving, "The Human Condition: A Feminine View" 40, no. 2 *Journal of Religion* (1960): 100–12.

15. Michele Saracino, "Moving Beyond the 'One True Story,'" in *Frontiers in Catholic Feminist Theology: Shoulder to Shoulder*, ed. Susan Abraham and Elena Precario-Foley (Minneapolis: Fortress Press, 2009), 18.

16. Richard Clifford and Khaled Anatolios, "Christian Salvation: Biblical and Theological Perspectives," *Theological Studies* 66 (2005): 739–69 at 757. This is the understanding of sin put forth by Athanasius, fourth-century Christian theologian and bishop of Alexandria.

17. Elizabeth (pseud.), interview by Mara Brecht, transcription from digital recording, Philadelphia, 1 August 2008.

18. Karl Rahner, *On Prayer* (New York: Paulist Press, 1968), 28.

BIBLIOGRAPHY

Ahmed, Leila. *A Border Passage: From Cairo to America—A Woman's Journey*. New York: Penguin, 2000.

———. "Early Feminist Movements in Turkey and Egypt." In *Muslim Women*, edited by Freda Hussain, 111–26. London and Sydney: Croom Helm, 1984.

———. *A Quiet Revolution: The Veil's Resurgence from the Middle East to America*. New Haven, Conn.: Yale University Press, 2011.

———. *Women and Gender in Islam: Historical Roots of a Modern Debate*. New Haven, Conn.: Yale University Press, 1992.

Amina (pseud.). Group interview by Jeannine Hill Fletcher and Mara Brecht. Transcription from digital recording. Radnor, Pa., 12 February 2009.

Amira (pseud.). Interview by Mara Brecht. Transcription from digital recording. Swathmore, Pa., 21 July 2007.

Anne (pseud.). Group interview by Jeannine Hill Fletcher and Mara Brecht. Transcription from digital recording. Radnor, Pa., 12 February 2009.

Antrobus, Peggy. *The Global Women's Movement: Origins, Issues, and Strategies*. London and New York: Zed Books, 2004.

Appadurai, Arjun. *Modernity at Large: Cultural Dimensions of Globalization*. Minneapolis: University of Minnesota Press, 1996.

Appiah, Kwame Anthony. *Cosmopolitanism: Ethics in a World of Strangers*. New York: Norton, 2006.

Aquino, Maria Pilar. "Feminist Intercultural Theology: Toward a Shared Future of Justice." In *Feminist Intercultural Theology: Latina Explorations for a Just World*, edited by Maria Pilar Aquino and Maria José Rosado-Nunes, 9–29. Maryknoll, N.Y.: Orbis, 2007.

Ava (pseud.). Interview by Mara Brecht. Transcription from digital recording. West Philadelphia, Pa., 20 July 2007.

———. Group interview by Jeannine Hill Fletcher and Mara Brecht. Transcription from digital recording. Radnor, Pa., 12 February 2009.

Barr, James. "Is God a Liar (Genesis 2–3)—And Related Matters." *Journal of Theological Studies* 57, no. 1 (2006): 1–22.

Beattie, Tina. *God's Mother, Eve's Advocate: A Marian Narrative of Women's Salvation*. New York: Continuum, 2002.

Beck, Ulrich. *Cosmopolitan Vision.* Translated by Ciaran Cronin. Cambridge, UK: Polity Press, 2006.

Berkeley, Kathleen C. *The Women's Liberation Movement in America.* Westport, Conn.: Greenwood Press, 1999.

Berner, Leila Gal. "Hearing Hannah's Voice: The Jewish Feminist Challenge of Ritual Innovation." In *Daughters of Abraham: Feminist Thought in Judaism, Christianity, and Islam,* edited by Yvonne Yazbeck Haddad and John L. Esposito, 35–49. Gainesville: University Press of Florida, 2001.

Bhabha, Homi. Keynote address to conference "Sex and Religion in Migration." Yale University, New Haven, Conn., 15 September 2005.

Bohache, Thomas. *Christology from the Margins.* London: SCM Press, 2008.

———. "Embodiment as Incarnation: An Incipient Queer Christology," *Theology and Sexuality* 10, no. 1 (2003): 9–29.

Borg, Marcus. "From Galilean Jew to Face of God: The Pre-Easter and Post-Easter Jesus." In *Jesus at 2000,* edited by Marcus Borg, 7–20. Boulder, Colo.: Westview Press, 1997.

Braaten, Carl E., and Robert W. Jenson, eds. *Mary, Mother of God.* Grand Rapids, Mich: Eerdmans, 2004.

Bradshaw, Sue. "Catholic Sisters in China: An Effort to Raise the Status of Women." In *Women in China: Current Directions in Historical Scholarship,* edited by Richard W. Guisso and Stanley Johannesen, 201–13. Youngstown, N.Y.: Philo Press, 1981.

Braude, Ann. "Brett, Mark. Review of *The Trial of Innocence: Adam, Eve and the Yahwist,* by Andre LaCocque. *Biblical Interpretation* 18 (2010): 479

———. ed. *Transforming the Faiths of Our Fathers: Women Who Changed American Religion.* New York: Palgrave Macmillan, 2004.

Brock, Rita Nakashima. "Feminist Theories." In *Dictionary of Feminist Theologies,* edited by Letty M. Russell and J. Shannon Clarkson, 116–20. Louisville: Westminster John Knox Press, 1996.

Butler, Judith. *Gender Trouble: Feminism and the Subversion of Identity,* 2nd ed. New York: Routledge, 1990.

———. *Undoing Gender.* New York: Routledge, 2004.

Bynum, Caroline Walker. *Jesus as Mother: Studies in the Spirituality of the High Middle Ages.* Berkeley: University of California Press, 1982.

Cady, Linell Elizabeth. "Identity, Feminist Theory, and Theology." In *Horizons in Feminist Theology: Identity, Tradition, and Norms,* edited by Rebecca S. Chopp and Sheila Greeve Davaney, 17–32. Minneapolis: Fortress Press, 1997.

Cady Stanton, Elizabeth. *Eighty Years and More: Reminiscences, 1815–1897.* Boston: Northeastern University Press, 1993.

———. *Elizabeth Cady Stanton as Revealed in Her Letters, Diary, and Reminiscences.* Edited by Theodore Stanton and Harriot Stanton Blatch. 2 vols. New York: Harper and Brothers Publishers, 1922; New York: Arno and New York Times, 1969.

———. "The Worship of God in Man." In *The World's Parliament of Religions: An Illustrated and Popular Story of the World's First Parliament of Religions, Held in Chicago in Connection with the Columbian Exposition of 1893,* edited by John Henry Barrows, 2:1234–36. Chicago: Parliament Publishing Company, 1893.

Cady Stanton, Elizabeth, et al. *The Woman's Bible.* 1895; reprint, North Stratford, N.J.: Ayer, 2002.

Carter, J. Cameron. *Race: A Theological Account*. Oxford and New York: Oxford University Press, 2008.

Chapin, Augusta J. Closing address to the Parliament. In *The World's Parliament of Religions: An Illustrated and Popular Story of the World's First Parliament of Religions, Held in Chicago in Connection with the Columbian Exposition of 1893*, edited by John Henry Barrows, 1:179. Chicago: Parliament Publishing Company, 1893.

———. Opening address to the 1893 World's Parliament of Religions. In *The World's Parliament of Religions: An Illustrated and Popular Story of the World's First Parliament of Religions, Held in Chicago in Connection with the Columbian Exposition of 1893*, edited by John Henry Barrows, 1:81–82. Chicago: Parliament Publishing Company, 1893.

Chodorow, Nancy Julia. "Gender, Relation, and Difference in Psychoanalytic Perspective." In *Feminist Social Thought: A Reader*, edited by Diana Tietjens Meyers, 7–21. New York and London: Routledge, 1997. First published in *Socialist Review* 9, no. 46 (1979): 51–69.

Christ, Carol. "Roundtable Discussion: Feminist Theology and Religious Diversity." *Journal of Feminist Studies in Religion* 16, no. 2 (2000): 79–84.

Christ, Carol, and Judith Plaskow, eds. *Weaving the Visions: New Patterns in Feminist Spirituality*. San Francisco: HarperSanFrancisco, 1989.

Chung Hyun Kyung. "Seeing the Religious Roots of Pluralism." *Journal of Ecumenical Studies* 34, no. 3 (Summer 1997): 399–402.

Chung Ok Lee. *Vision for a New Civilization: Spiritual and Ethical Values in the New Millennium*. New York/Iksan, Republic of Korea: Won Buddhism Publishing, 2000.

Clairmont, David. "On Hegemonies Within: Franciscan Missions and Buddhist Kings in Comparative Theological Contexts." In *The New Comparative Theology: Thinking Interreligiously in the 21st Century*, edited by Francis X. Clooney, 63–88. New York: T & T Clark, 2010.

Clark, Linda. "We Are Also Sarah's Children." *Drew Gateway* 48, no. 3 (1978): 11–37.

Clifford, Richard, and Khaled Anatolios. "Christian Salvation: Biblical and Theological Perspectives." *Theological Studies* 66 (2005): 739–69.

Clooney, Francis X. *Comparative Theology: Deep Learning across Religious Borders*. West Sussesx, UK: Wiley-Blackwell, 2010.

Coggins, R. J. *Samaritans and Jews: The Origins of Samaritanism Reconsidered*. Oxford: Basil Blackwell, 1975.

Congregation for the Doctrine of the Faith. "Letter on Certain Questions Concerning Eschatology." *Acta Apostolicae Sedis* 71 (1979), codice 35910–2, 17 May 1979.

Cooke, Miriam. *Women Claim Islam: Creating Islamic Feminism through Literature*. New York; London: Routledge, 2001.

Cooper, Sarah B. "Discussion of Woman as Religious Teacher." In *The World's Congress of Representative Women: A Historical Resume for Popular Circulation of the World's Congress of Representative Women, Convened in Chicago on May 15, and Adjourned on May 22, 1893*, edited by May Wright Sewall, 281–83. Chicago: Rand McNally, 1894, 242. Harvard University, Open Collections Program, www.ocp.hul.harvard.edu, http://pds.lib.harvard.edu/pds/view/2574452.

Copeland, M. Shawn. *Enfleshing Freedom: Body, Race, and Being*. Minneapolis: Fortress Press, 2010.

Cornell, M. Doretta. "Mother of All the Living: Reinterpretations of Eve in Contemporary Literature." *Crosscurrents* (Winter 2005): 91–107.

Cornille, Catherine. *The Im-Possibility of Interreligious Dialogue*. New York: Crossroad, 2008.

Corrington, Gail Paterson. "The Milk of Salvation: Redemption by the Mother in Late Antiquity and Early Christianity." *Harvard Theological Review* 82, no. 4 (October 1989): 393–420.

Cunningham, Sister Henrietta Marie. Personal papers, Maryknoll Archives, Ossining, N.Y.

Cyprian, Bishop of Carthage. "Epistle 61." In *The Ante-Nicene Fathers*, vol. 5, edited by Alexander Roberts and James Donaldson, 356–58. Grand Rapids, Mich: Eerdmans, 1951.

Daley, Brian E. *The Hope of the Early Church: A Handbook of Patristic Eschatology*. Cambridge: Cambridge University Press, 1991.

Dallavalle, Nancy. "Feminist Theologies." In *The Cambridge Companion to Karl Rahner*, edited by Declan Marmion and Mary E. Hines, 264–78. Cambridge: Cambridge University Press, 2005.

Daly, Mary. *Beyond God the Father: Toward a Philosophy of Women's Liberation*. 2nd ed. Boston: Beacon Press, 1985.

D'Angelo, Mary Rose. "Reconstructing 'Real' Women from Gospel Literature: The Case of Mary Magdalene." In *Women and Christian Origins*, edited by Ross Shepard Kraemer and Mary Rose D'Angelo, 105–28. New York and Oxford: Oxford University Press, 1999.

Davis, Sue. *The Political Thought of Elizabeth Cady Stanton*. New York: New York University Press, 2008.

Denton, Lynn Teskey. "Varieties of Hindu Female Asceticism." In *Roles and Rituals for Hindu Women*, edited by Julia Leslie, 211–231. Delhi: Motilal Banarsidass, 1992.

Desai, Manisha. "India: Women's Movements from Nationalism to Sustainable Development." In *Women's Rights: A Global View*, edited by Lynn Walter, 99–112. Westport, Conn.: Greenwood Press, 2001.

Descartes, René. *Discourse on Method and Meditations on First Philosophy*. Translated by Donald A. Cress. Indianapolis: Hackett, 1980.

Devi, Mahasweta. "Breast-giver." In *Breast Stories*, translated by Gayatri Chakravorty Spivak, 38–74. Calcutta: Seagull Books, 2010.

Dunning, Benjamin H. *Specters of Paul: Sexual Difference in Early Christian Thought*. Philadelphia: University of Pennsylvania Press, 2011.

Eastman, Annis F. F. "The Influence of Religion on Women." In *The World's Parliament of Religions: An Illustrated and Popular Story of the World's First Parliament of Religions, Held in Chicago in Connection with the Columbian Exposition of 1893*, edited by John Henry Barrows, 1:752–758. Chicago: Parliament Publishing Company, 1893.

Egnell, Helene. *Other Voices: A Study of Christian Feminist Approaches to Religious Plurality East and West*. Uppsala, Sweden: Studia Missionalia Svecana C, 2007.

Elena (pseud.). Interview by Mara Brecht. Transcription from digital recording. Philadelphia, Pa., July 21, 2007.

Elizabeth (pseud.). Interview by Mara Brecht. Transcription from digital recording. Philadelphia, Pa., 1 August 2008.

Feld, Merle. "We all Stood Together." Accessible at www.jwa.org.

Fishman, Sylvia Barack. *A Breath of Life: Feminism in the American Jewish Community*. New York: Free Press, 1993.

Ford, Bishop Francis X. "Retreat to MK Srs in Philippines." 1935. Ford Collection, File 2/15, Maryknoll Archives, Ossining, N.Y.

Fran (pseud.). Interview by Mara Brecht. Transcription from digital recording. Narbeth, Pa., 1 August 2008.

———. Group interview by Jeannine Hill Fletcher and Mara Brecht. Transcription from digital recording. Radnor, Pa., 12 February 2009.

Frankfort-Nachmias, Chava. "Israel: The Myth of Gender Equality." In *Women's Rights: A Global View*, edited by Lynn Walter, 127–39. Westport, Conn.: Greenwood Press, 2001.

Goldstein, Valerie Saiving. "The Human Condition: A Feminine View." *Journal of Religion* 40, no. 2 (April 1960): 100–12.

Grau, Marion. *Rethinking Mission in the Postcolony: Salvation, Society and Subversion.* New York: T & T Clark, 2011.

Griffiths, Morwenna. *Feminisms and the Self: The Web of Identity.* New York: Routledge, 1995.

Gruber, Mayer I. "The Status of Women in Ancient Judaism." In *Judaism in Late Antiquity: Where We Stand, Issues and Debates in Ancient Judaism*, part 3, vol. 2, edited by Jacob Nuesner and Alan J. Avery-Peck, 151–76. Leiden: Brill, 1999.

Gupta, Lina. "Affirmation of Self: A Hindu Woman's Journey" in *Women's Voices in World Religions*, edited by Hille Haker, Susan Ross, and Marie-Theres Wacker, 90–98. London: SCM Press, 2006.

Gutierrez, Gustavo. *A Theology of Liberation: History, Politics and Salvation.* Translated and edited by Caridad Inda and John Eagleson. Rev. ed. Maryknoll, N.Y.: Orbis, 1988.

Gutzler, Antoinette. "Reimagining the Body of Christ: Women's Body as Gospel Proclamation." In *The Body and Sexuality: Theological-Pastoral Perspectives of Women in Asia*, edited by Agnes M. Brazal and Andrea Lizares Si. 172–86. Manila: Ateneo de Manila University Press, 2007.

Haker, Hille, Susan Ross, and Marie-Theres Wacker, eds. *Women's Voices in World Religions.* London: SCM Press, 2006.

Hallstrom, Lisa Lassell. "Anandamayi Ma, the Bliss-Filled Divine Mother." In *The Graceful Guru: Hindu Female Gurus in India and the United States*, edited by Karen Pechilis, 85–118. Oxford: Oxford University Press, 2004.

Hannigan, Julia. Maryknoll China History Project. Interview by Sister Joanna Chan, 8 July 1980. Maryknoll Archives, Ossining, N.Y.

———. Maryknoll China History Project. Interview by Sister Joanna Chan . Transcript of third of three tapes. Monrovia, Calif., 4 August 1981. Maryknoll Archives, Ossining, N.Y.

Hartsock, Nancy. "The Feminist Standpoint: Developing the Ground for a Specifically Feminist Historical Materialism." In *Discovering Reality: Feminist Perspectives on Epistemology, Metaphysics, Methodology and Philosophy of Science*, edited by Sandra Harding and Merrill B. Hintikka, 283–310. 2nd ed. Norwall, Mass.: Kluwer Academic Publications, 2003.

Hassan, Riffat. "Feminism in Islam." In *Feminism and World Religions*, edited by Arvind Sharma and Katherine K. Young, 248–78. Albany: SUNY Press, 1999.

———. "The Issue of Woman-Man Equality in the Islamic Tradition." In *Eve and Adam: Jewish, Christian and Muslim Readings on Genesis and Gender*, edited by Kristen E. Kvam, Linda S. Schearing and Valarie H. Ziegler, 464–76. Bloomington: Indiana University Press, 1999. The essay originally appeared in *Women's and Men's Liberation: Testimonies of Spirit*, edited by Leonard Grob, Riffat Hassan, and Haim Gordin, 68–82. New York: Greenwood Press, 1991.

———. "Muslim Women in Post-Patriarchal Islam." In *After Patriarchy: Feminist Transformations of the World Religions*, edited by Paula M. Cooey, William R. Eakin, and Jay B. McDaniel, 39–64. Maryknoll, N.Y.: Orbis, 1991.

Heim, S. Mark. *Salvations: Truth and Difference in Religion.* Maryknoll, N.Y.: Orbis, 1995.

———. "Saving the Particulars: Religious Experience and Religious Ends." *Religious Studies* 36 (2000): 435–53.

Heng, Geraldine. "'A Great Way to Fly': Nationalism, the State, and the Varieties of Third-World Feminism." In *Feminist Genealogies, Colonial Legacies, Democratic Futures,* edited by M. Jacqui Alexander and Chandra Talpade Mohanty, 30–45. New York and London: Routledge, 1997.

Henrotin, Ellen Martin. Closing address to the Parliament. In *The World's Parliament of Religions: An Illustrated and Popular Story of the World's First Parliament of Religions, Held in Chicago in Connection with the Columbian Exposition of 1893,* edited by John Henry Barrows, 1:178. Chicago: Parliament Publishing Company, 1893.

Hick, John. *A Christian Theology of Religions: The Rainbow of Faiths.* Louisville: Westminster John Knox, 1995.

Hill Fletcher, Jeannine. "As Long as We Wonder: Possibilities in the Impossibility of Interreligious Dialogue." *Theological Studies* 68, no. 3 (September 2007): 532–54.

———. "Rahner and Religious Diversity." In *The Cambridge Companion to Karl Rahner,* edited by Declan Marmion and Mary E. Hines, 235–48. Cambridge: Cambridge University Press, 2005.

———. *Monopoly on Salvation? A Feminist Approach to Religious Pluralism.* New York: Continuum, 2005.

———. "Sisterhood Is Superfluous: Women in Interreligious Dialogue." In *The Blackwell Companion to Interreligious Dialogue,* edited by Catherine Cornille. Forthcoming 2013.

———. "Women's Voices in Interreligious Dialogue: A Look at the Parliament of the World's Religions." *Studies in Interreligious Dialogue* 16, no. 1 (2006): 1–22.

Hill Fletcher, Jeannine, Laura M. Taylor, and Elena Procario-Foley. "Ecclesiology Roundtable." In *Frontiers in Catholic Feminist Theology: Shoulder to Shoulder,* edited by Susan Abraham and Elena Procario-Foley, 215–21. Minneapolis: Fortress Press, 2009.

Hogan, Kevin. "Entering Into Otherness: The Postmodern Critique of the Subject and Karl Rahner's Theological Anthropology." *Horizons* 25, no. 2 (1998): 181–202.

Hoffmann, Paulita. Interview by author. Maryknoll residence, Ossining, N.Y., 7 December 2007.

———. Maryknoll China History Project. Maryknoll Archives, Ossining, N.Y.

Hom, Sharon K. "China: First the Problem of Rights and Law." In *Women's Rights: A Global View,* edited by Lynn Walter, 29–42. Westport, Conn.: Greenwood Press, 2001.

Homara (pseud.). Interview by Mara Brecht. Transcription from digital recording. Philadelphia, 16 December 2007.

Irigaray, Luce. *This Sex Which Is Not One.* Translated by Catherine Porther with Carolyn Burke. Ithica, N.Y.: Cornell University Press, 1985.

Jakobish, Doris. "Sikhism, Interfaith Dialogue and Women: Transformation and Identity." *Journal of Contemporary Religion* 21, no. 2 (May 2006): 183–99.

Joanne (pseud.). Interview by Mara Brecht. Transcription of digital recording. Philadelphia, 15 December 2007.

John Paul II, *Gratissimam Sane* (Letter to families). 2 February 1994. http://www.vatican.va/holy_father/john_paul_ii/letters/documents/hf_jp-ii_let_02021994_families_en.html.

Johnson, Elizabeth. *She Who Is: The Mystery of God in Feminist Discourse.* New York: Crossroad, 1992.

———. *Truly Our Sister.* New York, Continuum: 2006.

Jones, Camara Phyllis. "Levels of Racism: A Theoretic Framework and a Gardener's Tale." *American Journal of Public Health* 90, no. 8 (August 2000): 1212–15.

Jones, Serene. *Trauma and Grace: Theology in a Ruptured World.* Louisville: Westminster John Knox Press, 2009.

Kaying Diaries, Maryknoll Archives, Ossining, N.Y.

Kaufman, Gordon. *In Face of Mystery: A Constructive Theology.* Cambridge, Mass.: Harvard University Press, 1993.

Kazuko, Ono. *Chinese Women in a Century of Revolution, 1850–1950.* Edited by Joshua A. Fogel. Stanford, Calif.: Stanford University Press, 1989.

Keller, Catherine. *From a Broken Web: Separation, Sexism and Self.* Boston: Beacon Press, 1986.

——. "Returning God: The Gift of Feminist Theology." In *Feminism, Sexuality and the Return of Religion*, edited by Linda Martin Alcoff and John Caputo, 55–76. Indianapolis: Indiana University Press, 2011.

——. "Seeking and Sucking: On Relation and Essence in Feminist Theology." In *Horizons in Feminist Theology: Identity, Tradition, and Norms*, edited by Rebecca S. Chopp and Sheila Greeve Davaney, 54–78. Minneapolis: Fortress Press, 1997.

Kelsey, David. *Eccentric Existence: A Theological Anthropology.* 2 vols. Louisville: Westminster John Knox Press, 2009.

Kern, Kathi. *Mrs. Stanton's Bible.* Ithica, N.Y.: Cornell University Press, 2001.

Kettl, Sister Rosalia. Maryknoll China History Project. Interview by Sister Virginia Unsworth, 8 June 1981. Maryknoll Archives, Ossining, N.Y.

——. [Mary Martha Kettl], *One Inch of Splendor.* New York: Field Afar Press, 1941.

King, Sallie. "A Pluralistic View of Religious Pluralism," in *The Myth of Religious Superiority: Multifaith Explorations of Religious Pluralism*, edited by Paul Knitter, 88–104. Maryknoll, N.Y.: Orbis, 2005.

Kuhn, Thomas. *The Essential Tension: Selected Studies in Scientific Tradition and Change.* Chicago: University of Chicago Press, 1977.

——. *The Structure of Scientific Revolutions.* 2nd ed. Chicago: University of Chicago Press, 1970.

Khanna, Madhu. "A Conversation on Two Faces of Hinduism and their Implication for Gender Discourse." In *Women's Voices in World Religions*, edited by Hille Haker, Susan Ross, and Marie-Theres Wacker, 81–89. London: SCM Press, 2006.

Kiernan, Father Thomas V. "Chinese Sisters." *The Field Afar* (July–August 1936): 209.

Klein, Anne Carolyn. *Meeting the Great Bliss Queen: Buddhists, Feminists and the Art of the Self.* Boston: Beacon Press, 1995.

Korany, Hanna K. "The Position of Women in Syria." In *The World's Congress of Representative Women: A Historical Resume for Popular Circulation of the World's Congress of Representative Women, Convened in Chicago on May 15, and Adjourned on May 22, 1893*, edited by May Wright Sewall, 773–77. Chicago: Rand McNally, 1894. Harvard University, Open Collections Program, www.ocp.hul.harvard.edu, http://pds.lib .harvard.edu/pds/view/2574452.

Kuhl, Patricia. "A New View of Language Acquisition." Paper presented at "Auditory Neuroscience: Development, Transduction, and Integration," the National Academy of Sciences, 19–21 May 2000, Arnold and Mabel Beckman Center, Irvine, Calif., http://www .ncbi.nlm.nih.g.

Kumar, Radha. *The History of Doing: An Illustrated Account of Movements for Women's Rights and Feminism in India 1800–1990*. London and New York: Verso, 1993.

Kwok Pui-lan. *Chinese Women and Christianity 1860–1927*. Atlanta: Scholars Press, 1992.

Labidi-Maïza, Mehrézia. "My Father's Heir: The Journey of a Muslim Feminist" in *Women's Voices in World Religions*, edited by Hille Haker, Susan Ross, and Marie-Theres Wacker, 72–80. London: SCM Press, 2006.

Lande, Aasluv. "Recent Developments in Interreligious Dialogue." In *The Concept of God in Global Dialogue*, edited by Werner Jeanrond and Aasluv Lande, 32–47. Maryknoll, N.Y.: Orbis, 2005.

Lazarus, Josephine. "The Outlook of Judaism," in *The World's Parliament of Religions: An Illustrated and Popular Story of the World's First Parliament of Religions, Held in Chicago in Connection with The Columbian Exposition of 1893*, edited by John Henry Barrows, 1:705–15. Chicago: Parliament Publishing Company, 1893.

Levine, Amy-Jill. "Women in the Q Communit(ies) and Traditions." In *Women and Christian Origins*, edited by Ross Shepard Kraemer and Mary Rose D'Angelo, 150–70. New York and Oxford: Oxford University Press, 1999.

Liefels, Sister Mary Rose. "Roots in China." In *Creative Works*, 9–5. Maryknoll Archives, Ossining, N.Y.

Lindbeck, George. "Atonement and The Hermeneutics of Intratextual Social Embodiment." In *The Nature of Confession: Evangelicals and Postliberals in Conversation*, edited by Timothy R. Phillips and Dennis L. Okholm, 221–40. Downers Grove, Ill.: InterVarsity Press, 1996.

———. "Barth and Textuality." *Theology Today* 43 (1986): 361–76.

———. *The Nature of Doctrine: Religion and Theology in a Postliberal Age*. Louisville: Westminster John Knox Press, 1984.

Lipstadt, Deborah E. "Feminism and American Judaism: Looking Back at the Turn of the Century." In *Women and American Judaism: Historical Perspectives*, edited by Pamela S. Nadell and Jonathan D. Sarna, 291–308. Hanover, N.H.: University Press of New England/ Brandeis University Press, 2001.

Livingston, James C. and Francis Schüssler Fiorenza with Sarah Coakley and James H. Evans. *Modern Christian Thought Volume II: The Twentieth Century*. Upper Saddle River, N.J.: Prentice Hall, 2000.

Lernoux, Penny. *Hearts on Fire: The Story of the Maryknoll Sisters*. Maryknoll, N.Y.: Orbis, 1993.

M. Marcelline, Sister. Kaying Vicariate File, Maryknoll Archives, Ossining, N.Y.

Mary (pseud.). Group interview by Jeannine Hill Fletcher and Mara Brecht. Transcription from digital recording. Radnor, Pa., 12 February 2009.

Miles, Margaret R. *A Complex Delight: The Secularization of the Breast 1350–1750*. Berkeley: University of California Press, 2008.

Mollenkott, Virginia Ramey. *Omnigender: A Trans-religious Approach*. Rev. and exp. Cleveland: Pilgrim Press, 2007.

Morgan, Robin ed. *Sisterhood is Global: The International Women's Movement Anthology*. Garden City, N.Y.: Anchor/Doubleday, 1984.

Moss, Anna Mary. Achival Materials. Maryknoll Archives, Ossining, N.Y.

Murray, Pauli. *Pauli Murray: Selected Sermons and Writings*. Selected with an introduction by Anthony Pinn. Maryknoll, N.Y.: Orbis, 2006.

Narayanan, Vashudha. "Women of Power in the Hindu Tradition." In *Feminism and World Religions*, edited by Arvind Sharma and Katherine K. Young, 25–77. Albany, N.Y.: State University of New York, 1999.

Novick, Tzvi. "Pain and Production in Eden: Some Philological Reflections on Genesis iii 16." *Vetus Testamentum* 58 (2008): 235–244.

Nunes, Maria José F. Rosado. "Women's Voices in Latin-American Theology." In *Feminist Theology in Different Contexts*, edited by. Elisabeth Schüssler Fiorenza and M. Shawn Copeland, 3–17. London: SCM Press/Maryknoll, N.Y.: Orbis, 1999.

Oduyoye, Mercy Amba. *Beads and Strands: Reflections of an African Woman on Christianity in Africa*. Maryknoll, N.Y.: Orbis, 2004.

———. "Creation, Exodus and Redemption – an African Woman's Perspective on the Biblical Narrative" *Journal of African Christian Thought* 6, no. 1 (2003): 3–9.

O'Neill, Maura. *To Mend the World: Women in Interreligious Dialogue*. Maryknoll, N.Y.: Orbis, 2007.

Ono Kazuko. *Chinese Women in a Century of Revolution, 1850–1950*. Edited by Joshua A. Fogel. Stanford, Calif.: Stanford University Press, 1989.

Orevillo-Montenegro, Muriel. *The Jesus of Asian Women*. Maryknoll: N.Y.: Orbis, 2006.

Phan, Peter C. "Eschatology: Contemporary Context and Disputed Questions." In *Church and Theology: Essays in Memory of Carl J. Peter*, edited by Peter Phan, 241–75. Washington, D.C.: Catholic University of America Press, 1995.

Pinchman, Tracy. *Guests at God's Wedding: Celebrating Kartik Among the Women of Benares*. Albany: SUNY Press, 2006.

Pinn, Anthony. *Terror and Triumph: The Nature of Black Religion*. Minneapolis: Ausburg Fortress, 2003.

Plaskow, Judith. "Authority, Resistance, and Transformation: Jewish Feminist Reflections on Good Sex." In *The Coming of Lilith: Essays on Feminism, Judaism, and Sexual Ethics, 1972–2003*, edited with Donna Berman, 193–205. Boston: Beacon Press, 2005. Originally published in *Good Sex: Feminist Perspectives from the World's Religions*, edited by Patricia Jung, Mary Hunt, and Radhika Balakrishnan. New Brunswick, N.J.: Rutgers University Press, 2001.

———. "The Coming of Lilith: Toward a Feminist Theology." In *Womanspirit Rising: A Feminist Reader in Religion*, edited by Carol P. Christ and Judith Plaskow, 198–209. New York: Harper and Row, 1979.

———. "Sexual Orientation and Human Rights: A Progressive Jewish Perspective." In *The Coming of Lilith: Essays on Feminism, Judaism, and Sexual Ethics, 1972–2003*, edited with Donna Berman, 178–192. Boston: Beacon Press, 2005. Originally published in *Sexual Orientation and Human Rights in American Religious Discourse*, edited by Saul Olyan and Martha Nussbaum. Oxford: Oxford University Press, 1998.

———. *Standing Again at Sinai: Judaism from a Feminist Perspective*. San Francisco: HarperSanFrancisco, 1991.

Quinn, Philip L. and Kevin Meeker, eds. *The Philosophical Challenge of Religious Diversity*. New York and Oxford: Oxford University Press, 2000.

Raboteau, Albert J. *Slave Religion: The 'Invisible Institution' in Antebellum South*. Oxford and New York: Oxford University Press, 2004.

Rahner, Karl. *On Prayer*. New York: Paulist Press, 1968.

———. "Anonymous Christians." In *Theological Investigations*, translated by Karl-H. Kruger and Boniface Kruger. Volume 6. New York: Seabury Press, 1974.

———. "Christianity and the Non-Christian Religion." In *Theological Investigations*, translated by Karl-H. Kruger. Volume 5. London: Darton, Longman and Todd; Baltimore: Helicon Press, 1966.

———. "Church, Churches and Religions." In *Theological Investigations*, trans. David Bourke. London: Darton, Longman and Todd, 1973.

———. "The Dignity and Freedom of Man." In *Theological Investigations*, translated by Karl-H. Kruger. Volume 2. London: Darton, Longman and Todd, 1963.

———. *Foundations of Christian Faith: An Introduction to the Idea of Christianity*. Translated by William V. Dych. New York: Crossroad, 1994.

———. *Karl Rahner in Dialogue*. Edited by Paul Imhof and Hubert Biallowons. New York: Crossroad, 1986.

———. "The One Christ and the Universality of Salvation." In *Theological Investigations*, trans. David Morland. New York: Seabury Press, 1979.

Raphael, Melissa. *The Female Face of God in Auschwitz: A Jewish Feminist Theology of the Holocaust*. New York: Routledge, 2003.

Reinhartz, Adele. "Women in Judaism." In *Women's Voices in World Religions*, edited by Hille Haker, Susan Ross and Marie-Theres Wacker, 13–19. London: SCM Press, 2006.

Reklis, Kathryn. "A Sense of the Tragic in a Christian Theology of Freedom." *Theological Studies* 70 (2009): 37–60.

Rich, Adrienne. "Compulsory Heterosexuality and Lesbian Existence." *Signs* 5, no. 4 (Summer 1980): 631–60.

Rooke, Deborah W. "Feminist Criticism of the Old Testament: Why Bother?" *Feminist Theology* 15. No. 2 (2007): 160–74.

Rosen, Ruth. *The World Split Open: How the Modern Women's Movement Changed America*. New York: Penguin, 2001.

Rowe, Aimee Carrillo. *Power Lines: On the Subject of Feminist Alliances*. Durham and London: Duke University Press, 2008.

Rozenman, Elana, Ibtisam Mahameed, Zriek Randa Sabag, and Siham Halabi, "Peace-Building for Women—Taught by Middle East Interfaith Women." Panel presentation at the Parliament of the World's Religions, Barcelona, Spain, 10 July 2004.

Rudavsky, T. M. (Tamar). "To Know What Is: Feminism, Metaphysics, and Epistemology." In *Women and Gender in Jewish Philosophy*, edited by Hava Tirosh-Samuelson, 179–203. Bloomington: Indiana University Press, 2004.

Ruether, Rosemary Radford. *Sexism and God-Talk: Toward a Feminist Theology*. Boston: Beacon Press, 1983.

———. "Feminism and Jewish-Christian Dialogue." In *The Myth of Christian Uniqueness: Toward a Pluralistic Theology of Religions*, edited by John Hick and Paul F. Knitter, 137–48. Maryknoll, N.Y.: Orbis, 1987.

Russell, Letty M. and J. Shannon Clarkson, eds. *Dictionary of Feminist Theologies*. Louisville: Westminster John Knox Press, 1996.

Said, Edward. *Orientalism*. New York: Vintage Books, 1979.

Saracino, Michele. "Moving Beyond the 'One True Story.'" In *Frontiers in Catholic Feminist Theology: Shoulder to Shoulder*, edited by Susan Abraham and Elena Procario-Foley, 9–24. Minneapolis: Fortress Press, 2009.

Sarai (pseud.). Interview by Mara Brecht. Transcription from digital recording. Philadelphia, 1 August 2008.

Schüssler Fiorenza, Elisabeth. *In Memory of Her: A Feminist Reconstruction of Early Christian Origins*. New York: Crossroad, 1992.

——. *Bread Not Stone: The Challenge of Feminist Biblical Interpretation* Tenth-annivesary edition. Boston: Beacon Press, 1995.

——. "Feminist Hermeneutics," *Dictionary of Feminist Theologies*, edited by Letty M. Russell and J. Shannon Clarkson, 99–100. Louisville: Westminster John Knox Press, 1996.

Schüssler Fiorenza, Francis. "Systematic Theology: Task and Methods." In *Systematic Theology: Roman Catholic Perspectives*, edited by Francis Schüssler Fiorenza and John P. Galvin, 100–200. 2nd ed. Minneapolis: Fortress Press, 2011.

Seager, Richard Hughes. *The Dawn of Religious Pluralism: Voices from the World's Parliament of Religions, 1893*. LaSalle, Ill.: Open Court, 1993.

——. *The World's Parliament of Religions*. Bloomington and Indianapolis: Indiana University Press, 1995.

Sefcovic, Enid M.I. and Diane Theresa Bifano. "Creating a Rhetorical Home for Feminists in the 'Masters House' of the Academy: Toward a Gendered Taxonomy of Form and Content." *Women and Language* 27, no. 1 (Spring 2004): 53–62.

Sewall, May Wright, edited by *The World's Congress of Representative Women: A Historical Resume for Popular Circulation of the World's Congress of Representative Women, Convened in Chicago on May 15, and Adjourned on May 22, 1893*. Chicago: Rand McNally, 1894. Harvard University, Open Collections Program, www.ocp.hul.harvard.edu [http://pds.lib.harvard.edu/pds/view/2574452].

Sheridan, Sister Mary Imelda. Unpublished Talk on 'Direct Apostolate' (Kaying, China). Creative Works Box 14. Maryknoll Archives, Ossining, N.Y.

Sherman, Janann, edited by *Interviews with Betty Friedan*. Jackson, Miss.: University Press of Mississippi, 2002.

Siegel, Rachel Josefowitz. "'I Don't Know Enough': Jewish Women's Learned Ignorance." *Women in Judaism* 1, no. 1 (January 1997) 1–6. http://www.proquest.com/

Smith, Wilfred Cantwell. *The Meaning and End of Religion*. New York: Macmillan, 1962.

Sojourner Truth, "Ain't I a Woman?" Speech delivered at the Ohio Women's Rights Convention, 1851. Accessible at www.fordham.edu/halsall/mod/sojtruth-woman.html.

Sorabji, Jeanne. "Women of India." In *The World's Parliament of Religions: An Illustrated and Popular Story of the World's First Parliament of Religions, Held in Chicago in Connection with The Columbian Exposition of 1893*, vol. 2, edited by John Henry Barrows, 1037–1038. Chicago: The Parliament Publishing Company, 1893.

Spivak, Gayatri Chakravorty. "'Breast-giver': For Author, Teacher, Sublatern, Historian. . . ." In *Breast Stories* (Mahasveta Devi), translated and with introductory essays by Gayatri Chakravorty Spivak, 75–133. Calcutta: Seagull Books, 2010.

Stork, Helene. "Mothering Rituals in Tamilnadu: Some Magico-Religious Beliefs." In *Roles and Rituals for Hindu Women*, edited by Julia Leslie, 89–106. Delhi: Motilal Banarsidass Publishers, 1992.

Sullivan, Francis. *Salvation Outside the Church? Tracing the History of the Catholic Response*. New York: Paulist Press, 1992.

Sun Ai Lee. "Untitled." In *Eve and Adam: Jewish, Christian and Muslim Readings on Genesis and Gender*, edited by Kristen E. Kvam, Linda S. Schearing and Valarie H. Ziegler, 420–421. Bloomington: Indiana University Press, 1999. Originally published in *The Bible through Asian Eyes, edited by* Masao Takenaka and Ron O'Grady, 24. Aukland, New Zealand: Pace Publishing and the Asian Christian Art Association, 1991.

Suriya, Lady Linchee. "Women in Agriculture in Siam." In *The World's Congress of Representative Women: A Historical Resume for Popular Circulation of the World's Congress of Representative Women, Convened in Chicago on May 15, and Adjourned on May 22, 1893,* edited by May Wright Sewall, 765–769. Chicago: Rand McNally, 1894. Accessible via Harvard University's 'Open Collections Program' www.ocp.hul.harvard .edu, http://pds.lib.harvard.edu/pds/view/2574452.

Szold, Henrietta. "What has Judaism Done for Woman?" In *The World's Parliament of Religions: An Illustrated and Popular Story of the World's First Parliament of Religions, Held in Chicago in Connection with The Columbian Exposition of 1893,* edited by John Henry Barrows, 2:1052–56. Chicago: Parliament Publishing Company, 1893.

Taumoepeau, Mele and Ted Ruffman. "Mother and Infant Talk About Mental States Relates to Desire Language and Emotion Understanding." *Child Development* 77 (March–April 2006): 465–481.

Taylor, Charles. *Sources of the Self: The Making of Modern Identity.* Cambridge, Mass.: Harvard University Press, 1989.

Taylor, Laura. "Redeeming Christ: Imitation or (Re)citation?" in *Frontiers in Catholic Feminist Theology: Shoulder to Shoulder,* edited by Susan Abraham and Elena Procario-Foley, 119–140. Minneapolis: Fortress Press, 2009.

Thomas Aquinas. *Summa Contra Gentiles,* vol. 2. Translated by Anton C. Pegis. Notre Dame, Ind.: University of Notre Dame, 1976.

Tilley, Terrence W. *The Disciples' Jesus: Christology of Reconciling Practice.* Maryknoll, N.Y.: Orbis, 2008.

Tillich, Paul. *Dynamics of Faith.* New York: Harper and Brothers, 1958.

Townes, Emilie. *Womanist Ethics and the Cultural Production of Evil.* New York: Palgrave Macmillian, 2006.

Trinh T. Minh-ha, *Woman-Native-Other: Writing Postcoloniality and Feminism.* Bloomington: Indiana University Press, 1989.

Troch, Lieve. "Swimming like Salmons Against the Stream: Some Reflections on Interreligious Communication from a Feminist Perspective." In *ESWTR Yearbook: Feminist Perspectives in Pastoral Theology,* 99–110. Leuven: Peeters, 1998.

Tropper, Aram. "Jewish Life in Late Antiquity." *Journal for the Study of Judaism in the Persian, Hellenistic, and Roman Period* 37, no. 3 (2006): 299–343.

Van den Bogaerde, Beppie. "The Role of Language Input in Acquisitions Theory." In *Input and Interaction in Deaf Families* (LOT Dissertation Series 35), Netherlands Graduate School of Linguistics, http://www.lotpublications.nl/publish/articles/000464/bookpart .pdf.

Voss Roberts, Michelle. "Gendering Comparative Theology." In *The New Comparative Theology: Thinking Interreligiously in the 21st Century,* edited by Francis X. Clooney, 109–28. New York: T & T Clark, 2010.

Walsh, J. E. *Mission Manual of the Vicariate of Kongmoon (South China).* Hong Kong: Nazareth Press, 1937.

Ward Howe, Julia. "What Is Religion?" In *The World's Parliament of Religions: An Illustrated and Popular Story of the World's First Parliament of Religions, Held in Chicago in*

Connection with The Columbian Exposition of 1893, edited by John Henry Barrows, 2:1250–51. Chicago: Parliament Publishing Company, 1893.

Waters, Sr., Kenneth L. "Saved Through Childbearing: Virtues as Children in 1 Timothy: 15–22." *Journal of Biblical Literature* 123, no. 4 (2004): 703–35.

Wiest, Jean-Paul. *Maryknoll in China: A History, 1918–1955.* Armonk, N.Y.; London: M.E. Sharpe, 1988.

Williams, Delores S. "Black Women's Surrogacy Experience and the Christian Notion of Redemption." In *After Patriarchy: Feminist Transformations of the World's Religions*, edited by Paula M. Cooey, William R. Eakin, and Jay B. McDaniel, 1–14. Maryknoll, N.Y.: Orbis, 1991.

Williams, Fannie Barrier. "What Can Religion Further Do to Advance the Condition of the American Negro?" In *The World's Parliament of Religions: An Illustrated and Popular Story of the World's First Parliament of Religions, Held in Chicago in Connection with The Columbian Exposition of 1893*, edited by John Henry Barrows, 2:1114–15. Chicago: The Parliament Publishing Company, 1893.

Wire, Antoinette Clark. *The Corinthian Woman Prophets: A Reconstruction through Paul's Rhetoric.* Minneapolis: Fortress Press, 1990.

Wittig, Monique. *The Straight Mind and Other Essays.* Boston: Beacon Press, 1992.

Wollstonecraft, Mary. *A Vindication of the Rights of Woman.* 1792. Electronic Text Center, University of Virginia Library, http://etext.virginia.edu/toc/modeng/public/WolVind .html.

Young, Pamela Dickey. *Christ in a Post-Christian World: How Can We Believe in Jesus Christ When Those Around Us Believe Differently—Or Not At All?* Minneapolis: Fortress Press, 1995.

INDEX

Bordering Religions / *Concepts, Conflicts, and Conversations*